Bought – GN –

March 18, 1983

UNITED NATIONS DECISION MAKING

UNITED NATIONS DECISION MAKING

by

Johan Kaufmann

SIJTHOFF & NOORDHOFF   1980
Alphen aan den Rijn, The Netherlands
Rockville, Maryland, USA

ISBN 90 286 0410 3

Library of Congress Catalog Card Number: 80-50455

Third, fully revised edition of John G. Hadwen and Johan Kaufmann, *How United Nations Decisions Are Made.*

Printed in The Netherlands.

Table of Contents

Preface

When in 1958 John Hadwen, then first secretary of the Canadian Mission to the United Nations, and I ventured to write *How United Nations Decisions Are Made,* we were treading largely unexplored ground. We were the first, or at least among the first, to explore the dynamics of United Nations decision making, as distinguished from formally describing United Nations procedures. The book had a certain impact, and a revised edition came out in 1962.

Twenty odd years have passed. The world has changed, and with it the United Nations. Membership stands at 152. Colonies have virtually disappeared. Groups of nations, operating separately from individual governments, have increasingly become autonomous participants in United Nations decision making. Problems related to the growth of developing countries have become paramount in terms of the attention they receive in the various United Nations bodies. The workload of the U.N. General Assembly becomes heavier and heavier (the thirty-third session of the General Assembly, supposed to have ended by Christmas 1978, had to be extended to 29 January 1979!). Special sessions of the General Assembly on particular subjects are held increasingly frequently. Special United Nations conferences on new or "rediscovered" issues have become a normal feature. The decision-making process at the United Nations has been influenced by all these factors, and others, such as the rise of new participants in decision making, including both governmental and non-governmental organizations.

For several years our publishers had encouraged the preparation of a new edition, and so had numerous colleagues and friends. Since John Hadwen, saddled with other responsibilities, found himself unable to participate, I unwisely undertook to prepare the new edition. Unwisely, because the task was very much heavier and more time-consuming than I had anticipated. Although the elements influencing the United Nations decision-making process twenty years ago still exist, the new factors, some of which I have just indicated, required more attention and research than I had thought. I found it necessary to revise the structure of the book thoroughly. The original edition was very much influenced by the experiences preceding the establishment of the U.N. Special Fund in 1958. The present book covers the Security Council and the General Assembly in some detail, while the old edition was centered on the Second (Economic and Financial) Committee of the General Assembly. Certain portions of *How United Nations Decisions Are Made* (second revised edition of 1962), including three case studies, have been incorporated in the present book.

I found it preferable to divide the material in three parts. Part I analyzes the decision-making processes in the General Assembly, the Security Council, and the Economic and Social Council with related organs. Part II covers the various elements of decision making, the organization and methods of delegations, and the tactics behind United Nations procedures. Part III offers a number of case studies, in addition to examples and smaller case studies spread throughout the book. The reader is referred to chapter 1 for more details on the various chapters.

I have focussed on decision making. This book must therefore not be seen as a sort of handbook of United Nations facts, even though an effort has been made to cover recent developments. Facts change rapidly at the U.N., and only a periodical review such as is provided by the *United Nations Yearbook*, by the annual *Issues before the General Assembly* (published by the United States Association for the United Nations) and similar publications can keep up with the continuously changing scene.

A number of persons at permanent missions to the United Nations in New York and Geneva, at the U.N. Secretariat in New York and Geneva, and at the Netherlands Ministry of Foreign Affairs have assisted me in various ways. In order not to saddle them with any responsibility their names remain unmentioned. Their help is gratefully acknowledged.

Dr. Davidson Nicol, Executive Director of UNITAR, and Dr. Robert S. Jordan, at the time Director of Research at UNITAR, have given constant encouragement and put services of UNITAR at my disposal. As a result, Ms. Margaret M. Croke and Dr. Suzanne E. Valters have given valuable assistance. My profound gratitude goes to Dr. Valters who has reviewed every draft chapter, corrected errors in language, fact and structure, and made constructive suggestions. Mr. Jean Gazarian has helped to correct certain drafts. I am indebted to

Ambassador C.W.A. Schurmann for library research in Geneva. Mr. H.D. Ponsen has helped with certain data. Professor Leon Gordenker has reviewed the entire draft in its pre-final stage. I am particularly grateful for his suggestions on the structure of the book. All remaining errors are of course my responsibility.

My special thanks go to Ms. Elisabeth Lieve whose typing and handwriting-deciphering capabilities were able to produce typescripts at record speed.

A special word of thanks is due to Professor D. Durrer; the rest period he prescribed after an illness made it possible to finish this book at a more leisurely pace than would otherwise have been possible. In this connection I am also indebted for wise counsel to Professor A. Querido.

Work on this book started in New York, during my tenure as permanent representative of The Netherlands at the United Nations, and continued, with long interruptions, in Tokyo, Hakoñe, and The Hague. It was finished in Amsterdam and Gstaad. Without the constructive combination of both encouragement and discouragement of my wife I could not have completed the work on this book, combined as it was with a full-time job. Finally, I express appreciation to the publishers, Sijthoff & Noordhoff, for their suggestions on numerous points, and for their patience.

Gstaad/Tokyo, January 1980   Johan Kaufmann

Abbreviations

ACABQ	Advisory Committee on Administrative and Budgetary Questions
ACC	Administrative Committee on Coordination
ANC	African National Congress
ASEAN	Association of South East Asian Nations
CDF	Capital Development Fund
CIEC	Conference on International Economic Co-operation
CPC	Committee for Programme and Coordination
EC	European Communities
ECA	Economic Commission for Africa
ECE	Economic Commission for Europe
ECLA	Economic Commission for Latin America
ECOSOC	Economic and Social Council
ECWA	Economic Commission for Western Asia
EEC	European Economic Community
EPC	European Political Cooperation
EPTA	Expanded Programme of Technical Assistance
ESCAP	Economic and Social Commission for Asia and the Pacific
FAO	Food and Agriculture Organization of the United Nations
GA	General Assembly of the United Nations
GAOR	General Assembly Official Records
GATT	General Agreements on Tariffs and Trade
IAEA	International Atomic Energy Agency
IBRD	International Bank for Reconstruction and Development
ICAO	International Civil Aviation Organization
ICSAB	International Civil Service Advisory Board
IDA	International Development Association
IDB	Industrial Development Board

IFALPA	International Federation of Airline Pilots Associations
IFC	International Finance Corporation
IFDA	International Foundation for Development Alternatives
IIAW	International Research and Training Institute for the Advancement of Women
ILO	International Labour Organisation
IMCO	Inter-Governmental Maritime Consultative Organization
IMF	International Monetary Fund
ITU	International Telecommunication Union
JIU	Joint Inspection Unit of the United Nations
NGO	Non-governmental organization
OAS	Organization of American States
OAU	Organization of African Unity
OECD	Organization for Economic Co-operation and Development
OEEC	Organization for European Economic Co-operation
PAC	Pan Africanist Congress of Azania
PLO	Palestine Liberation Organization
RIO	Foundation Reshaping the International Order
SALT	Strategic Arms Limitation Talks
SG	Secretary-General
SUNFED	Special United Nations Fund for Economic Development
SWAPO	South West African Peoples Organization
TAB	Technical Assistance Board
UNCDF	United Nations Capital Development Fund
UNCITRAL	United Nations Commission on International Trade Law
UNCTAD	United Nations Conference on Trade and Development
UNDOF	United Nations Disengagement Observer Force
UNDP	United Nations Development Programme
UNDRO	Office of the U.N. Disaster Relief Coordinator
UNEP	United Nations Environment Programme
UNESCO	United Nations Educational, Scientific and Cultural Organization
UNFDAC	United Nations Fund for Drug Abuse Control
UNFICYP	United Nations Force in Cyprus
UNFPA	United Nations Fund for Populations Activities
UNHCR	Office of the United Nations High Commissioner for Refugees

UNICEF	United Nations Children's Fund
UNIDO	United Nations Industrial Development Organization
UNIFIL	United Nations Interim Force in Lebanon
UNITAR	United Nations Institute for Training and Research
UNMOGIP	United Nations Military Observer Group in India and Pakistan
UNRISD	United Nations Research Institute for Social Development
UNRWA	United Nations Relief and Works Agency for Palestine Refugees in the Near East
UNSO	United Nations Sudano-Sahelian Office
UNTSO	United Nations Truce Supervision Organization
UNU	United Nations University
UPU	Universal Postal Union
WEO	Western European and other countries
WFC	World Food Council
WFP	World Food Programme
WHO	World Health Organization
WIPO	World Intellectual Property Organization
WMO	World Meteorological Organization
WFUNA	World Federation of United Nations Associations

Chapter 1

Introduction

This chapter first discusses the objectives and organization of this book and then some general factors influencing United Nations decision making. The reader is also referred to the United Nations Charter, Annex I to this book (pp. 225-246). The Charter remains the best source for the overall objectives of the United Nations, and for a description of its principal organs and their powers.[1]

1. Objectives and Organization of this Book

Like its predecessor, *How United Nations Decisions Are Made*, this book is focussed on decision-making processes, both formal and informal, in the United Nations. In the last chapter, "The Future of U.N. Decision Making: Some Concluding Observations", a certain amount of evaluation is undertaken, and some suggestions to improve the decision-making processes are put forward.

The main body of the book is divided into three parts: Part I describes and analyzes the main procedures and decision-making processes of the three principal United Nations organs: the General Assembly (chapter 2), the Security Council (chapter 3), and the Economic and Social Council and related organs (chapter 4).

I have sketched the paramount position of the General Assembly, with an overview of the characteristics of such things as the general debate, the General Committee, the Credentials Committee and each of the seven Main Committees in which the bulk of the General Assembly work is done. The analysis of the Security Council endeavors to highlight its unique role as a conflict solver, with the increasing importance of consensus type decision making. The analysis of the Economic and Social Council shows why and how this organ could not attain the objectives set forth in the U.N. Charter: lack of confidence of a majority of the U.N. membership and a tendency to shift important matters either to non-U.N. bodies or to newly established organizations, such as the U.N. Conference on Trade and Development.

Part II, "Dynamics of United Nations Decision Making", provides a survey and an analysis of the various factors, elements and procedures which together determine the decision-making process. Chapter 5, "Elements of Decision Making", is divided into three sections. First, some new developments are discussed: the rise of operational programs, the increased use of ad hoc global conferences under United Nations auspices, and the significance of special sessions of the General Assembly. Second, the role of groups is analyzed, with special reference to the Group of 77 and the European Communities. The United Nations decision making roles of non-governmental organizations and of liberation movements are indicated.

The organization and work methods of delegations are set forth in chapter 6. The difference between a permanent mission and a delegation is explained; the role of parliamentary and other public members of delegations to the General Assembly is described.

Chapter 7 delves deeper into the procedures and tactics of United Nations decision making. The resolution-making and voting process, the use of various tactical moves, the significance of speeches, and the role of committee officers and their election receive attention in this chapter. The meaning of consensus and pseudo-consensus, and of various types of votes is also discussed.

Examples and smaller case studies are interspersed throughout the book. For example, chapter 3 contains a case study of the role of the President of the Security Council.

Part III contains three categories of case studies. First, chapter 8 presents six "success stories":

—the mediating role of presiding officers, with two examples: the first substantive session of the U.N. Disarmament Commission (May/June 1979), and the 1971 plenary session of the Economic Commission for Europe;
—an initiative on the question of torture successfully managed by the two initiating countries (The Netherlands and Sweden) in the General Assembly sessions of 1974 and 1975;
—the story of fast action, in the wake of a hijacking incident, crowned with the adoption, at the 1977 session of the General Assembly, of a resolution on the safety of international civil aviation;
—an initiative of the Secretary-General to convene an urgent meeting on refugee problems;

—a detailed negotiating story on the question of how financial contributions to a U.N. program, i.e., to the U.N. Special Fund, should be used (1959).

Next, chapter 9 analyzes two "failure stories":

"Summitry at the First Part of the Fifteenth Session of the General Assembly (1960)" shows how an important political initiative had to be withdrawn as a consequence of successive difficulties. "An Initiative that Failed: Immediate Needs as a Result of Economic and Other Emergency Situations" analyzes how a constructive and seemingly well-conceived proposal, after ups and downs over a period of three years, had to be taken back.

Thirdly, chapter 10 shows how failure can be turned into success: the ambitious proposals of the late 1940s and the 1950s for the creation of a large U.N. capital development fund (SUNFED) failed; on the other hand, the pressures to establish SUNFED gave birth to two alternative institutions: the U.N. Special Fund (later merged with the Expanded Program of Technical Assistance into the U.N. Development Programme), and, after all, a capital development fund, but one geared to financing small projects not financed elsewhere in the U.N. system and endowed with—as yet—modest resources.

Chapter 11, "The Future of U.N. Decision Making: Some Concluding Observations", does not endeavor to sum up everything, nor does it offer hard and fast conclusions. It does, however, offer some suggestions for improvements in the decision-making process at the United Nations.

I have to emphasize again that the book deals with decision making. There has been no attempt to transform it into a kind of handbook on United Nations facts. However, I have made an effort to take into account important recent developments.

I have devoted separate chapters to three of the six principal organs of the United Nations: the General Assembly, the Security Council and the Economic and Social Council, but not to the three others mentioned in Art. 7 of the U.N. Charter: the Trusteeship Council, the International Court of Justice, and the Secretariat. The Secretariat is referred to in practically every chapter, with special emphasis on the role of the Secretary-General. In chapter 11 some further attention is given to the Secretariat and the Secretary-General, in connection with the confidence factor and with recruitment policies.

The International Court of Justice, headquartered in The Hague, The Netherlands, is the principal judicial organ of the United Nations.

Its Statute forms an integral part of the U.N. Charter. Since it is not an intergovernmental decision-making organ, the Court is not analyzed in this book.[2]

As to the Trusteeship Council, the success of the decolonization process, especially since the adoption of General Assembly resolution 1514 (XV) (1960) on the Declaration on the Granting of Independence to Colonial Countries and Peoples, has strongly decreased its significance. The parity of countries administering trust territories and other countries in the membership had to be abandoned: as of 1980 it consists of only five members: the United States as administering member, and China, France, the United Kingdom and the Soviet Union as non-administering members.

The Special Committee on the Implementation of the Declaration on Decolonization, created in 1961, with 24 members, for many years under the dynamic leadership of S. Salim, ambassador of Tanzania to the United Nations, and president of the thirty-fourth session of the General Assembly, has actively "accompanied" and encouraged the decolonization process. As of 1980 there are only a few territories, mostly small island territories, left with colonial status.

The relationships between the various U.N. organs and the specialized agencies can be gleaned from Chart 1, the United Nations System.

Finally, I wish to stress that on purpose this book, like its precursor, *How United Nations Decisions Are Made*, has been kept eminently practical, without any attempt to develop a theoretical framework.[3] It would have been tempting to do so, and perhaps needs to be done. Whether it can be done is something else, because decision making at the United Nations is in constant evolution, and cannot be strapped into a rigid theory.

2. Some General Factors Influencing United Nations Decision Making

2.1. *The Purposes of the United Nations*

The United Nations is recognized to have a variety of general purposes which may be grouped under the following headings:

—the promotion of international cooperation on specific issues;
—the peaceful settlement of disputes between members and the provision of peace-keeping machinery;

Chart 1. The United Nations System

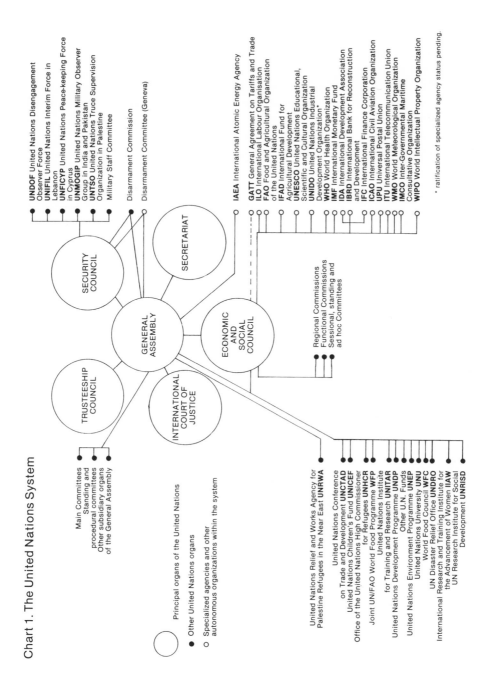

—the promotion of economic development of developing countries through a number of technical assistance and aid programs;
—the combatting of racial discrimination and the safeguarding of human rights;
—the promotion of the right of self-determination and the elimination of colonialism;
—the collection and dissemination of information;
—the elaboration of internationally recognized rules, and verification of compliance with these rules;
—the provision of an international meeting place.

The United Nations has been successful in conducting programs designed to meet specific international problems which are not susceptible to national or regional action. It has collected funds for these internationally agreed objectives and in the social and economic fields has a long list of accomplishments to its credit. When the nations of the world recognize a common objective of a specific kind the United Nations provides a useful forum and administrative framework for the pursuit of this objective. Its capacity for constructive action of this type is a direct function of the willingness of individual governments to undertake such action together. In fact it is difficult for the United Nations to promote any successful action unless there is approximate unanimity on the issue among the members of the international community of nations. In all cases the basic limitation on the extent of international cooperation remains the degree to which individual states are willing to work with others and at times to submerge and adapt their own national interests in relation to the general international good. This principle applies to both the economic and political fields.

2.2. *Dispute Settlement*

Disputes among U.N. members are generally settled in the United Nations only if international assistance is regarded by both parties as helpful, or if the parties are responsive to world opinion as expressed through the U.N. "A government that changes its policy after a U.N. vote is not bowing to a mathematical law. It is accepting the fact that it cannot afford to antagonize any further those elements in the hostile majority whose friendship, support, or at least tolerance are essential to it."[4] Furthermore, "if two or more governments really wish to settle a quarrel in a dignified way without losing face, the U.N. can provide the necessary facilities."[5]

Apart from the Security Council, whose role in the pacific settlement of disputes is spelled out in chapter VI of the U.N. Charter (see Annex I), settlements of disagreements between governments can be facilitated by:

—the Secretary-General. Successive Secretaries-General have exercised their good offices, either according to an explicit mandate (such as given by the Security Council to Secretary-General Waldheim in the Cyprus conflict), or informally "behind the scenes". In some cases the Secretary-General appointed a special representative, e.g., Mr. G. Jarring for the Middle East conflict.

—U.N. Panels for Inquiry and Conciliation. Under General Assembly resolution 268D (III) of 1949, each Member State can designate five persons well-fitted to serve as members of commissions of inquiry and conciliation. No panel has ever been constituted.

—the physical presence at U.N. sessions of representatives, perhaps cabinet ministers, of parties to a dispute. During General Assembly sessions, contacts can be established unobtrusively.

—the General Assembly can exercise a harmonizing influence (see also p. 16). A typical example was the conflict between Bangladesh and India on the use of the water of the Ganges river. Bangladesh obtained the inscription as a separate agenda item at the thirty-first session of the General Assembly (1976) of its complaint against India. The feeling of a no doubt overwhelming majority of delegates was that direct negotiations between the two parties could solve the problem. An informal request by Bangladesh for mediation by the European Communities, then chaired by The Netherlands, met with a negative response. The non-aligned countries, through a contact group consisting of Algeria, Egypt, Guyana, Sri Lanka and the Syrian Arab Republic, were able to negotiate agreement of Bangladesh and India to a text for a draft consensus decision of which the essence was the agreement of the two governments to negotiate in order to solve the dispute. The decision was unanimously adopted (No. 31/404). Within a year India and Bangladesh were able to reach a mutually satisfactory solution.

—A further contribution to facilitating dispute settlement is provided by the fact-finding procedure laid down in General Assembly resolution 2329 (XXII) of 1967. Pursuant to this resolution the Secretary-General has prepared "a register of experts in legal and other fields, whose services the States parties to a dispute may use by agreement for fact-finding in relation to the dispute." Each Member State was invited to nominate up to five of its nationals to be included in such a register.

This procedure was the result of an initiative of The Netherlands going back to the seventeenth General Assembly session (1962). The new procedure was backed by two studies of the Secretary-General, and an inquiry among Member States. Lukewarm support by many, and opposition by others had produced the modest result of a register of experts. Unfortunately, this facility has not been used (as of 1 January 1980), sharing the fate of the Panels for Inquiry and Conciliation mentioned earlier. The conclusion seems to be that any fact-finding under United Nations auspices, whether by the Secretary-General, a specially designed person or group of persons, or by a Security Council mission, can only be brought about as the result of a completely ad hoc negotiation in relation to each particular case with the assent of all concerned, and without reference to any previously established general procedure.[6]

2.3. *Collection of Information*

Another important function of the U.N. is the collection and distribution of economic, statistical and other information. Some of this information is valuable to governments, especially of the smaller or developing countries, in interpreting international trends affecting their own national policies. Such data are also necessary for the creation of a sense of international community. Without some common factual language the international community cannot conduct programs or develop long-term attitudes of international cooperation.

In many cases Secretariat reports include valuable suggestions or proposals on specific problems or issues. One of the most important is the annual *Report of the Secretary-General on the Work of the Organization* (formerly the Introduction to the Report on the Work of the Organization), in which the Secretary-General not only reviews the principal developments but also puts forward his personal views.

2.4. *Exchange of Views*

The United Nations is frequently described as a body whose primary justification is that it provides for an exchange of views between governments. One of the difficulties of the U.N., however, is that the views expressed by any one government at the U.N. are transmitted to other governments mainly in an indirect manner through the reports of permanent missions or of delegations. U.N. official records receive only haphazard attention in the national capitals of member governments and seldom have an effect on national political attitudes. The degree of importance attached to the United Nations frequently depends on the size and/or degree of development of a particular Member State; the significance of the U.N. as an international forum looms larger for smaller states.

A further difficulty for the United Nations as a forum for the exchange of views lies in the fact that each issue tends to be isolated from other related political and economic questions. Each issue is treated separately on the agenda and each country has a different set of problems in which it is interested. Indeed, some delegations specifically endeavor to separate problems in which they face disagreeable choices from problems with which they have no special difficulties.

There are, of course, "general debates" and opportunities for *tours d'horizon* where a more comprehensive outlook prevails. However, when there is a series of different problems between governments, these problems are sometimes combined in bilateral negotiations outside the United Nations so as to secure overall agreement. This is not to say that there is no relation at all between items on the agenda of U.N. meetings, but rather to suggest that in the United Nations the relation between problems is frequently less close than between problems considered in bilateral discussions. For example, in the First (Political and Security) Committee of the General Assembly, all agenda items on disarmament and arms control are grouped together in a single general discussion. Yet each draft resolution on a disarmament issue is considered separately, and "package deals" are exceptional.

2.5. *Bilateral Contacts*

Since propaganda practised at the United Nations scarcely penetrates to the public of other countries, countries do not "get to know each other" through the United Nations, although their representatives do, in a way which in the long run may affect national policies. In many eyes the personal relationships established at the United Nations have as much, if not greater, importance than the formal decisions which are reached. Personal contacts at the U.N. can promote useful decisions both within the Organization's framework and outside it; the bilateral meetings referred to later (p. 105) also play an important part in this respect. When Dag Hammarskjöld was Secretary-General, he stressed that contacts in the rooms and the lobbies of the United Nations "do represent... an attempt at a meeting of minds, and they are... very often influenced by a spirit of personal confidence, even if the general temperature... is characterized by, so to say, official lack of confidence."[7]

When senior representatives of the countries of the world gather regularly as they do at U.N. meetings, it has to be expected that some problems not directly related to the U.N. agenda will be discussed, and occasionally settled.

For example, the Berlin blockade was lifted in May 1949 largely as a result of negotiations initiated through personal contacts at U.N. headquarters. An informal exchange of views between United States and Soviet representatives, when they were in New York for the General Assembly, led to further intergovernmental meetings which resulted in an end to the blockade.

When, after President Sadat's visit to Jerusalem in November 1977, the permanent representatives of Egypt and Israel wanted to meet personally—for the first time since both countries had been represented at the U.N.—under conditions of confidentiality, the meeting was arranged at the home of a mutually trusted permanent representative of a smaller Western country. On that occasion the Ambassador of Egypt handed an official invitation to Israel to participate in peace talks in Cairo; the next day the Israeli Ambassador transmitted his government's positive reply in the same way.

Through participation in the work of the United Nations, Member States may develop recognizable characteristics in international affairs. Governments are required to express opinions and to take positions, at least by voting, on a wide range of international problems which without the United Nations might not have concerned them. Under these circumstances, the U.N. can be said to provide one of the means by which countries develop a sense of identity and independent political attitudes on international issues.

2.6. *Self-Interest*

National delegations are created to represent their own country's self-interest which may be furthered or hindered by U.N. discussion of various issues. A country's national self-interest may be aided by public discussion on one subject but not on another. The decision to put forward an item for consideration by the United Nations may depend on the willingness of the country concerned to discuss similar items which might be brought forward by others. Countries may have some central issue of special concern to them which for U.N. purposes determines their position on many other U.N. issues.

The national self-interest of a Member State may involve the use of the U.N. in the hope of securing political advantage. The United Nations is one of the most important avenues of the world in which a nation's prestige in relation to other governments is raised or lowered. A country can build up its influence in the United Nations to be used in pursuit of its own objectives in the future.

For many delegations certain issues before the U.N. are of little direct interest, yet some of these delegations continue to work for generally agreed conclusions. Perhaps they do so out of a sense of international responsibility, perhaps out of a desire to exercise diplomatic talents, perhaps for the satisfaction of controlling the destinies of others without damage to themselves, and perhaps because they do not wish to see the U.N. fail in any task. The achievement of internationally agreed decisions on international questions is in itself a suitable goal.

A delegation cannot generally defeat a proposal merely by voting it down but must bring forward a counter-proposal. A delegation with ideas reflecting its concept of the role which international action can play has a major advantage over a delegation without ideas or with ideas but no corresponding instructions.

A delegation which is present to defend itself when attacked, can, if it conducts itself moderately, obtain better long-term results in terms of its country's position in international affairs than if it is absent from the U.N. or does not participate in the debate in question.

For many countries events outside the sphere of activity of the U.N. may be of primary concern and their delegations at the United Nations are instructed to ensure that U.N. action does not disturb current or projected non-U.N. negotiations. Governments will therefore react positively or negatively to a given U.N. proposal, depending on their assessment of the role which the U.N. should play in that particular situation. When smaller countries present draft resolutions requesting faster or specific results of the Strategic Arms Limitation Talks (SALT) between the Soviet Union and the United States, these two powers unite in trying to obtain texts which will interfere minimally with these sensitive negotiations.[8]

There is, of course, a natural temptation to direct policies and programs through familiar channels that avoid the interposition of world institutions. In the short run those channels seem to be more manageable or more in accord with what are thought to be realistic politics. Governments may undertake to support the United Nations in principle and may wish and intend to do so; however, a great majority of the important international issues are discussed and disposed of bilaterally or through international channels other than the U.N. (i.e., within the framework of the General Agreement on Tariffs and Trade, the Organization for Economic Cooperation and Development, the Organization of American States, the Organization of African Unity, the League of Arab States, etc.).[9] Thus the United Nations channel is only one of a variety of channels available for the consideration of international problems, and it is not always considered to be the best. It has, however, a number of unique features, including almost universal participation and equality of voting, if not of influence, for all members.

Many newly independent countries have few foreign embassies in their capitals, and have themselves only a few embassies abroad. For them the United Nations is not only an important means for developing a sense of identity, but also for establishing direct contact with a large number of other governments.

One of the chief dangers to the United Nations, in particular the General Assembly, is its irrelevancy. The institution's relevancy will gradually decline unless nations bring to it not only the issues in which they expect to use the U.N. as a propaganda forum to pressure others, but also the issues on which international cooperation for long-term purposes is desirable, even if in the short run national self-interest might appear to be served best by action outside the U.N. Unless the United Nations is regarded by its members as a normal channel for the consideration of international issues, and not as an abnormal channel used only in emergencies, its value will certainly diminish.

2.7. *Public Opinion*

The influence of public opinion on U.N. proceedings is felt at various levels.

On very important occasions the presence of an audience adds somewhat to the atmosphere of a U.N. meeting and may affect the style of the speakers. Normally, however, the presence of the public at U.N. meetings does not affect debates except to remind delegates that their speeches are a matter of public record. There is little difference between the conduct of public and private meetings of United Nations bodies. A private meeting of a United Nations body, usually called a closed meeting, is a formal meeting but without the presence of the public or the press and in some cases without the admittance of delegates whose countries are not members of the body in question. In any case, a large, or even a small U.N. meeting can rarely be truly private, even if the public is excluded, since the practices of delegations concerning the release of information, including that relating to private

12

meetings, differ greatly. To ask for a private meeting of a United Nations organ presumes difficulties and arouses suspicion. For these reasons, only very small committees or very technical committees meet often without the general public in attendance. However, the Security Council does hold frequent informal consultations, which are tantamount to a closed meeting. For the purpose of electing the Secretary-General the Security Council meets in a formal closed meeting (see chapter 3, p. 50).

Sometimes decisions in the United Nations are affected by reports in the New York newspapers. *The New York Times*, for example, is read by all United Nations General Assembly delegations. This fact is chiefly a matter of timing, since frequently there is not sufficient time for newspapers outside New York to publish reports on one day's business early enough to affect the following day's business, particularly if there is a language barrier or a substantial difference in time zones. With the rapid advances of modern communications techniques, however, this situation may be changing.

The presence of correspondents from the home countries of delegates is of considerable importance for delegation attitudes. It is through these correspondents that a government's policy as expressed in the United Nations becomes known in the home country. News reports sent from New York can have a significant value in determining national policies if they create a reaction in public opinion which in turn affects the government and its representatives at the United Nations.

A few delegations hold periodic press conferences and briefings. Others hold only very occasional press conferences, and some delegations hold none, relying for their press relations on personal contacts. Press coverage may assist a delegation in making its position known to other delegations and their governments and in affecting domestic public opinion. On balance, however, it is better for a delegation to circulate information to other delegations through personal contacts than through the press.

There are also other channels through which the United Nations and its work become better and more widely known. Among these are the U.N. Department of Public Information as well as the radio and television coverage provided by other public and private agencies. In addition, non-governmental organizations have been playing an increasingly large role in enhancing public awareness of issues before the United Nations, particularly in regard to the problems of international economic and social development. The work of these various information components tends, however, to have a long-term rather than a short-term influence on the decision-making process in the United Nations.

The publicity provided through these channels also creates pressure on all delegates to achieve constructive results. As greater publicity is given to U.N. actions, so blame and credit for its success and failure is more widely assigned. However, even here, the short-term effects of publicity on particular U.N. decisions are seldom evident.

While press, radio and television coverage of the United Nations provides opportunities for greater public understanding of the Organization, there is a natural bias on the part of various communications media towards reporting controversy. As a result, publicity is generally given to the drama of conflicts at the U.N. This publicity may even increase the scope of these conflicts. Harmful publicity may also have a countervailing effect on the willingness of governments to have their problems discussed in the United Nations.

Increasingly, the U.N. Department of Public Information (DPI) is instructed by General Assembly resolutions to give special attention to specific matters, such as *apartheid*, the Year of the Child (1979), and the rights of the Palestinians. For economic and social questions DPI has a special division which started out as a semi-autonomous Center for Economic and Social Information (CESI). This Center was subsidized by The Netherlands and other governments.

It has also been suggested that wide publicity may lead to over-simplification and exaggeration; Dag Hammarskjöld once commented that "it must be said that public debates in the United Nations can just as readily be used to make a propaganda case for home consumption... as for a genuine step toward peaceful accommodation. The public conception of the peace-making role of the United Nations also tends to be distorted, because it is so largely based on reports of these debates which emphasize the conflicts that make news." Mr. Hammarskjöld also commented that "insofar as United Nations debates are fully and fairly reported, the possibilities are increased for giving to the public an opportunity to appraise national policies as expressed in these debates and to arrive at an objective opinion concerning them."[10]

2.8. *Moral Pressures*

Individual delegations are frequently instructed to take action for what could be described as moral reasons, and there are a great variety of moral concepts represented at the United Nations which must be taken into account. Governments and their delegations are of course composed of individuals whose judgments and recommendations are often affected by moral considerations. However, while delegations may take a position largely for moral reasons on one particular issue, they are unlikely to be influenced chiefly by a fixed set of moral principles on all U.N. issues. National self-interest cannot always be established as arising from moral principles on which there is widespread individual, national, or international agreement. It is necessary to avoid the delusion that the U.N. represents the moral conscience of the world. It does not fulfil such a function although it frequently aspires to do so on human rights and certain other matters.

On a number of issues in the past there has been a general sense of moral approval or revulsion which has had a substantial effect on the actions of the United Nations. Certainly each year, for instance, many governments pass through a crisis of conscience in respect of the various human rights and related issues, such as problems with regard to refugees.

The United Nations is, of course, a non-religious organization. The moment of silence at the opening of each session of the General Assembly and the existence of a meditation room at U.N. headquarters are signs of the willingness of the U.N. Organization to recognize the existence of abstract moral precepts. A U.N. system of ethics is contained in the U.N. Charter and also in various resolutions of or (draft) treaties prepared by the General Assembly, the Economic and Social Council, the Commission on Human Rights, the Commission on the Status of Women and other U.N. bodies which deal in one way or another with moral problems. Religious or other bodies cannot regard the U.N. as providing a direct opportunity for pressure towards particular moral goals, since delegates represent in the final analysis their governments, not themselves. From any one moral standpoint, the history of the U.N. cannot be considered to have followed a consistently moral course since its establishment. This history represents, however, the best that could be accomplished on each subject at each time by an international agency, taking into account the extent to which governments were prepared to cooperate in the U.N. and to support its decisions. There is no ground for complacency in viewing the "moral" record of the U.N. Equally there is no ground for indignation. It takes individuals a long time to develop moral codes of action to which they adhere; it would take international organizations composed of Member States with such a wide variety of cultural and religious traditions a long time during a period of relative peace to develop international standards of ethical conduct, if indeed these are possible. In progressing towards such a goal, the U.N. wil continue to take decisions which are compromises and which from a moral point of view will satisfy few individuals.[11]

2.9. *The Pressures towards ''Compromise''*

The existence of many divisions and tensions in the United Nations often creates the need for what may be called a ''fire brigade'', now often called ''bridge-builders'', consisting of a group of countries in a position to help to promote agreement when a breakdown in negotiations has occurred. The team may be different for each particular problem, but a ''fire brigade'' of ''middle-group'' delegations, willing to assume some responsibility, is necessary on many issues. However, the ''fire brigade'' technique has suffered considerably from the ''group-to-group'' negotiating system which has become the dominant feature of economic-oriented negotiations. If ''group-to-group'' negotiations fail, as has happened frequently in UNCTAD, it may be too late for an ad hoc ''fire brigade'' to take over successfully.

The task of the compromisers is made easier by the pressures towards agreement which are characteristic of many international gatherings and certainly of the United Nations. The fact that the U.N. can only make recommendations to governments, and that these recommendations will carry maximum weight if adopted unanimously, constitutes a powerful force towards the negotiation of compromise solutions acceptable to everybody. Towards the end of a session lack of time and the desire of delegates to go home may also be an incentive towards compromise. Sometimes it is true that unanimous decisions merely conceal differences of opinion and defer action. A decision adopted by a majority vote calling for vigorous action may exercise greater influence on the governments which were in the minority than a watered down compromise version. In each U.N. debate a balance must be struck between the views of delegations urging drastic action and the views of delegations opposed to dramatic action on pragmatic grounds. Each issue and each debate require a different diplomatic technique and a different solution. When this fact is recognized and accepted, appeals for ''U.N. action'' will be made more responsibly than they have at times been made in the past.

Sir Leslie Munro, then President of the General Assembly, stated in a press conference on the third emergency special session of the Assembly (1958), which dealt with Middle East questions, that he ''attributed the success of Arab Governments in reaching an agreement, unanimously endorsed by the Assembly, to the harmonizing influence of the Assembly itself.''[12] In the U.N., countries are almost forced to accept some reasonable compromise on issues concerning them if their valid public objections are met. Objections which cannot be expressed publicly in the U.N. seldom have much force. The drafting and nego-tiating of a compromise solution to a U.N. problem is a time-consu-ming and often thankless task but some delegation is always ready to try. In fact there are sometimes so many compromise solutions sug-gested that an agreed solution may well be hindered for that reason alone. While compromisers are necessary, at the U.N., as elsewhere, too many cooks can spoil the broth.

To fulfil the role required of a ''bridge-builder'' or a member of the ''fire brigade'' a delegation must have wide political acceptability, be well informed, enjoy the confidence of countries directly involved in the disputed issue, be strongly supported by its national government, and in some cases represent a country capable of contributing finan-cially or otherwise to the implementation of U.N. decisions. The task of obtaining majority support in the U.N. is becoming increasingly difficult and complex as its size increases. Middle power nations can become continuously active on most U.N. issues as professional go-betweens. This can result in the assumption of financial and political responsibilities which are serious in relation to the capacities of their national governments. The philosophy of the middle power has been described by Sidney Smith, Foreign Minister of Canada at the time:

The assumption of greater responsibility is perhaps good for the souls of the middle powers. It has been all too easy for us to belabour the Great Powers and find in their sins the causes of all our trouble. It is not infrequently the irresponsibility of a lesser power which has involved the United Nations in a crisis, and we should bear in mind that such irresponsibility inevitably encourages the Great Powers to assume greater authority. The lesser powers are not wiser or more virtuous just because they are smal-ler. Nevertheless our lack of the capacity for global aggression and our limited involve-ment in world affairs does give us the chance to play a peace-making role which is denied by circumstances to the Great Powers.[13]

There have been several analyses of the changed positions of the Great Powers in the United Nations as it is now constituted. Already in a 1958 article concerning the position of the United States, a writer com-mented: ''Where once we could dictate on the East River, we must now bargain and compromise. In brief, we can no longer afford to *demand* what we want; we must *bargain* for it. Our solo power has been progressively fused into a complex decision-making apparatus jointly operated by a large group of friends, near-friends and those whom we hope to make our friends."[14] Following the idea to its logical conclusion, another author suggests the following four precepts applicable to the Great Powers and no doubt to others: "Let the moral position be sound; let our allies be consulted as in a true partnership; let our colleagues be persuaded of the essential correctness of our position when this is possible... But let leadership also be enhanced by learning to lose with grace."[15]

These comments from 1958 remain equally valid in the 1980s. In the U.N. large countries, including the two Super Powers, can only achieve results if they can convince a majority of the U.N. members of the correctness of their positions.

"Great Power" now rests with the Group of 77 (see pp. 98-100). Since that Group alone constitutes a majority, it can, in effect, force through any decision which it wants. However, the Group of 77 has gradually realized that such abuse of its power may lead to counter-productive results, and it has shown an increased willingness to negotiate towards achieving consensus.

On balance, the pressures towards compromise in the U.N. represent healthy influences. They have softened or turned aside national passions which could otherwise have caused yet another crisis in the continuous series of crises since the end of the Second World War.

2.10. *Interaction between U.N. Debates and Government Action*

It is believed that on a number of issues U.N. discussion on a regular basis has over a period of time caused particular governments to take action which they might not otherwise have taken. The U.N. debates on Cyprus over the years probably contributed to the agreement between the United Kingdom, Greece, and Turkey, which was signed in 1959 and implemented in 1960. If Cyprus, Greece and Turkey eventually reach agreement on the future of the island, it will be due in no small measure to the continuing involvement of the Security Council and the General Assembly, to the U.N. peace force in Cyprus (UNFICYP) which has prevented hostilities, and especially to the mediating work of the Secretary-General of the United Nations and of his personal representative on the island.

Another example lies in the fact that the concept of equal pay for women has now been accepted in many countries perhaps earlier than might have been the case had the United Nations not debated the subject.

On the other hand, the value of this type of indirect pressure from the United Nations may be offset by the occasions in which the U.N. rubs salt into old wounds or aggravates political disputes. The United Nations is a forum for the expression of national pride and constitutes a body in which that national pride can also be embarrassed. It is difficult to draw up a balance sheet, and reach a total for or against the U.N. on this score.

The very existence of the United Nations creates the necessity for decisions. There can be few international issues on which the U.N. does not have some influence, if only because the parties to a dispute must decide whether to take the issue to the U.N. or not. Most U.N. proposals originate as a result of a complex series of decisions by individual governments in which domestic political considerations, timing, the international political climate, the potential reaction of other governments and some sort of estimate of the cost and trouble of an initiative versus its potential benefits, all play their part.

The fact that U.N. meetings are held at regular intervals forces governments to take definite positions, if only because once a meeting begins something must be done, and if A does not take the initiative B will. National self-interest, however, is not necessarily expressed in consistent or continuous policies, since governments change or adapt themselves to changes in domestic opinion which are frequently unpredictable. These circumstances are bound to affect their positions in the United Nations and their ability to influence U.N. decisions.

The regularity of U.N. meetings also means that many problems may be given continuity of international treatment. Without the United Nations, individual issues might have to be made the subject of a specific international meeting after which they would remain dormant or ignored until some authority succeeded in promoting another international meeting.

On the more difficult issues a U.N. debate is frequently regarded as a last resort. Indeed, at times the threat of possible discussion of an issue in the U.N. has been sufficient to promote bilateral discussions between governments concerned. As Article 33 of the Charter provides: ''The parties to any dispute, the continuance of which is likely to endanger the maintenance of international peace and security, shall, first of all, seek a solution by negotiation, enquiry, mediation, conciliation, arbitration, judicial settlement, resort to regional agencies or arrangements, or other peaceful means of their own choice.''

The forces against international action through the United Nations are substantial. It has to be demonstrated that it is in the national self-interest to submerge national policies in favor of international policies. The onus of proof is generally on those who propose a U.N. action. It is relatively easy not to take action in the U.N. It is far from easy to explain why U.N. action is required on a particular issue.

Furthermore, the United Nations is often only a court of last resort. As Secretary-General Waldheim stressed: "We have seen, for instance, in regional conflicts that one party or another involved has not wanted to go to the United Nations as long as it was winning. When it started to lose, it suddenly came to us. It was then somewhat disappointed because we could not immediately solve the problem."[16]

One characteristic which the initiators of U.N. action must take into account is the fact that, if it is at times difficult to get a debate started in the U.N., it is also frequently difficult to get it stopped. Many issues appear to be with the U.N. indefinitely either for political reasons and/ or because of the long-term nature of the problem. U.N. bodies like other organizations may develop vested interests which prevent early disengagement even when such action might be justified.

It is unfortunate that the effects of U.N. decisions are felt much more in countries with freedom of the press, and with some form of parliamentary democracy than in other countries where there are no public channels through which U.N. decisions can be brought to bear on governments. Some critics have complained that the U.N. punishes those countries which support it and leaves unpunished those which hypocritically participate, ignoring, if it suits them, any unacceptable U.N. decision.

From one point of view the U.N. is illogical, a large and a small state having theoretically, if not practically, the same voice in U.N. affairs. The U.N. has no overall administrative powers and any one country can create an impasse by ignoring or rejecting U.N. decisions of special concern to it. Some have done so but in the long run even these have found attendance at U.N. sessions preferable to leaving their positions completely unrepresented. The authority of the U.N. may be elusive, yet it is impressive. As one U.N. diplomat has stated: "It smacks of rhetoric to say that the United Nations is a forum for the conscience of the world. Let us state more modestly that it is a sounding board for the opinion of a great many nations in the world, and if that opinion is strong enough and united enough, it cannot fail to have its influence..."[17]

Notes to chapter 1

1. The best comment on the U.N. Charter remains:
L.M. Goodrich, E. Hambro and A.P. Simons, *Charter of the United Nations: Commentary and Documents,* 3rd rev. ed. (New York: Columbia University Press, 1969).

2. The reader interested in the International Court of Justice is referred to:

E. McWhinney, *The World Court and the Contemporary International Law-Making Process* (Alphen aan den Rijn: Sijthoff & Noordhoff, 1979), VII + 219 pp.

Shabtai Rosenne, *The World Court: What It Is and How It Works.* 3rd rev. ed. (Leiden, Dobbs Ferry, N.Y.: Sijthoff, Oceana Publications Inc., 1973), 252 pp.

S. Rosenne (ed.), *Documents on the International Court of Justice,* revised edition (Alphen aan den Rijn: Sijthoff & Noordhoff, 1979).

Leo Gross, *Review of the Rôle of the International Court of Justice,* American Journal of International Law, Vol. 66, No. 3, July 1972, pp. 479-490.

Edvard Hambro, "Some Observations on the International Court of Justice after Thirty Years," in: *Studi in onore di Giorgio Balladore Pallieri,* vol. 2 (Milano, 1978), pp. 306-333.

Philip C. Jessup, *Do New Problems Need New Courts?—Comments by Salo Engel, John R. Freeland (and) Leo Gross—Discussion,* American Journal of International Law, Vol. 65, No. 4, September 1971: Proceedings of the American Society of International Law at its sixty-fifth annual meeting, Washington, D.C., 29 April-1 May 1971, pp. 261-268, 275-285.

Manfred Lachs, *La Cour internationale de la Justice dans le monde d'aujourd'hui,* Revue belge de droit international, Vol. XI, 1975-2, pp. 548-561.

Hermann Mosler, "Problems and Tasks of International Judicial and Arbitral Settlement of Disputes Fifty Years after the Founding of the World Court," in: *Judicial Settlement of International Disputes. International Court of Justice—Other Courts and Tribunals— Arbitration and Conciliation. An International Symposium,* pp. 3-15.

Kotaro Tanaka, *The Character of World Law in the International Court of Justice,* Japanese Annual of International Law, No. 15, 1971, pp. 1-22.

3. Johan Kaufmann, *Conference Diplomacy* (Leyden, Dobbs Ferry: A.W. Sijthoff, Oceana Publications Inc., 1970) provides a systematic overview of multilateral diplomacy covering not only the United Nations, but also the specialized agencies.

4. *The Economist* (London), 13 April 1957, p. 110.

5. *New York Times,* 21 January 1958.

6. On dispute settlement see: K. Venkata Raman, *Dispute Settlement Through the United Nations,* published under the auspices of the U.N. Institute for Training and Research (UNITAR) (Dobbs Ferry, Oceana, 1977); also: B.V.A. Röling, *International Law and the Maintenance of Peace,* Netherlands Yearbook of International Law, Vol. IV, 1973.

7. Press Conference, 5 February 1959.

8. See Alva Myrdal, *The Game of Disarmament* (New York: Pantheon Books, 1976), passim. See also: William Epstein, *The Last Chance, Nuclear Proliferation and Arms Control* (New York: The Free Press, 1976).

9. On the relations between regional organizations and the United Nations, see Berhanykun Andemicael (ed.), *Regionalism and the United Nations* (Dobbs Ferry, Alphen aan den Rijn: Oceana Publications Inc., Sijthoff & Noordhoff, 1979).

10. Dag Hammarskjöld, "The Element of Privacy in Peace-Making," *U.N. Review* (New York), March 1958.

11. U Thant has described the moral influences on his perception of the role of the Secretary-General; see U Thant, *View from the UN* (New York: Doubleday, 1978), chapter II. For a variety of insights into the relationships between moral issues and the U.N., see Robert Muller, *Most of All, They Taught Me Happiness* (Garden City: Doubleday, 1978).

12. *New York Times,* 23 August 1958.

13. GAOR, 13th session, 1958, 759th plenary meeting.

14. Urban G. Whitaker, Jr., "U.S. at the U.N.: The Burden of Friendship," *Nation* (New York), 4 October 1958.

15. Robert E. Riggs, *Politics in the United Nations, a Study of United States Influence in the General Assembly* (Urbana: Illinois University Press, 1958), p. 180.

16. Press Conference, SG/SM/2676, 15 February 1979. On the legal effects of U.N. resolutions see: J. Castañeda, *Legal Effects of United Nations Resolutions* (New York: Columbia University Press, 1969).

17. C.W.A. Schurmann, GAOR, 11th session, 584th plenary meeting, 20 November 1956.

Part One

Three Principal United Nations Organs: General Assembly, Security Council, Economic and Social Council

Chapter 2

World Meeting Place:
The General Assembly

1. Introductory Observation

The General Assembly is one of the six principal organs established under the Charter of the United Nations (the others are the Security Council, the Economic and Social Council, the Trusteeship Council, the International Court of Justice, and the Secretariat). Because of the universality of its membership, the wide scope of its agenda, its supervisory role in relation to other U.N. organs, its budget-making powers, and the continuing desire, in spite of criticism, of statesmen of all countries to attend its sessions, the General Assembly can be rightly called *the* principal organ of the United Nations. The General Assembly comes closest to the idea of a world parliament. Yet its powers are limited, in most cases confined to recommendations which can be ignored even by those who voted in their favor. As any parliament, the General Assembly reflects the strengths and weaknesses of its members, which are the Member States of the United Nations, 152 as of January 1980.

The role and position of the General Assembly have been aptly characterized as follows:

The United Nations General Assembly represents the organized views of more governments on more subjects than any periodic gathering in the world. It focusses the attention of many private groups in many countries on the business of international cooperation. Its recommendations make waves—sometimes ripples, sometimes great splashes—in the capitals and the countrysides. Its agenda always contains both the unconquered difficulties of past years and the new issues of recent weeks. It includes business as serious as the nuclear arms race and as distant as outer space, as heartrending as the plight of desperate refugees and as controversial as the ceaseless struggles of the Middle East. The General Assembly pronounces its opinions, whether measured and thoughtful or impulsive and overwrought, on these and a hundred other issues. It also serves as housekeeper and supervisor for the tentacular United Nations system. In both symbolic and practical senses, it presides over the daily difficulties of a world which has little inclination to honor any single conscience or to speak with one voice.[1]

The General Assembly "may discuss any questions or any matters" within the scope of the U.N. Charter, with the exception only that the General Assembly is not supposed to make recommendations with regard to any "dispute or situation" under active consideration in the Security Council (Articles 10 and 12 of the Charter).

The rules of procedure of the General Assembly are reproduced in Annex II.

2. Types of General Assembly Session

The *regular session* of the General Assembly commences the third Tuesday in September (rule 1) and has, except in the beginning when the building in New York was not completed, always met in New York, at U.N. Headquarters. Proposals to have it meet elsewhere (under rule 4) run into logistical difficulties (see p. 132).

Special sessions have been called from time to time by the General Assembly itself (rule 7) and have been held on economic subjects, disarmament, etc. (for examples see pp. 81, 147). A special session can also be requested by a majority of the members of the U.N. or by the Security Council (rule 8a). The sixth special session (1974) was thus requested on the initiative of Algeria, with the support of a large number of developing nations.

An *emergency special session* can be convened (rule 8b) at the request of a majority of the U.N. members or at the request of the Security Council "on the vote of any nine members thereof", so that the veto does not apply. This procedure is based on the Assembly's "Uniting for Peace" resolution (377A [V]) of November 1950. In that year the Security Council, after an initial decision on U.N. forces for Korea had been possible because the Soviet Union had boycotted the Council, ran into vetos by the Soviet Union on two subsequent occasions that year, both also on Korea. Hence the Assembly's decision to provide for an emergency procedure. An emergency session must be convened within 24 hours after the request by the Security Council or by the membership majority. The emergency procedure was applied five times in the period 1951-1967, and then again in 1980 after the veto by the Soviet Union of a resolution requesting the withdrawal of Soviet armed forces from Afghanistan.

3. The General Debate

After a number of formal decisions (opening of the session, election of the President, election of the chairmen of the Main Committees, admission of any new Member State) the plenary of the General Assembly spends three weeks on a "general debate". This is in fact a series of monologues in which each head of delegation, usually the foreign minister, undertakes a *tour d'horizon* of the current state of the world's problems as seen in the light of his government's policy. There is a debate to the extent that the "right of reply" is frequently exercised (see p. 136). Attendance at the general debate tends to be poor, except when a speech is made by the head of delegation of a major power, or when somebody deemed to be a celebrity takes the floor. Yet there is fierce competition to be inscribed on a particular day, and even at a particular time (number two in the morning for example) for this general debate. This inscription is done with the Secretariat, on a certain day some three weeks before the opening of the General Assembly session. Physically strong permanent mission members are assigned for this task, which often means standing in line for a long time. Some diplomats have themselves locked in the building the previous evening, in order to be number one or two the next morning at 9 a.m. when inscription starts. There is still considerable haggling for the "right place" in the general debate, and delegations will make deals, if necessary, to try to achieve what they want.

During the general debate, but also all along during the General Assembly session, heads of state or government are allowed time, outside the Assembly's agenda, to "address the General Assembly." Such speeches can be delivered in the language of the country involved even if that is not a working language of the United Nations, provided a text in one of the working languages is made available to the Secretariat. The same facility may be accorded to a head of delegation during the general debate (but not on other occasions).

4. The General Assembly and its Committees

The General Assembly has two procedural committees, the General Committee (also known informally as the Steering Committee, or, after its French name, the Bureau) and the Credentials Committee, and seven substantive or Main Committees (see Chart 2).

Article 22 of the United Nations Charter empowers the General As-

Chart 2. The structure and subsidiary bodies of the General Assembly

THE GENERAL ASSEMBLY

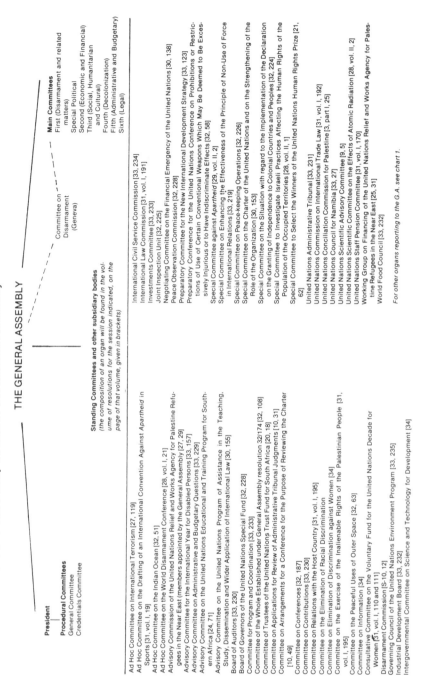

President

Procedural Committees
General Committee
Credentials Committee

Committee on Disarmament (Geneva)

Main Committees
First (Disarmament and related matters)
Special Political
Second (Economic and Financial)
Third (Social, Humanitarian and Cultural)
Fourth (Decolonization)
Fifth (Administrative and Budgetary)
Sixth (Legal)

Standing Committees and other subsidiary bodies
(the composition of an organ will be found in the volume of resolutions for the session indicated, on the page of that volume, given in brackets)

Ad Hoc Committee on International Terrorism [27, 119]
Ad Hoc Committee on the Drafting of an International Convention Against *Apartheid* in Sports [31, vol. I, 19]
Ad Hoc Committee on the Indian Ocean [32, 51]
Ad Hoc Committee on the World Disarmament Conference [28, vol. I, 21]
Advisory Commission of the United Nations Relief and Works Agency for Palestine Refugees in the Near East (members appointed by the General Assembly [27, 29]
Advisory Committee for the International Year for Disabled Persons [33, 157]
Advisory Committee on Administrative and Budgetary Questions [33, 229]
Advisory Committee on the United Nations Educational and Training Program for Southern Africa [24, 71]
Advisory Committee on the United Nations Program of Assistance in the Teaching, Study, Dissemination and Wider Application of International Law [30, 155]
Board of Auditors [33, 230]
Board of Governors of the United Nations Special Fund [32, 228]
Committee for Program and Coordination [33, 233]
Committee of the Whole Established under General Assembly resolution 32/174 [32, 108]
Committee of Trustees of the United Nations Trust Fund for South Africa [20, 18]
Committee on Applications for Review of Administrative Tribunal Judgments [10, 31]
Committee on Arrangements for a Conference for the Purpose of Reviewing the Charter [10, 49]
Committee on Conferences [32, 187]
Committee on Contributions [33, 230]
Committee on Relations with the Host Country [31, vol. I, 195]
Committee on the Elimination of Racial Discrimination
Committee on the Elimination of Discrimination against Women [34]
Committee on the Exercise of the Inalienable Rights of the Palestinian People [31, vol. I, 195]
Committee on the Peaceful Uses of Outer Space [32, 63]
Committee on Information [34]
Consultative Committee on the Voluntary Fund for the United Nations Decade for Women [31, vol. I, 110 and 111]
Disarmament Commission [S-10, 12]
Governing Council of the United Nations Environment Program [33, 235]
Industrial Development Board [33, 232]
Intergovernmental Committee on Science and Technology for Development [34]

International Civil Service Commission [33, 234]
International Law Commission [31, vol. I, 191]
Investments Committee [33, 233]
Joint Inspection Unit [32, 225]
Negotiating Committee on the Financial Emergency of the United Nations [30, 138]
Peace Observation Commission [32, 228]
Preparatory Committee for the New International Development Strategy [33, 123]
Preparatory Conference for the United Nations Conference on Prohibitions or Restrictions of Use of Certain Conventional Weapons Which May Be Deemed to Be Excessively Injurious or to Have Indiscriminate Effects [32, 58]
Special Committee against *Apartheid* [29, vol. II, 2]
Special Committee on Enhancing the Effectiveness of the Principle of Non-Use of Force in International Relations [33, 219]
Special Committee on Peace-keeping Operations [32, 226]
Special Committee on the Charter of the United Nations and on the Strengthening of the Role of the Organization [30, 153]
Special Committee on the Situation with regard to the Implementation of the Declaration on the Granting of Independence to Colonial Countries and Peoples [32, 224]
Special Committee to Investigate Israeli Practices Affecting the Human Rights of the Population of the Occupied Territories [28, vol. II, 1]
Special Committee to Select the Winners of the United Nations Human Rights Prize [21, 62]
United Nations Administrative Tribunal [33, 231]
United Nations Commission on International Trade Law [31, vol. I, 192]
United Nations Conciliation Commission for Palestine [3, part I, 25]
United Nations Council for Namibia [33, 27]
United Nations Scientific Advisory Committee [9, 5]
United Nations Scientific Committee on the Effects of Atomic Radiation [28, vol. I, 170]
United Nations Staff Pension Committee [31, vol. I, 170]
Working Group on Financing of the United Nations Relief and Works Agency for Palestine Refugees in the Near East [25, 31]
World Food Council [33, 232]

For other organs reporting to the G.A. see chart 1.

sembly to establish such subsidiary organs as it deems necessary for the performance of its functions, for example the Special Committee on the Situation with regard to the Implementation of the Declaration on the Granting of Independence to Colonial Countries and Peoples.

The main Secretariat officials assisting the plenary meetings of the General Assembly are the Secretary-General and the Under-Secretary-General for Political and General Assembly Affairs. The latter also assists the General Committee and the Credentials Committee.

4.1. *The General Committee and the Question of Rotation of Committee Chairmanships*

The General Committee consists of 29 members, namely the President of the General Assembly (who serves as its Chairman), the chairmen of the seven substantive or Main Committees, and the vice-presidents of the General Assembly, whose number is 21. The number òf vice-presidents was increased from 17 to 21 by the General Assembly at its thirty-third session in 1978, and as a result the pattern of distribution of the chairmen and the vice-presidents was adjusted (General Assembly resolution 33/138). Of the seven chairmen of the Main Committees two are to come from African states, one each from the groups of Asian states, Eastern European states, Latin American states, and Western European or other states, while one chairmanship rotates every alternate year among the group of Asian states and the group of Latin American states. The 21 vice-presidents of the General Assembly are distributed as follows: 6 from African states, 5 from Asian states, 1 from Eastern European states, 3 from Latin American states, 2 from Western European or other states, and 5 from the permanent members of the Security Council (China, France, the Union of Soviet Socialist Republics, the United Kingdom and the United States of America). This adds up to 22; however, the region from which the President of the Assembly comes loses one vice-presidency.

Prior to the thirty-third session the Asian states and the much more numerous African states had been considered as one group. However, the Asian group communicated to the other groups that it would like to negotiate about the distribution of the chairmanships and, in general, about its share of various seats. The immediate reason for this was that at the elections for the International Law Commission in 1976 the Asian group lost one seat, because an informal arrangement on the distribution by groups was in fact not confirmed in the actual election. Various groups are not totally happy about the share of chairmanships they obtain. Efforts have been made to arrive at a systematic rotation for several years, so as to predetermine which group would provide the chairman of each committee. These efforts have not yet been successful.

4.2. *The General Committee and the Agenda of the General Assembly*

The main tasks of the General Committee are (a) to recommend to the plenary an agenda for each regular session, including recommendations on newly proposed agenda items,[2] (b) to recommend which agenda items should be allocated to each of the committees and to the plenary, and (c) to recommend measures for the organization of work. Also, in accordance with the Rules of Procedure of the Assembly, the General Committee at the beginning of each session sets a closing date for the session.

The Committee must approve, or modify, the draft agenda which is submitted to it by the Secretary-General. The "draft agenda" consists of (a) items on the provisional agenda (rules 12 and 13), (b) supplementary items (rule 14), and (c) additional items (rule 15). Any item proposed for inclusion in the agenda has to be accompanied by an explanatory memorandum and, if possible, by basic documents or by a draft resolution. Occasionally, a delegation opposing inscription will wish its views registered. However, a vote on the inscription is rarely requested. Most delegations follow a policy of permitting inscription of almost any item. Thus, inscription of an item proposed by Grenada for the thirty-second session, on "coordinating and disseminating of the results of research into unidentified flying objects and related phenomena" may have caused raised eyebrows, but passed without a vote.

The allocation to committees occasionally gives rise to fierce discussion. For example, in recent years the delegation of Turkey has opposed the allocation of the Cyprus item directly to the plenary saying this would deny the Turkish Cypriot community an equal hearing with the Greek Cypriot community. In its opinion discussion in the plenary, with provision for statements in the Special Political Committee by representatives of the two communities, permitted only a perfunctory hearing of the representatives of the Turkish Cypriot community while it permitted the Greek Cypriots the opportunity to argue their case with two voices.

There is a tendency to deal with agenda items deemed very important directly in plenary meetings. In 1960, of 92 items 24 or 26% were dealt with in plenary, whereas in 1978 of 129 items 35 or 27% were dealt with in plenary; thus there is hardly any change. For many, the plenary discussion is supposed to bestow a prestige of its own on the discussion of the item in question.[3]

The agenda items on Cyprus, the Middle East, Namibia, and *apartheid* in South Africa, have thus been dealt with in plenary in recent years. Whether this really has afforded higher prestige, or has elevated the level of debate, is open to question. But at the United Nations, as elsewhere, this is largely a matter of perception.

4.3. *The Credentials Committee*

The Credentials Committee consists of 9 members. The United States, the Soviet Union and China are traditionally members; the other seats are divided between the various groups. There is no fierce competition to be a member of the Credentials Committee; the Secretariat negotiates with the future members on behalf of the President of the Assembly to achieve a fair composition. The members are appointed on the nomination of the temporary President (see rule 30 of the Rules of Procedure), before the election of the President of the session. All recommendations of the Credentials Committee are submitted to the plenary session, and occasionally are the subject of debate and voting.

It is through an attack on the credentials that the membership rights of certain members have been challenged. Such attacks have taken place in the Credentials Committee in regard to the credentials of South Africa, Chile and Israel. In the case of South Africa, the Credentials Committee rejected the credentials of that government in 1974 and again in 1979. South Africa in the meantime had not presented its credentials nor tried to participate in Assembly deliberations. On the whole, however, most Member States of the U.N. support what is the generally accepted doctrine, i.e., that as long as the credentials of a delegation have been duly issued by the government in power, the U.N. has no business in challenging the legitimacy of the government itself.

4.4. *Participants in the General Assembly*

In the early days of the U.N. nobody doubted that the only official participants in the work of the General Assembly were Member States (leaving aside the important role of the Secretary-General and his staff). Non-member states could be present as "observers". To become an observer a state had an exchange of correspondence with the

Secretary-General. Observership implied that the country in question was given a reserved seat (in practice several seats) at the side of the plenary General Assembly Hall, had facilities to receive public U.N. documents, and was listed under the appropriate heading in the book listing permanent missions. In the course of time several intergovernmental organizations have received special status, giving them the right to observe General Assembly sessions.

As a result there are the following categories (January 1980):

—Member States (152);
—Observers Non-member states: 'the Democratic People's Republic of Korea, the Holy See, Monaco, Republic of Korea, Switzerland;
—Specialized agencies and other autonomous parts of the U.N. system;
—Intergovernmental organizations which have received a standing invitation to participate in the sessions and the work of the General Assembly as observers: the Agency for Cultural and Technical Cooperation, the Commonwealth Secretariat, the Council for Mutual Economic Assistance, the European Economic Community, the Islamic Conference, the League of Arab States, the Organization of African Unity, the Organization of American States;
—Other organizations which have received a standing invitation to participate in the sessions and the work of the General Assembly as observers: the Palestine Liberation Organization (PLO), the South West Africa People's Organization (SWAPO).

Non-governmental organizations have no official status in observing the General Assembly (contrary to the Economic and Social Council where they have an accepted status, see chapter 4). Yet several non-governmental organizations play an important part in the decision-making process of the General Assembly. This is particularly so for human rights questions.

5. The First (Disarmament and related matters) Committee

The First Committee deals with political and security matters. Its agenda used to cluster around three series of subjects: disarmament, outer space, and miscellaneous political and security items. On the recommendation of the tenth special session of the General Assembly on disarmament of 1978 it was decided, at the 1978 regular session of the General Assembly, to have the First Committee deal exclusively with disarmament and arms control, and related international security items.

At the thirty-third regular session there was a total of 18 items allocated to the First Committee, of which 17 dealt with disarmament issues. The Report of the Committee on Disarmament (formerly the Conference of the Committee on Disarmament), a Geneva-based non-U.N. committee reporting to the General Assembly, is traditionally one of the main substantive reports before the First Committee, and gives ample opportunity for delegations to comment on a great variety of matters.

On disarmament questions there are no clear-cut lines between nations, such as the North-South schism[4] which is evident in the Second Committee. As of 1980, the divisions run roughly as follows:

—those who want to put a total end to the proliferation of nuclear arms, versus those who want to condition this on a more adequate provision of nuclear resources for peaceful purposes (as more or less promised in the Non-Proliferation Treaty);
—those (mostly smaller powers) who want to achieve fast progress in the real decrease of nuclear and other massive destruction arms versus those who want to go very carefully, and therefore presumably slowly (mainly the two Super Powers, the United States and the Soviet Union).

The First Committee also deals with the implementation of the Declaration on the Strengthening of International Security (General Assembly resolution 2734 [XXV]).

Under the category "miscellaneous political and security items" the First Committee has, at recent sessions, often considered various items proposed by the Soviet Union, one of which concerned a possible Treaty on the Non-Use of Force in International Relations. The Committee also dealt for many years with the controversial question of Korea, which, since 1976, is no longer on the Assembly's agenda.

The atmosphere of the First Committee is business-like, with emotions rarely flashing. On disarmament questions numerous differently composed small informal groups, reflecting the various interests at stake, are created spontaneously to try to reach agreement on mutually acceptable draft resolutions and for other similar purposes.

The main Secretariat officials assisting the First Committee are the Under-Secretary-General for Political and Security Council Affairs and the Assistant Secretary-General for Disarmament. The First Committee, as all other Main Committees, has a secretary, usually a high official of the Secretariat, who plays a pivotal role in organizing the work of the Committee, providing for information and documentation, etcetera.

6. The Special Political Committee (SPC)

This Committee, originally named the Ad Hoc Political Committee, was created in 1956 as a permanent organ to alleviate the task of the First Committee.
Traditional agenda items are:

—the report of the U.N. Scientific Committee on the Effects of Atomic Radiation;
—reports of the U.N. Relief and Works Agency for Palestine Refugees in the Near East (UNRWA);
—review of the question of peace-keeping operations (on which a Special Committee of government representatives reports);
—report of the Special Committee to investigate Israeli practices affecting human rights of the population of the occupied territories.

Certain political questions that may be added to the Assembly's agenda on the proposal of a country or group of countries are also allocated to the Special Political Committee.
The Question of Cyprus used to be dealt with in the SPC, but lately it has been allocated to the plenary. However, as previously noted, hearings are held in the SPC to give the Turkish and Greek communities a chance to express their views. As they are not Member States of the U.N., and do not have observer status, they cannot speak in plenary session.
The policies of *apartheid* of the Government of South Africa, an item which is currently discussed in the plenary, also used to be dealt with in the SPC. However, representatives of organizations having a special interest in the question of *apartheid* are still heard in the SPC.
As of 1978, agenda items dealing with questions related to outer space have been transferred to the SPC, so that the First Committee could devote itself to disarmament issues. The debates on outer space tend to be uncontroversial, although below the surface some deeper disagreements are noticeable. For example, on such questions as the use of satellites for direct television broadcasting or for remote sensing, there are nations which believe that such activities should be possible with a minimum of restriction, while other states feel strongly that such

activities must be subjected to specific national control.

In addition, starting in 1978, the item "Questions relating to information" was transferred from the Fifth Committee to the SPC.

Since the SPC is a political committee, it is not surprising that political controversies are normal in it.

The main Secretariat officials assisting the Committee are the Under-Secretaries-General for Special Political Affairs and the Commissioner-General of UNRWA.

7. The Second (Economic and Financial) Committee

The Second Committee of the General Assembly is the paramount U.N. body in the field of international cooperation on economic subjects. Major new initiatives are taken in it, or are consecrated by its approval when submitted by other bodies, such as the Economic and Social Council, or the UNCTAD Conference, or the ad hoc U.N. conferences on certain subjects such as population, food, environment, water, etc. Although the Second Committee, in spite of the increased U.N. membership, has continued the practice of a general debate, sometimes under a particular agenda item suitable for this purpose, it has also continued to provide sufficient opportunities for informal negotiations. Most of the negotiations are between the Group of 77 and either the developed countries as a whole, or some particular subgrouping of the developed countries. The informal negotiations among members of the Second Committee are usually carried out under the chairmanship of one of its vice-chairmen.[5]

Some of the main questions dealt with by the Second Committee are:

—the international development strategy for the U.N. Second Development Decade (resolution 2626 [XXV]);[6]
—promulgation of a Charter of Economic Rights and Duties of States (resolution 3281 [XXIX]);
—the decision to establish a committee of the whole to overview progress in the establishment of a new international economic order (resolution 32/174);
—preparations for an international development strategy for the Third U.N. Development Decade (resolution 33/193);
—restructuring of the economic and social sectors of the United Nations system (resolution 32/197);

—comprehensive policy review of United Nations operational activities for development (resolution 33/201).

The Second Committee also acts as the final reviewing body for the activities of numerous U.N. funds, programs, and institutions, including the U.N. Development Programme, the U.N. Children's Fund, the U.N. Environment Programme, the Office of the U.N. Disaster Relief Coordinator, the U.N. University, the U.N. Institute for Training and Research, the U.N. Industrial Development Organization (UNIDO) (which is in the process of becoming a U.N. specialized agency, as a result of which it will be independent from the General Assembly), and the U.N. Conference on Trade and Development (UNCTAD).

The principal Secretariat officials assisting the Second Committee are the Director-General for Development and International Economic Cooperation, the Under-Secretary-General for International Economic and Social Affairs, the Under-Secretary-General for Technical Cooperation and Development, and the Assistant Secretary-General of the Office of Secretariat Services for Economic and Social Matters.

8. The Third (Social, Humanitarian and Cultural) Committee

This Committee has traditionally given a large amount of its time to human rights questions. In the early years it was heavily involved in the drafting of the Human Rights Covenants: each session considered some articles.[7]

Some important questions before the Third Committee are:

—elimination of all forms of racial discrimination (on which the Committee on the Elimination of Racial Discrimination reports); Decade for Action to Combat Racism and Racial Discrimination;
—alternative approaches and ways and means within the U.N. system for improving the effective enjoyment of human rights and fundamental freedoms. Under this heading various proposals and suggestions have been made, including the creation of a post of U.N. High Commissioner for Human Rights;
—world social development;
—torture and other cruel, inhuman or degrading treatment or punishment; rights of detained persons;

—status and implementation of the International Covenants on Human Rights;
—policies and programs relating to youth;
—U.N. Decade for Women;
—activities of the U.N. High Commissioner for Refugees.

On many questions political debates break out in the Third Committee. The Committee has more women delegates accredited to it than any of the other Main Committees and hence is also referred to as the "ladies committee".[8] The atmosphere in the Third Committee is congenial and more than elsewhere, those who have engaged in fierce debate in the Committee will later join in a friendly gathering. Certain personalities with a great reputation, such as Mrs. Roosevelt (United States), Professor Cassin (France), and Professor Beaufort (The Netherlands), put their stamp both on the style and content of the Third Committee's work.

Increasingly, human rights issues dominate the proceedings of the Third Committee. The Western democracies, including Japan, defend the classical full enjoyment of human rights, as enshrined in the U.N. Covenants, and argue that the U.N. has extensive responsibilities in this regard. On the other hand, the Soviet Union and its allies contend that the U.N. has a more specific role "firstly by combatting gross, massive and systematic violations of human rights, and secondly by drafting international conventions and agreements in that field." (Ambassador O. Troyanovsky of the Soviet Union in the Third Committee on 24 November 1978) The first category is defined by the Soviet Union as "aggressions, colonialism, fascism, racism, *apartheid* and suppression of national liberation movements. Flagrant instances of such violations are the current situation in southern Africa, the situation in the Arab territories occupied by Israel, in Chile, etc." However, Ambassador Troyanovsky also stated that "... it had also been recognized [at the 1945 San Francisco Conference on International Organizations at which the United Nations Charter was signed] that, if violations of human rights created a situation that threatened peace or impeded the implementation of the Charter, they ceased to be the exclusive affair of each State."[9]

The fact that a long-standing proposal to appoint a U.N. Commissioner for Human Rights has failed to obtain sufficient support, might indicate that the viewpoint of the majority of the U.N. Member States is closer to that of the Soviet Union than to the Western point of view.

The principal Secretariat officials assisting the Third Committee are the Under-Secretary-General for Political and General Assembly Affairs, the Assistant Secretary-General for Social Development and Humanitarian Affairs, the U.N. High Commissioner for Refugees, and the Director of the Division of Human Rights.

9. The Fourth (Decolonization) Committee)

This Committee used to be one of the most important, charged as it was with overseeing the process of decolonization, especially after the adoption of the Declaration on the Granting of Independence to Colonial Countries and Peoples (resolution 1514 [XV] of 14 December 1960) which gave a big impetus to that process.

In recent years the Committee has declined in importance, firstly because the process of decolonization is largely completed, and secondly because certain items which used to be on its agenda, such as the question of Namibia, are now dealt with in plenary session.

One of the main items remains the report of the Special Committee on the Situation with regard to the Implementation of the Declaration on the Granting of Independence to Colonial Countries and Peoples (usually referred to as the Committee of Twenty-four).

Other recent important items on its agenda have been:

—the question of East Timor;
—the question of Southern Rhodesia;
—U.N. Educational and Training Programme for Southern Africa.

The principal Secretariat official assisting the Fourth Committee is the Under-Secretary-General for Political Affairs, Trusteeship and Decolonization.

10. The Fifth (Administrative and Budgetary) Committee

This Committee is very important because its decisions are required to keep the U.N. functioning. Its main agenda item is undoubtedly the U.N. program budget. This is now approved on a biennial basis, with certain adjustments after the first year of the biennium. Other important agenda items of the Fifth Committee are:

—the scale of assessments for the apportionment of the expenses of the U.N.;

—administrative and budgetary coordination of the U.N. with the specialized agencies;
—personnel questions, including the issue of equitable geographic distribution of professional posts in the U.N. Secretariat (elaborate statistics are distributed, and numerous complaints by countries that are or feel "under-represented" are expressed in the Committee), and that of measures to increase the number of women in the professional category in the U.N. system;[10]
—the financing of U.N. peace-keeping operations (UNDOF, UNIFIL, UNFICYP, etc.).

The Fifth Committee is one of the least "politicized" committees. Budgetary and management specialists of the permanent missions, or specialists in this field from the capitals, occupy its seats. The Fifth Committee is advised, in written reports, by a number of expert bodies, in the first place the Advisory Committee on Administrative and Budgetary Questions (ACABQ), now consisting of 16 members, who are elected by the General Assembly after having been nominated as candidates by their respective countries. They are supposed to serve in an individual capacity, rather than as representatives of their governments. ACABQ gives advice on all budgetary and related proposals of the Secretariat. Other expert bodies are:

—the Committee on Contributions (which makes recommendations on the scale of assessments);
—the International Civil Service Commission (which makes recommendations with a view to the development of a single unified international civil service in the U.N. system);
—the Joint Inspection Unit (consists of a group of independent inspectors, who report on various organizational and programmatic questions that the Unit has investigated often on its own initiative):
—the Board of Auditors;
—the Joint Staff Pension Board.

The main Secretariat officials assisting the Fifth Committee are the Under-Secretary-General for Administration and Management, the Under-Secretary-General for Conference Services and Special Assignments, the Assistant Secretary-General for Financial Services, the Assistant Secretary-General for Personnel Services, the Assistant Secretary-General for General Services, and the Assistant Secretary-General for Program Planning and Coordination.

11. The Sixth (Legal) Committee

This Committee is composed of legal experts, sometimes scholars of great repute. Some of the most learned and profound speeches made in the United Nations can therefore be heard in this Committee. The atmosphere is usually serene, and tempers rarely flare, except perhaps when advice on some particularly difficult issue before some other committee is asked. The principal expert body from which the Sixth Committee receives reports is the International Law Commission, a body of 25 independent experts elected by the General Assembly. Other reporting bodies are the U.N. Commission on International Trade Law, the Committee on Relations with the Host Country (which deals with relations between Member States and the United States; no similar body exists with regard to relations between Member States and Switzerland, host to the U.N. Office at Geneva), and the Special Committee on the Charter of the United Nations and the Strengthening of the Role of the Organization. The latter Committee is presumed to be temporary. It was created in 1974, after a debate in which many Member States expressed dissatisfaction on a number of things, including the composition of various organs, especially the Security Council and the Economic and Social Council as laid down in the U.N. Charter. Charter revision is a long and difficult process; the compromise reached in 1974 was that not only Charter revision, but also ways and means to change things (called "strengthening") without Charter amendment, should be looked at. As of 1979 the Committee had not reached agreement on any specific recommendation.

On the Secretariat side the Legal Counsel is the principal Secretariat official participating in the work of the Sixth Committee; he is often called upon to introduce an agenda item, or to give advice and comments.

12. Procedure

The progress of the work of the Main Committees of the General Assembly is discussed once a week at a meeting of an informal coordination committee. This committee, which consists of the secretaries of the Main Committees, is presided over by the Under-Secretary-General for Political and General Assembly Affairs. The progress of work of the Assembly is also reviewed at a luncheon meeting hosted, usually on a weekly basis, by the President of the General Assembly, and attended by the chairmen of the seven Main Committees.

The procedure followed by each Main Committee, while not identical, usually consists of a general debate, either on each individual item or on a series of items, followed by presentation and discussion of the texts of draft resolutions and possible amendments thereto, vote or decision on the various drafts, and explanations of the vote (for details, see chapter 7). The rapporteur of the committee, with the aid of the Secretariat, then prepares a report to the General Assembly, usually on the action taken in connection with each item but sometimes with regard to several items, and containing the recommendation of the committee with regard to the particular item or items. The General Assembly in plenary session takes its decisions about resolutions on the various items on the basis of these reports and any supplementary discussion. All resolutions, even when approved by a Main Committee, are considered to be draft resolutions until they have been adopted by the plenary General Assembly.

Notes to chapter 2

1. Leon Gordenker, "Reflections on the General Assembly," *Issues before the 34th General Assembly of the United Nations 1979-1980* (New York: United Nations Association of the United States of America, 1979).

2. The Rules of Procedure of the General Assembly provide in Part II that the provisional agenda for a regular session should be drawn up by the Secretary-General and communicated to the members of the United Nations at least 60 days before the opening of the session. Any member or principal organ of the United Nations or the Secretary-General may, at least 30 days before the date fixed for the opening of a regular session, request the inclusion of a supplementary item in the agenda. Additional items of an important and urgent character, proposed for inclusion in the agenda less than 30 days before the opening of a regular session or during a regular session may only be placed on the agenda if the General Assembly so decides by a majority of the members present and voting.

3. As early as 1949, the General Assembly approved various recommendations made by the Special Committee on Methods and Procedures of the General Assembly, including the suggestion that certain questions should be considered directly in plenary in order to lighten the task of any given Main Committee, to give greater solemnity and publicity to the discussion of the item, to deal with questions the essential elements of which were already known to the Assembly because of previous discussion, to reduce repetition of debate, and to shorten the duration of the Assembly session (Rules of Procedure of the General Assembly, A/520/Rev. 13, Annex II). The recommendations of the old Special Committee on methods and procedures of the General Assembly are reproduced as annexes I and II (not reprinted in this book) of doc. A/520, rev. 13, Rules of Procedure of the General Assembly. Annex V to that docu-

ment reproduces the Conclusions of a newer Special Committee on the Rationalisation of the Procedures and Organisation of the General Assembly, approved in 1971 (G.A. resolution 2837 [XXVI]).

4. The term "North-South" is used to denote the developed countries of the "North" and the developing countries of the "South".

5. In December 1971, at its twenty-sixth session, the General Assembly decided to amend its Rules of Procedure, inter alia to increase to two the number of vice-chairmen for each Main Committee.

6. The goals, targets and policy measures of the international development strategy for the Second United Nations Development Decade contained in resolution 2626 (XXV) were complemented at the sixth special session, in May 1974, by the adoption of the Declaration and Program of Action on the Establishment of a New International Economic Order (resolutions 3201 [S-VI] and 3202 [S-VI]), at the twenty-ninth session, in December 1974, by the adoption of the Charter of Economic Rights and Duties of States (resolution 3281 [XXIX]), and at the seventh special session, in September 1975, by the adoption of a resolution on Development and International Economic Cooperation (resolution 3362 [S-VII]).

7. On United Nations involvement with human rights questions see: Moses Moskowitz, *International Concern with Human Rights* (Dobbs Ferry: Oceana, 1974).

8. It is perhaps worth noting that the Committee is only a "ladies committee" in comparison with the other Main Committees where women are few and far between. At the thirty-third session a total of 471 persons were named to the Third Committee as "representative", "alternate", or "adviser". Of these, 130 or 38% were women. 94 countries, or 64%, gave men alone the title of "representative" in the Third Committee. 58 countries, or 39.5%, were represented solely by men in the Third Committee.

9. For these statements by the Soviet Union, see GAOR, thirty-third session, Third Committee, Summary Records, A/C.3/33/SR.56.

10. The U.N. system is the term used to denote the United Nations plus all the specialized agencies.

Chapter 3

Preserving the Peace:
The Security Council

The Security Council is the organ charged under the Charter (Article 24) with the "primary responsibility for the maintenance of international peace and security"; it may act with regard to (1) the peaceful settlement of disputes and (2) acts with respect to threats to the peace, breaches of the peace and acts of aggression. The Council has undergone important changes in its methods of functioning and of decision making since its inception. These changes are only partially linked to the increase in membership from 11 to 15, which took place on 1 January 1966 following amendment of the Charter which came into effect 31 August 1965.

Conduct of business in the Security Council, in particular voting, is prescribed in the United Nations Charter; Article 27 on voting provides the following:

1. Each member of the Security Council shall have one vote.
2. Decisions of the Security Council on procedural matters shall be made by an affirmative vote of nine members.
3. Decisions of the Security Council on all other matters shall be made by an affirmative vote of nine members including the concurring votes of the permanent members; provided that, in decisions under Chapter VI, and under paragraph 3 of Article 52, a party to a dispute shall abstain from voting.

The most conspicuous element is the veto on substantive decisions, contained in paragraph 3, for each of the five permanent members of the Security Council; the permanent members, specified in Article 23, are China, France, the Union of Soviet Socialist Republics, the United Kingdom of Great Britain and Northern Ireland, and the United States of America.

Soon after the Second World War in the early years of the functioning of the Security Council, the voting provisions of the third paragraph of Article 27 led to consultations among the veto-holding powers as to whether an abstention by one of those permanent members did or did not mean that the required affirmative vote was lacking. It was agreed that "common sense" required that an abstention or non-participation in the vote should be construed as a form of concurrence.[1]

The practice of voluntary abstention by the permanent members has diminished the potential destructive influence of the veto.

Prior to the enlargement of the Security Council from 11 to 15 the majority requirement was seven, which meant that a combined abstention of the five permanent members would have been tantamount to a rejection of a proposal. Disunity of the Great Powers never made this happen. The present requirement of a majority of nine out of fifteen means that all five permanent veto-holding members could abstain (along with one other member) and yet a proposal or draft resolution could be adopted. In this sense the enlargement has meant a small contribution to the democratization of the Council.[2]

In addition, under the provisions of Article 27(3) a party to a dispute shall abstain from voting. The question was left unanswered, however, as to what was meant by the concept "dispute" which was undefined in the Charter. The result has been that governments have rarely brought a "dispute" to the attention of the Council, but usually referred to a "situation" or some other similar term.

In the period 1946-1964 the work of the Council was heavily influenced by the Cold War. Initiatives were taken without the participation of the President of the Council, who rotates from month to month according to the English alphabet. "Often an element of surprise was sought by one side or another as a debating tactic in the Council."[3]

The Council, during this period, was frustrated by 108 vetoes (103 by the U.S.S.R., a large number of these being on applications for admission to membership) by one or more of the five permanent members. Surprise action could occasionally overcome a threatened veto such as occurred during the walkout of the Soviet Union from the Council in January 1950—in protest against the presence of a representative of Taiwan—which made it possible to adopt later in the year resolutions permitting United Nations intervention in the Korean conflict.

Another device for getting around the veto has been action under the "Uniting for Peace" resolution which the General Assembly adopted in 1950.[4] If the Security Council is deadlocked by a lack of unanimity among its permanent members, the Assembly may consider the matter immediately and make recommendations. If the Assembly is not in session, any nine members of the Council or a majority of U.N. members may request an emergency special session[5] (see p. 26).

Since 1964 there has been a gradual evolution away from confrontational voting towards consensus-reaching methods, and, in this connection, towards a greater emphasis on private meetings of various kinds before the public debate begins.

In this process of consensus-seeking the President of the Council is playing an increasingly important role. It is now current practice that as soon as a question is brought before the Security Council (usually upon the complaint of one or more of the parties concerned in a conflict) the President will engage in confidential consultations, which will relate both to the procedure, including the timing of dealing with the question, and to the substance of the matter, in particular various possible options for acceptable Security Council action or non-action.

The consultations of the President of the Security Council will involve several or all of the following:

a. *Consultations with the Secretary-General*
The Secretary-General is bound to be the main source of objective information on any question. If the situation involves an item already on the list of matters of which the Security Council is seized, there is usually some Secretariat report (examples: the question of Cyprus, peace-keeping forces in the Middle East). The Secretary-General can also provide, if necessary, guidance to the President as to whom he might usefully consult. In this respect a problem may arise when a new item comes up.

b. *Consultations with the parties to a conflict*
This is obviously one of the most important types of consultations to be undertaken. It is not always obvious who are the parties to a conflict, especially if they are non-governmental entities (e.g., liberation movements, with sometimes more than one claiming to be the "authentic" representative).

c. *Consultations with one or several of the permanent members of the Security Council*
The President will wish to be certain that no veto will be cast by one of the permanent members of the Council, or, in a positive sense, that the permanent members will all go along with, or at least not oppose, a consensus solution.

d. *Consultations with one or more of the non-permanent members of the Security Council*
Among these, the group of non-aligned countries, to the extent that it is represented on the Council, is especially significant. Occasionally,

45

e.g., on questions related to southern Africa, other members wait until the non-aligned nations have drafted a text. In other cases, especially those coming back periodically, such as the Cyprus question, the President will attempt to negotiate on the basis of the text of the resolution adopted some six months earlier.

e. *Consultations with regional groups*
Among these groups, the African group, which usually has three members on the Council, is especially important, both because it is the most numerous group in the United Nations (as of 1 January 1980: 49 members, roughly one-third of the U.N. membership) and because several of the important issues before the Council relate to Africa (e.g., Namibia, Southern Rhodesia, *apartheid* in South Africa).

f. *Consultations with liberation and similar movements*
These are now in some cases treated on a basis similar to that of a state party to a conflict. They have also been allowed to participate in the discussion of a question before the Council. The Palestine Liberation Organization (PLO), for example, has been invited to participate with the same rights as a Member State invited under rule 37 (see p. 49). On the other hand, the African National Congress (ANC), the Pan Africanist Congress of Azania (PAC), and the South West Africa People's Organization (SWAPO) have been invited to participate under rule 39 which refers to "other persons, whom [the Council] considers competent for the purpose, to supply it with information or give assistance in examining matters within its competence."

The functioning of the President of the Security Council can be illustrated with the following sequence of events in October 1977.[6]

In the wake of renewed violence in South Africa, in response both to the death of the nationalist Steve Biko on 12 September 1977 and to measures taken by the South African government against certain organizations and publications on 20 October 1977 which reflected that nation's continuing *apartheid* policies, the African delegations at the United Nations began pressing for new and vigorous Security Council action. The African members hoped that the emerging policy of the new Carter administration would mean a United States position that would now be more responsive to African wishes on the issue.

The Council still had before it four draft resolutions which its African members had submitted earlier in the year. The African starting position was to have these four resolutions adopted by the Council. Under these draft resolutions, the Security Council would, in essence:

46

—impose a mandatory embargo on the delivery of arms to South Africa for an indefinite period;
—call on South Africa to implement all previous U.N. resolutions before a certain date;
—request all nations to discontinue loans and investments to South Africa;
—put on the record once again its disapproval of *apartheid*.

The President of the Council for the month of October, Ambassador R. Jaipal (India), started out by encouraging the Western members of the Security Council—the United States, the United Kingdom, France, Canada, and the Federal Republic of Germany—to meet with the African members of the Council as well as with other leading African delegates which were not at that time members of the Security Council. These meetings produced no middle ground between the positions of the African delegations and the Western nations. The Africans continued to stand by the four draft resolutions, while the Western nations, although sympathetic to the idea of a mandatory arms embargo, did not wish to see Chapter VII of the Charter invoked in a manner which might lead to a further extension of the application of that Chapter to economic sanctions. The Western nations, therefore, proposed a formulation which avoided stating that the situation in South Africa constituted a threat to international peace and security; instead it stated that the acquisition of arms and related matériel by South Africa constituted a threat to international peace and security.

The Council President then took a calculated risk. He decided to draft a compromise resolution, which became known as the "Indian draft". This draft which called for a renewable six-months arms embargo against South Africa was disliked by the Western members and frowned upon by African delegations; however, none of them rejected it. Following further consultations, the five Western delegations decided to table a draft of their own, which was based largely on the Indian draft. The essence of this draft consisted of a six-months embargo; however, it did not refer explicitly to Chapter VII of the Charter. The six months' provision was incorporated in an attempt to protect the future veto-power of the United States, the United Kingdom, and France.

The African delegations were disappointed that the arms embargo was limited to six months and that Chapter VII was not mentioned. Logic was on their side: either South Africa would modify its *apartheid* policies, and the arms embargo would be lifted even before the expiration of the six-months period, or South Africa would continue its *apartheid* policies, in which case the Western powers would have to agree to an extension of the embargo.

In the meantime, however, the African nations, faced with the uncertainty of what limits the Western powers, in particular the United States, were willing to accept, decided to have the four draft resolutions put to the vote. Only one, Security Council document S/12309/Rev. 1, which condemned the South African policy of *apartheid* in general terms (Security Council resolution 417 of 31 October 1977) was adopted unanimously. The other three were all vetoed by three permanent members: the United States, the United Kingdom, and France, a negative vote by any one of these three nations being sufficient to prevent adoption. Further intensive negotiations on a compromise text on the arms embargo continued and finally achieved a positive result. The Western nations agreed to an indefinite arms embargo under Chapter VII.

In the last phases of these informal consultations a great deal of attention had been given to the exact scope of the arms embargo. For example, would the embargo cover not only new but also existing licensing arrangements to manufacture arms in South Africa? Would equipment for police forces be included? The results of these negotiations are reflected in paragraphs 2 and 3 of the resolution and are not without ambiguity. Initially, the Secretary-General was entrusted with the execution of the resolution embodying the embargo; subsequently, however, a committee of the whole was established to monitor compliance with the embargo (S/RES/421 [1977] of 9 December 1977).

The actual adoption of the agreed resolution (S/RES/418 [1977]) took place on 4 November 1977 under the President for that month, Ambassador Kikhia of Libya, by a show of hands, on the proposal of the representative of India, the previous month's President. This method was chosen, rather than that of noting a consensus and declaring the resolution adopted without actual vote, in order to demonstrate that all members explicitly agreed with the resolution as adopted.

The adoption of the resolution was generally acclaimed as an historic event. As Secretary-General Waldheim said:

We have today clearly witnessed an historic occasion. The adoption of this resolution marks the first time in the 32-year history of our Organization that action has been taken under Chapter VII of the Charter against a Member State. It is not my purpose to seek to determine whether the Council's decision by itself is adequate to secure its objectives. However, it is abundantly clear that the policy of *apartheid* as well as the measures taken by the South African Government to implement this policy are such a gross violation of human rights and so fraught with danger to international peace and security that a response commensurate with the gravity of the situation was required. It is also significant that this momentous step is based on the unanimous agreement of the Council members. Thus we enter a new and significantly different phase of the long-standing efforts of the international community to obtain redress of these grievous wrongs.[7]

The above case indicates that under the right circumstances the President of the Security Council can play an eminently useful role. Among the requirements are the right temperament, a grasp of the underlying elements including the real positions of the parties concerned—the real positions often not being identical to those proclaimed in public speeches—and a willingness to aim for the highest common denominator among various positions. Or, as one former President of the Security Council has described it: ''The qualities ideally required of a Council President... are patience, tact, firmness and even ruthlessness, sensitivity to atmosphere, evenhandedness and considerable endurance.''

Contrary to the General Assembly and the Economic and Social Council, whose presidents are normally dissociated from their own delegation activities and in any case do not deliver statements for their countries, in the Security Council the President continues to represent his country during the month of his presidency. This has the advantage that he can be in more direct touch with day-to-day developments, but it may also lead to a certain amount of confusion as to whether the President is acting as presiding officer, or as his country's representative. When Ambassador Andrew Young (United States) met with the representatives of the Palestine Liberation Organization on 26 July 1979 to discuss the possible postponement of a Security Council debate scheduled for August on the question of Palestinian rights, it seemed to many that this was a normal thing to do for the person who was the incoming President of the Council as from 1 August 1979. The United States government, however, saw the encounter as a non-permitted meeting; the uproar in its aftermath led to Young's resignation.

While the Security Council has gradually shown a return to consensus-building methods and a greater emphasis on informal, closed consultations of various kinds, at the same time its public meetings on many questions have drifted towards what might be called a ''mini-General Assembly'' situation; rule 37 of the provisional rules of procedure, permitting an ''invitation'' to any member of the United Nations when the Security Council considers that its interests are specially affected, is frequently invoked by a great many countries; such an invitation when requested has rarely been rejected.[8] As a result in some of the debates on questions concerning the Middle East or southern Africa in the period 1975-1979 the number of participating non-members exceeded that of the fifteen Council members.

The Security Council shares with the General Assembly the responsibility for three important functions: (1) the admission of new members, and (2) the appointment of the Secretary-General, both of which require a positive recommendation of the Security Council and are subject to the provisions of Article 27(3), i.e., the veto, and (3) the election of members of the International Court of Justice.

Although admission to membership seems, in most cases, to have become almost automatic in the past two decades, delays have occurred in certain cases—Angola, Bangladesh, and Viet Nam—because of the initial opposition from a permanent member. Major differences among the permanent members precluded the admission of all but a small number of new members in the period 1946-1955 until the stalemate was finally broken by a "package deal".

The appointment of the Secretary-General is the result of considerable negotiations and bargaining to find a candidate generally acceptable not only to the permanent members but also to the rest of the Organization's membership. The recommendation of a candidate for the Secretary-Generalship is the only instance where the Security Council is required to hold closed meetings; however, leaks invariably occur, so that the names of the leading candidates as well as the number of vetoes against a particular candidate are widely publicized.

The Security Council has an important role, jointly with the General Assembly, in the election of members of the International Court of Justice. Each candidate must receive the absolute majority of votes of the Security Council (the veto does not apply), and of the General Assembly.

Some functions foreseen in the Charter, however, do not at present fill the Security Council's agenda. It does not deal with the "regulation of armaments" as provided under Article 26 nor has it held more than one of the periodic meetings on a ministerial or similar level as foreseen in Article 28. Such meetings were vigorously recommended by the Canadian Foreign Minister in his statement during the general debate of the thirty-second session of the General Assembly, and had also been advocated several times by the late Secretary-General U Thant.

For the future one can only speculate on the role of the Council. The present trend towards informal procedures is promising. The Security Council, by tradition, by its composition, and by the seriousness with which it is taken by all concerned, remains the only specific U.N. organ equipped to deal with international political emergencies, including the establishment and possible continuation of U.N. peace-keeping forces in a number of crisis areas.

Notes to chapter 3

1. See Sydney Bailey, "New Light on Abstentions in the UN Security Council," *International Affairs* (London), October 1974.

2. The ten non-permanent members of the Council are elected by the General Assembly as follows: 5 from the African and Asian states, 1 from East European states, 2 from Latin American states, and 2 from Western European and other states (see G.A. resolution 1991 A [XVIII], 19 December 1963).

3. Statement by Secretary-General Waldheim to a UNITAR Symposium, November 1977, U.N. Press Release SG/SM/2504, 18 November 1977.

4. G.A. resolution 377 (V), 3 November 1950.

5. There have been emergency special sessions of the General Assembly on the following issues: 1956, Suez; 1956, Hungary; 1958, Lebanon; 1960, Congo; 1967, Middle East; 1980, Afghanistan.

6. This case study is based on a speech delivered by the Permanent Representative of India, Ambassador R. Jaipal, before a UNITAR Seminar on the Presidency of the Security Council, 18-20 November 1977.

7. *Security Council Official Records,* 32nd year, 2046th meeting, 4 November 1977.

8. For a few exceptions, see Sydney D. Bailey, *The Procedure of the U.N. Security Council* (Oxford: Clarendon Press, 1975), p. 147.

The Elusive Quest for World Economic Policies: The Economic and Social Council and Related Bodies

1. The Economic and Social Council (ECOSOC)

The "principal organ" under the Charter for decisions in the economic and social field is the Economic and Social Council (see Chart 3). The Charter assigns specific responsibilities to the Council for advancing international cooperation in economic, social and humanitarian matters on which it reports annually to the General Assembly. The Economic and Social Council also acts in response to specific requests by the Assembly. Article 60 of the Charter provides that the powers of the Council are exercised "under the authority of the General Assembly." In addition, the Council is responsible for the overall coordination of the various organizations in the United Nations system working in the economic, social, and human rights fields. The coordinating role of the Council was recently re-emphasized in the recommendations of the Ad Hoc Committee on the Restructuring of the Economic and Social Sectors of the United Nations system (see General Assembly resolution 32/197, annex [20 December 1977]).

The plenary of the Council often initiates debates on major issues, although most problems are referred to one of the Council's three sessional committees for discussion and recommendations. These sessional committees often reflect the decision-making patterns of their Assembly counterparts in terms of agenda items discussed. The First (Economic) Committee reflects those of the Second Committee of the General Assembly, the Second (Social) Committee those of the Assembly's Third Committee, while the Third (Policy and Program Coordination) Committee has some affinity with the Fifth Committee.

The recommendations of these committees are usually accepted by the Council. A matter would be reopened for discussion in the plenary sessions only if a delegation felt strongly about a particular problem on which it was defeated in committee. The sessional committees have the same membership as the Council, and the same government represen-

Chart 3. The structure of ECOSOC

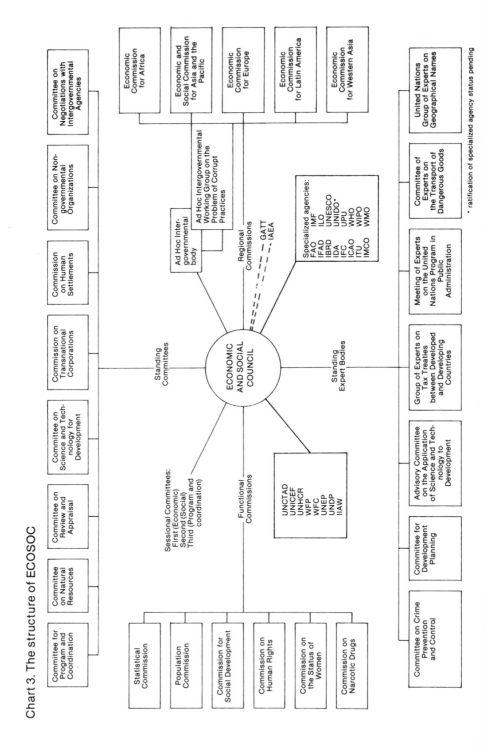

* ratification of specialized agency status pending

54

tatives frequently assume responsibility for items through the various stages of Council consideration.

The chairman of each of the sessional committees occasionally plays an important role in arriving at compromise solutions. The President of the Council may also exercise a leadership role in negotiations to achieve consensus on important resolutions. His influence, as of every chairman, is also of significance in matters where the choice of timing and voting is important.

An essential decision-making characteristic in the Economic and Social Council, as in most economic bodies in the United Nations, is the juxtaposition of the developing countries, operating through the Group of 77, and the much looser group of developed countries. The developed countries—apart from the socialist countries of Eastern Europe—often are not agreed on a course of action, or such a course is only arrived at after great difficulty. Some Western countries, such as the Nordic group and The Netherlands, often side with the Group of 77 in terms of philosophy on the new international economic order and occasionally on specific draft resolutions.

The role of the Secretariat is two-fold: substantive and technical support. The substantive aspect involves writing reports required by the Economic and Social Council and its subsidiary bodies as well as working with the President of the Council and delegations during the sessions. The technical aspect involves the essential role of efficiently servicing the meetings; this can in itself have an influence on timing, and thereby on the contents of the decision-making process, if the Secretariat has to arbitrate on conflicting demands for meeting space and interpretation services. The Secretariat is also important for its role in submitting estimates of financial implications which can, on occasion, influence the proceedings decisively.

One of the fundamental difficulties for the Economic and Social Council has been that, while many programs and other detailed questions are discussed by the Council, a number of other major problems have often been handled in other bodies. For example, during the early years of the Council's existence, major economic issues of worldwide significance were dealt with, whether within or outside formal meetings, in other fora, some of them outside the United Nations system such as the Organization for European Economic Cooperation (OEEC), later the Organization for Economic Cooperation and Development (OECD) and the General Agreement on Tariffs and Trade (GATT). Within the U.N. system such issues were taken up in the International Bank for Reconstruction and Development or in the International Monetary Fund.

This trend of discussing important economic questions in other bodies has continued; the focus of these discussions within the United Nations has increasingly been in the General Assembly. A major factor behind this development was the growth in numbers and influence of the developing countries in the United Nations since the 1960s. They tended to bypass the Economic and Social Council, because the Council's composition, from its point of view, was not representative; it had only 18 members until 1965, while by then the total U.N. membership had already reached 117. Many developing countries, therefore, preferred to pursue various economic objectives in the Second Committee of the General Assembly in which they were all represented. Uninhibited by any Charter provision as exists in relation to the Security Council, the General Assembly can and does take jurisdiction over ECOSOC affairs at any time.

Furthermore, starting in 1964, the U.N. General Assembly began to organize world conferences on economic and social matters outside the framework of the Economic and Social Council, and then subsequently created new bodies whose mandates overlapped with those of the Council. These new organs came under the General Assembly rather than the Economic and Social Council (although they usually report to the Assembly through the Council) and in some cases had their own separate secretariats. These organs were also often backed by powerful groups of countries or specific interest groups focusing on a new problem which took the limelight away from the Council. The United Nations Conference on Trade and Development (UNCTAD), established in 1964, the United Nations Industrial Development Organization (UNIDO), established in 1966, the United Nations Environment Programme (UNEP), established in 1972, and the World Food Council, established in 1974, are typical examples. In the cases of UNCTAD and UNIDO an additional reason for the establishment of separate bodies with separate secretariats was the dissatisfaction of the developing countries with the Department of Economic and Social Affairs in New York which—they felt—took a too conservative point of view. The developing countries wanted the new bodies to have their "own" secretariats which reflected their views on economic and social issues.

In addition, several specialized agencies, such as the International Labour Organization (ILO) and the Food and Agricultural Organization (FAO) were and continue to be involved in major economic policy issues.

56

With the increase in the membership of the Economic and Social Council in 1965 from 18 to 27, and then to 54 in 1973, a major stumbling block on the path of greater relevance of the Council was removed.[1] It could no longer be argued that the Council was unrepresentative of the total U.N. membership. In the meantime, however, the new organs, mainly the UNCTAD Conference and Board, the UNIDO Conference and Board, and later the UNEP Council had carved out their policy functions; they, of course, had no inclination to transfer anything back to the Economic and Social Council.

A further development has been that the General Assembly held special sessions on major questions of economic policy, namely the sixth (1974) and seventh (1975) special sessions. Another special session is planned for 1980 to assess the progress made in the various forums of the United Nations system in the establishment of a new international economic order and to take appropriate action for the promotion of development of developing countries, including the adoption of a new international development strategy for the 1980s.

This tendency towards focusing much more of the discussion of major economic issues in the General Assembly is continuing. For example, at the thirty-second session of the General Assembly, the crucial question as to what body would "monitor" (a vague word used intentionally as a compromise between "supervise" and "follow") the various negotiations related to a new international economic order throughout the U.N. system was decided in favor of a new ad hoc committee of the whole (i.e., open to any Member States desirous of participating) (G.A. resolution 32/174, 19 December 1977). The Assembly thus bypassed the Council which was relegated to a relatively minor role. The creation of this committee seemed to indicate that a majority of U.N. Member States still believed that the Council was not capable of dealing with delicate aspects of economic questions.

At the thirty-third session of the General Assembly the preparation of a new international development strategy was entrusted to a preparatory committee also open to the participation of all states, and responsible to the General Assembly, although it was instructed to report to the Assembly through the Council (G.A. resolution 33/193, 29 January 1979).

Another problem for the Economic and Social Council has been the question of the Council's efficiency. The two principal sessions of the Council, in the spring in New York and in the summer in Geneva, have been increasingly filled with a large variety of agenda items which are in themselves not unimportant, but which contribute to a lack of proper focus in the Council. While the Council, in accordance with the Charter, should deal with all world economic problems and coordinate joint planning on a U.N. system-wide basis, it has done so only sparingly.

One proposal to make the Council more efficient has been that it should abandon the two large sessions each year and instead institute a system of shorter subject-oriented sessions. This idea is enshrined in the resolution on restructuring the economic and social work of the United Nations, adopted at the thirty-second session of the General Assembly (32/197), but is only very gradually, if at all, being put into practice (see pp. 66-69).

There is also a problem as to what kind of delegates a government should send to ECOSOC. Its tasks may be too broad for specialists and too specialized for many members of permanent missions or from U.N. departments in the foreign ministries. Given the length of the two main annual sessions (at least a full month each) governments are reluctant to send high level specialists for any length of time. Efforts to convene ECOSOC on the ministerial level for a few days have failed most of the time.

Although the real or presumed inefficiency of the Economic and Social Council is certainly part of the story, the reluctance of governments to engage in global international economic cooperation, with some delegation of powers to a supra-national authority, is another factor. While the United Nations, in particular the General Assembly, continues to be an important forum for the discussion of international economic issues, governments frequently prefer to pursue their endeavors in smaller groupings. For example, it is well known that certain branches of the United States Government concerned with economic matters, such as the Treasury Department and the economic departments of the State Department, prefer bodies over which they exercise more control in terms of United States positions than is often the case in most United Nations fora.

Thus it seems that, in terms of the practice of the last decades, the Economic and Social Council has been relegated to a relatively limited role, administering and supervising—with varying degrees of effectiveness—a host of detailed programs; trying to provide for coordination between these programs as well as providing coordination of the work of its own subsidiary bodies; and providing for general debates —but rarely policy action—on world economic and social issues. These in themselves are honorable, and indeed useful and indispensable functions, but not what was intended by the United Nations Charter in terms of overall policy.

2. Functional Commissions, Standing Committees, Standing Expert Bodies

These bodies (see Chart 3) conduct and supervise, on a continuing basis, the technical work of the United Nations in specialized fields.

All of the Functional Commissions have country memberships —Member States being elected by the Council—which have been and continue to be determined by more or less regional or political distribution of seats among U.N. members. The terms of reference of most of the commissions require the Secretary-General to consult with the governments selected before the representatives are nominated and confirmed by the Council. The aim is to secure balanced representation of expertise in the various fields of a particular commission's competence.

The standing committees are intergovernmental bodies which assist the Economic and Social Council in providing policy guidance and in making policy recommendations. The standing expert bodies are composed of experts who provide advice to the Council and its subsidiary intergovernmental bodies. Where the Council's standing bodies have individuals as members, they are in some cases elected by the Council; in other cases they are appointed by the Council upon the recommendation of the Secretary-General.

3. Regional Commissions

A parallel part of this general structure are the regional commissions (see Chart 3). These bodies were established to encourage the regional sharing of experience regarding common problems, the cooperative study of regional economic issues, and the preparation of action on the regional level. Normally the detailed work of these bodies does not directly affect the discussions in the Economic and Social Council or in the General Assembly. On political issues the regional commissions usually follow patterns established in the General Assembly. Their budgets are approved by the Fifth Committee of the General Assembly, and they report annually to the Secretary-General through the Executive Secretary of each regional commission. Although the secretariats of the commissions are formally part of the U.N. Secretariat with headquarters in New York, the regional commissions tend to lead independent lives. Decision making in the regional commissions is normally done by consensus; acrimonious debate and voting are exceptional.

For purposes of coordination there is an annual debate in the Economic and Social Council on the functions of the regional commissions and on their performance, with increasing emphasis on the decentralization of many activities to the regional commissions.

The governments which are members of the regional commissions have become justifiably proud of their activities and of their secretariats. This is reflected in the growing desire to have resolutions of the General Assembly or of the Economic and Social Council "recognize" or "give due regard to" or "take into account" the work (often preceded by "valuable") being done by the regional commissions. This satisfaction is also reflected in consistent proposals to decentralize a number of U.N. headquarters functions to the regional commissions, including operational activities. These proposals are backed by the developing countries which feel that they have more direct control over the activities of the regional commissions. Some developed countries have been less enthusiastic about decentralization because of the resulting overlapping of work and redundancies in staffing.

4. The U.N. Conference on Trade and Development (UNCTAD)

The U.N. Conference on Trade and Development (UNCTAD), established by the General Assembly (G.A. Resolution 1995 [XIX]), was a reflection of the wish of the developing countries to have their "own" organization as well as their own secretariat, rather than to have to work through the "old-fashioned" Economic and Social Council (then still composed of only 18 Member States). For some countries the desire to bypass GATT was also a motive for setting up UNCTAD. The plenary of UNCTAD has met, after the initial conference in Geneva (1964), in New Delhi (1968), Santiago (1972), Nairobi (1976), and Manila (1979).

The structure of UNCTAD is summarized in Chart 4. Decision making is very much based on negotiations between the Western market economy countries, referred to in UNCTAD as "Group B"[2] and the developing countries, aligned in the "Group of 77". Occasionally, however, in UNCTAD, like in any other body, some countries may present a common point of view not stereotyped on the basis of "Group B versus Group of 77". This happened at the fourth UNCTAD Conference in Nairobi in 1976 when The Netherlands and 19 other countries joined in a common statement, delivered by Minister Pronk of The Netherlands, to express basic agreement with the

Chart 4. The structure of UNCTAD

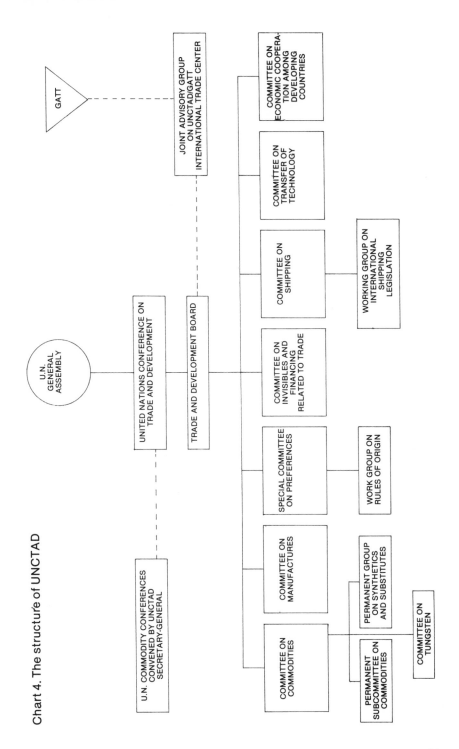

Group of 77 on the idea of an Integrated Commodities Program, including a Common Fund. The "fundamental principles" for such a fund to stabilize earnings of developing countries from raw materials have been agreed upon in 1978 following negotiations between industrialized and developing countries under the auspices of UNCTAD.

Speeches are often delivered in UNCTAD by spokesmen for Group B or the Group of 77. Negotiations are similarly carried out on a group basis, and have often led to the phenomenon of "maximum demand clashes with minimum offer", since each group tended to cluster its position around its extremists: the Group of 77 asking for the maximum, Group B offering the minimum. Lately, however, the insight has developed that such positioning does not lead to any compromise results. Consequently, it can now be said that group positions in UNCTAD are often close to what can be called the "median" position of each group. There is also a greater tendency for delegations from different groups to get together quite informally on a self-constituted basis, or semi-formally, perhaps either urged by the chairman or following some consultation in and between the formal groups. Such subgroups can more easily find middle ground and open the way towards some consensus decision. UNCTAD has become a significant negotiating body for certain trade, shipping and aid issues, usefully complementing GATT and other bodies.

The General Assembly resolution under which UNCTAD was constituted (G.A. resolution 1995 [XIX]) provided for an unprecedented "conciliation procedure" to facilitate compromise before voting. The essence of the procedure is that a predetermined minimum number of members of an UNCTAD organ may request postponement of voting, if necessary, until the next session. During the interval a conciliation committee, which must include representatives of countries particularly interested in the matter under dispute, would endeavor to resolve the matter. The conciliation committee is appointed by the President of the Conference or by the Chairman of the Board. Within the conciliation committee, there is no voting. This UNCTAD procedure,[3] however, has never been used. Perhaps this fact demonstrates that informal conciliation procedures are better than formal ones.

5. The Specialized Agencies

Related to the United Nations, in particular to the Economic and Social Council, are the specialized agencies (in alphabetical order):

FAO	Food and Agricultural Organization
IBRD	International Bank for Reconstruction and Development
ICAO	International Civil Aviation Organization
IDA	International Development Association
IFAD	International Fund for Agricultural Development
IFC	International Finance Corporation
ILO	International Labour Organisation
IMCO	Inter-Governmental Maritime Consultative Organization
IMF	International Monetary Fund
ITU	International Telecommunication Union
UNESCO	United Nations Educational, Scientific and Cultural Organization
UNIDO	United Nations Industrial Development Organization
UPU	Universal Postal Union
WHO	World Health Organization
WIPO	World Intellectual Property Organization
WMO	World Meteorological Organization

IAEA is an agency established "under the aegis of the United Nations;" it reports annually to both the United Nations General Assembly and the Economic and Social Council.[4] The United Nations Industrial Development Organization (UNIDO), which has been an organ of the General Assembly since 1966, is slated to become a specialized agency.[5] There also exists an Interim Commission for the International Trade Organization. An international trade organization has never come into existence. The Interim Commission is headed by the Director-General of the General Agreement on Tariffs and Trade (GATT) who is a member of the Administrative Committee on Coordination (ACC). GATT does not submit an annual report to the Economic and Social Council, although it is considered a de facto specialized agency (footnote to the title of section III of Annex to G.A. resolution 32/197).

Unlike the regional and functional commissions, the specialized agencies are not part of the United Nations Organization, although they report annually to the Economic and Social Council and are members of the ACC. Some of the agencies were established prior to the United Nations or even to the League of Nations. Each agency has an agreement with the United Nations on relations between the two organizations.

Although the International Monetary Fund (IMF) and the International Bank for Reconstruction and Development (IBRD) together with its affiliates, the International Development Association (IDA) and the International Finance Corporation (IFC), are legally described as specialized agencies and have a relationship agreement with the United Nations, they are, in fact, somewhat different. These agencies are supervised by governing bodies in which voting rights are weighted according to a member country's share in the capital of each organization. The conduct of business is largely in the hands of the management, which reports to the Executive Directors and to the full governing bodies. The annual reports of these agencies are referred to the Economic and Social Council for information and as a basis for a Council debate once a year.

Over a period of time what has been termed "the specialized agency sovereign equality complex" has developed. Most of the difficulties between the specialized agencies and the United Nations arise in determining the fields of jurisdiction of each agency and coordinating efforts in the same field. One of the major problems is that frequently within national governments there is insufficient coordination between officials responsible for representation in the different organizations. For example, in some governments, delegates appointed by a ministry of agriculture to serve as representatives at meetings of the Governing Body of the Food and Agricultural Organization do not always accept guidance from foreign offices, even on general political issues. Some doctors and meteorologists, furthermore, appear to have considered that they are not subject to any general direction in their participation in meetings of WHO and WMO. Foreign offices do not always control, to put it mildly, the international actions of other departments. As a consequence, officials of the United Nations and of the specialized agencies sometimes receive contradictory instructions from governing bodies which yet have very similar governmental memberships.

It has also happened that the Director-General of an agency took action designed to promote better coordination, only to be overruled by governments. Thus, when in 1968 Mr. A. Boerma, then Director-General of FAO, proposed to transfer FAO's Regional Office for Africa from Accra to Addis Ababa, seat of the U.N. Regional Commission for Africa, and to appoint the Executive Secretary of ECA as FAO

Regional Director for Africa, he met with a flat refusal on the part of governments represented at the African Regional Conference of FAO, mostly representatives of ministries of agriculture, who were afraid that FAO might be losing its independence. The FAO Council then endorsed the decision[6] of the Regional Conference.

6. Coordination

Some of the difficulties encountered during the initial years on "coordination between the U.N. and the specialized agencies" have disappeared as a result of strenuous efforts of a number of United Nations organs and persons (including former Under-Secretaries General M. Hill and C.V. Narasimhan), and because a "live and let live" attitude seems gradually to have prevailed. The main bodies involved in coordination are:

1. The Economic and Social Council's sessional committee on coordination, called the Policy and Programme Coordination Committee. It discusses annual reports, as well as a special oral report by the executive head of each specialized agency. It also handles miscellaneous coordination issues.

2. The Economic and Social Council's standing Committee for Programme and Coordination (CPC). This Committee, initially chaired by P. Hansen, who became later on Assistant Secretary-General, has done a pioneering job in developing the "biennial programming" concept and its contents; it looks in depth at programs of the United Nations and of the specialized agencies, all of which have related programs. The CPC is now also a subsidiary body of the General Assembly, an important evolution in terms of dealing with joint planning.

3. The Advisory Committee on Administrative and Budgetary Questions (ACABQ) (see p. 39) has often touched on program coordination between the United Nations and the specialized agencies, and issues an annual report on the situation.

4. The Administrative Committee on Coordination (ACC), chaired by the Secretary-General of the United Nations, consists of all the executive heads of the specialized agencies with occasional participation of the heads of related organs and programs of the United Nations system. It meets twice a year. It takes care of coordination between the various secretariats on program and administrative matters. Efforts to give the ACC more ambitious tasks, e.g., as an advisory committee to governments or as a sort of "world cabinet" have not succeeded.[7]

7. Restructuring of the U.N. Economic and Social Sectors

A major new effort is currently underway to improve cooperation and coordination within the United Nations system in regard to development questions and policies—that is, the effort embodied in the resolution on restructuring the economic and social sectors of the U.N. system referred to earlier in this chapter (G.A. resolution A/RES/32/197).

This resolution was prepared, over a period of two years, by an ad hoc committee of the General Assembly, created by the seventh special session (resolution 3362 [S-VII] of 16 September 1975). The Committee was open-ended; in fact roughly half the U.N. membership participated. It was chaired by K.K.S. Dadzie (then Permanent Representative of Ghana to the U.N. office in Geneva and since 1978 the first incumbent of the newly created post of Director-General for Development and International Economic Cooperation). Throughout its life the Committee labored with a severe handicap: the developing countries strongly felt that progress on restructuring the economic and social sectors should go hand in hand with progress on various substantive matters, such as commodity problems, transfer of resources, etc. Since there was very little progress on these issues, no haste was necessary in the question of restructuring. This view clashed with that of the developed countries, most of whom felt that the request from the seventh special session should be seen as valid in itself, even though it was part of the resolution dealing with a new international economic order as a whole. This confrontational situation resulted in very slow progress of the Ad Hoc Committee's work. Numerous informal contact group sessions hardly resulted in any quicker action. According to most participants it was mostly due to the strenuous efforts of chairman Dadzie (recognized in para. 1 of resolution 32/197) that a compromise result was achieved. Ambassador Dadzie kept proposing, in a low keyed manner, compromise formulas, many of which found their way into the finally adopted resolution.

The impetus for the restructuring effort derives from the widely held view that the system had become increasingly fragmented with a detrimental effect on coherence and coordination and a resulting inability to respond adequately to the wishes of the international community.

The restructuring effort which is addressed to all sectors dealing with economic and social questions is regarded as an opportunity to make the system more efficient and cost-effective through improving its internal management. In addition, developing countries view the restructuring effort as a means of expanding their influence and of making the system more responsive to the wishes of a majority of Member States, especially toward the goal of promoting the requirements of the Declaration and Programme of Action for a New International Economic Order.

The role of the General Assembly as the principal forum for policy making and for the establishment of over-all strategies, policies and priorities of the system as a whole has been re-emphasized.

The Economic and Social Council has the role of monitoring and evaluating those strategies, policies and priorities established by the General Assembly, of ensuring over-all coordination of activities of organizations within the U.N. system, and of undertaking comprehensive reviews of organizational activities in the U.N. system.

The resolution lays down, in effect, the optimum level for interaction between the Secretariat and governments at all levels of activity —global, regional and national, in the latter case with the aim of better coordination of U.N. organizations involved in development assistance at the country level.

At the Secretariat level, the post of Director-General for Development and International Economic Cooperation has been created to assist the Secretary-General in carrying out his responsibilities in the economic and social fields. The Director-General is seen as having a catalytic role in ensuring that all elements of the United Nations conform to the policy guidelines established by the General Assembly. Among his duties are that of ensuring effective leadership and over-all coordination in the U.N. system with the goal of achieving a multidisciplinary approach to the problem of development on a system-wide basis. He is also responsible for coordination within the Secretariat itself by establishing policy-related guidelines for all services and organs in the economic and social fields.

At the intersecretariat level, the ACC is responsible for inter-agency coordination. Here the Director-General also has a role to play, since he would be designated by the Secretary-General to chair ACC meetings over which the Secretary-General is unable to preside. He is also to oversee the functioning of the subsidiary bodies of the ACC.

Progress in implementing the "restructuring resolution" has been slow on the inter-governmental scale, but rather fast as far as the Secretariat is concerned. The Economic and Social Council has extensively discussed a revamping of its work methods, and has adopted modest improvements. On the question of subject-oriented shorter sessions no progress was made, so that as of 1980 ECOSOC still has two long annual sessions. As regards operational activities, the idea of "a single governing body responsible for the management and control, at the inter-governmental level, of United Nations operational activities for development" (which, in any case, as para. 35 of resolution 32/197 stipulates, excludes the United Nations Environment Programme, the United Nations Children's Fund and the World Food Programme) has not advanced. The machinery of the Administrative Committee on Coordination has been simplified: as of 1979 some 30 subsidiary bodies were replaced by three committees: one organizational committee and two consultative committees, one dealing with program and related matters, and the other with operational activities.

On behalf of the Secretariat, resolution 32/197 has described various functions in the economic and social sectors, indicating certain "clusters" for which separate organizational entities should exist. Prior to the restructuring there were the following main Secretariat functions in the economic and social sector of the U.N. Secretariat (leaving aside autonomous activities, such as UNDP, UNICEF, etc.):

—the Under-Secretary-General for Economic and Social Affairs;
—the Assistant Secretary-General for Social Development and Humanitarian Affairs;
—the Under-Secretary-General for Coordination and Inter-Agency Affairs;
—the Under-Secretary-General for the Department of Technical Cooperation for Development.

While the post of Under-Secretary-General for Coordination and Inter-Agency Affairs was abolished, the following new leading functions were added as a result of the restructuring:[8]

—the Director-General for Development and International Economic Cooperation;
—the Assistant Secretary-General for the Office of Secretariat Services for Economic and Social Matters;
—the Assistant Secretary-General for the Office for Development Research and Policy Analysis;
—the Assistant Secretary-General for the Office for Program Planning and Coordination;
—the Assistant Secretary-General and Deputy to the Under-Secretary-General of the Department for Technical Cooperation for Development.

Whether this new machinery will turn out to be efficient, or, on the contrary, too cumbersome to work with, time will tell.

Notes to chapter 4

1. The pattern of distribution of membership was specified in General Assembly resolution 2847 (XXVI) of 20 December 1971, as follows: 14 from African states, 11 from Asian states, 10 from Latin American states, 13 from Western European and other states, and 6 from Eastern European states.

2. The groups are listed in the original UNCTAD resolution of the General Assembly for purposes of electing specified numbers of countries to the UNCTAD Board:

Group A—Asian and African countries (plus Yugoslavia);
Group B—Western European and other countries (such as Australia, Canada, New Zealand, United States of America);
Group C—Latin America;
Group D—Socialist countries of Eastern Europe.

3. A similar conciliation procedure was recommended by the Group of 25 Experts on the Structure of the United Nations System. They proposed "negotiating groups" for the General Assembly and the Economic and Social Council of "manageable size" (10 to 30 members) which "would operate on the basis of unanimity." (*A New United Nations Structure for Global Economic Cooperation.* New York: United Nations, 1975). This proposal, however, was not accepted by the General Assembly. On the UNCTAD conciliation mechanism see Diego Cordovez, "The Making of UNCTAD," *Journal of World Trade Law*, vol. 1, no. 3, 1967. For an analysis of the first UNCTAD Conference of 1964, see A.S. Friedeberg, *The United Nations Conference on Trade and Development of 1964* (Rotterdam: Universitaire Pers, 1968).

4. The U.N. Charter confers certain powers on U.N. organs vis-à-vis the specialized agencies. Thus, under art. 17 the General Assembly may make recommendations to the agencies on their administrative budgets. Art. 63 stipulates that ECOSOC may coordinate the activities of the agencies through consultation with and recommendations to the agencies. At the time that the constitution of the International Atomic Energy Agency was negotiated, issues related to nuclear energy were considered too delicate to risk "meddling" by the United Nations in the affairs of IAEA; hence formal specialized agency status was avoided.

5. In April 1979 a Conference of Plenipotentiaries, held in Vienna, adopted UNIDO's Constitution clearing the way for UNIDO to become the seventeenth U.N. specialized agency. Entry into force is, however, delayed until at least 80 states have deposited instruments of ratification, acceptance or approval.

6. See Martin Hill, *The United Nations System: coordinating its economic and social work* (Cambridge: Cambridge University Press, 1968), p. 58. This work has an extensive and penetrating discussion of the problems of coordination in the U.N. system. For decision making in the specialized agencies see: Robert Cox, Harold K. Jacobson, Gerard Curzon, Victoria Curzon, Joseph S. Nye, James P. Sewell, and Susan Strange, *The Anatomy of Influence: Decision Making in International Organization* (New Haven: Yale University Press, 1973). Also: Henry G. Schermers, *International Institutional Law,* 2 vols. (Leyden: A.W. Sijthoff, 1972).

7. For a survey of these efforts, see J. Berteling, "Inter-Secretariat Co-ordination in the United Nations System," in H. Meijers and D. Vierdag (eds.), *Essays on International Law and Relations in Honour of A.J.P. Tammes* (Leiden: Sijthoff, 1977). The work

and the problems of the ACC are discussed extensively in Hill, op. cit., and in Mahdi Elmandjra, *The United Nations System, an Analysis* (London: Faber and Faber, 1973). For a comprehensive analysis of the activities of the United Nations and the specialized agencies see: Harold K. Jacobson, *Networks of Interdependence* (New York: Knopf, 1979).

8. Some of these posts existed in more or less the same form before, but were occupied by individuals with a lower official rank.

Part Two

Dynamics of United Nations Decision Making

Chapter 5

Elements of Decision Making

1. Some New Developments

If we compare the situation in 1980 with that of 1960, when the previous version of this book was written, several important developments have taken place:

—"operational programs", i.e., programs of economic or related assistance to developing countries, have greatly expanded;
—global conferences or permanent machinery, both under U.N. auspices, are increasingly being used to deal with certain world-wide issues which do not lend themselves to handling by a single agency;
—special sessions of the General Assembly are being held on particular subjects; for example, to further a "new international economic order", to establish a "new international development strategy", or to consider questions of disarmament;
—new entities, either governmental (Group of 77, non-aligned movement, European Communities) or non-governmental, have come into being and grown in importance;
—the decolonization process is virtually complete, with the U.N. membership at 50% over the level of 1960, or tripled as compared to 1946;
—the Cold War, which used to dominate many areas of U.N. decision making, has been replaced by a variety of divisive elements which differ from issue to issue; on most economic issues the juxtaposition of developed and developing countries is of paramount importance.

The problem of the economic development of developing countries, although identified with remarkable foresight in the United Nations Charter, has gradually attracted the increasing attention of the world community and of the United Nations to the point that more than 80% of the resources of the United Nations system are now devoted to issues of economic development. It seems possible to distinguish the following periods marking approaches to this question:

1945-1964: Charity

Although generalization is often dangerous, one can say that the period from 1945 to 1964 was one of "benign neglect". The problems of the developing countries were seen mostly as a question of charity, and economic questions were dealt with in a technical and fragmented manner. Yet, the total flow of aid from developed to developing countries, in proportion to the developed countries' gross national product, was higher than in subsequent years!

The First U.N. Development Decade, which followed a keynote speech by President Kennedy to the sixteenth session of the General Assembly (1961) constituted a "conscience-raising exercise".[1]

1964-1973: Increasing Interest

The year of the first UNCTAD Conference, the United Nations Conference on Trade and Development, 1964, was a kind of turning point. The first UNCTAD Conference meant the beginning of collective bargaining on development issues. The developing countries organized what is still called the Group of 77, although it currently has 118 members. They presented a common front vis-a-vis an often divided, and certainly surprised and hesitant, group of Western and other industrialized countries.

Fundamental problems of the developing countries were further analyzed, both by scholars and by governments. It was perceived, for instance, that one must not concentrate everything on a single sector such as industry, but that one must rather look—in any country or region—at the entire actuality of economic development. It was recognized that emphasis must be given to various qualitative factors, including the quality of education, of health systems, and of public administration. Awareness also grew that more must be done for the poorest group of countries, and for the poorest people within developing nations. The resolution on the International Development Strategy for the Second United Nations Development Decade (G.A. resolution 2626 [XXV] of 24 October 1970) was a first effort to codify commitments of the rich to the poor countries.

74

The genesis of the third period can be traced to 1973. The traumatic events of the Middle East war of October 1973, including the actions of the Organization of Petroleum Exporting Countries (OPEC), came as a rude awakening to a Western world which had come to rely on inexpensive and constant flows of oil. October 1973 also meant the beginning of a sharper and more self-reliant attitude of the developing countries and the adoption of tougher bargaining tactics. Increasingly, demands were heard for a new international economic order that developing countries hoped would bring a redistribution of economic wealth and power.

2. Operational Programs

The focus on the problem of development of developing countries was accompanied by an enormous rise in the U.N. system of operational activities designed to assist the economic growth of developing countries. In successive waves, beginning with the regular (1950), later the Expanded Program of Technical Assistance (1953), followed by the U.N. Special Fund (1959), and the subsequent merger of the Expanded Program and the Special Fund into the U.N. Development Program (UNDP) (1966), these activities grew—taking into account only the UNDP system—from about $20 million in 1950 to over $600 million in 1979. Although the UNDP was supposed to serve as an integrating agency for all pre-investment activities, there has been a tendency to establish separate new funds for specific purposes.

Issues within UNDP and other United Nations assistance programs have mostly revolved around two central questions:

—to what extent should the assistance to countries be influenced by centrally agreed priorities, including those which can be derived from U.N. General Assembly and Economic and Social Council recommendations, rather than by requests from countries?
—to what extent should programs be administered by specialized agencies and others as agents for the central financing body, such as UNDP, and to what extent should the central body exercise various kinds of supervision and control over the executing agents?

During the early years of the U.N. assistance programs, in particular during the period of the existence of the Expanded Program of Techni-

75

cal Assistance, the specialized agencies agreed on pre-determined shares of the annually available fund. This encouraged "specialized agency salesmanship" in convincing certain countries to undertake various projects, so that the agencies could fill their quotas. Dissatisfaction with this situation led to the setting up, at the beginning of 1959, of the U.N. Special Fund, whose assistance was based exclusively on the merits of individual projects.[2] When the Special Fund and the Expanded Program of Technical Assistance merged into the U.N. Development Programme, the problems related to the above-mentioned two issues initially created an atmosphere of uncertainty and confusion. As a result of dissatisfaction with this state of affairs, Sir Robert Jackson was commissioned to write a "hard-hitting" report on the capacity of UNDP to make effective use of its present resources and on its capacity to administer a program twice as large within five years. His report[3] recommended sweeping reforms. Therefore, the General Assembly in 1970 redefined the structure and activities of UNDP (resolution 2688 [XXV] of 1970).

The Special Fund and EPTA components were completely merged. Included among the reforms were the putting into effect of a U.N. Development Cooperation Cycle, based on country programs and requests. The decision of UNDP's Governing Council in 1971, usually referred to as the "consensus", enshrined this concept in the form of "Indicative Planning Figures" (IPF). Based on GNP, population, and other economic indicators, a figure is arrived at as to the proportion of UNDP assistance to be allocated to a particular country. These "Indicative Planning Figures" involve overall national development programs based on five-year cycles, and have come to be presumed entitlements of countries to receive aid totalling the amounts of the IPF. UNDP's role is thus essentially limited to screening out bad projects, and to seeing to it that those which are subsidized are effectively implemented. There is, therefore, little margin for real policy guidance in terms of following globally set priorities. This problem became particularly evident when certain Western governments tried, in the General Assembly, in the Economic and Social Council, as well as in the UNDP Governing Council, to get more attention for a "basic needs strategy", under which assistance should be given on a priority basis to countries and to groups of people within countries clearly deficient in the satisfaction of basic needs such as food, health, education, etc. The developing countries vigorously and successfully opposed such well-meant guidance, claiming that they themselves would be able to determine through which programs, projects and policies, the basic needs of their populations could be met.

On the question of centralization versus decentralization in conceiving and executing projects, UNDP and its predecessors, the Special Fund and the Expanded Program of Technical Assistance, have tried to conform to the concept laid down in their statutes, of making maximum use of the specialized agencies as executing agents. However, UNDP itself has developed a sizeable bureaucracy which keeps track of projects and supervises the executing agents.

The main decision-making organ of UNDP is its Governing Council, with 48 members elected by the Economic and Social Council. It is justly proud of its decision-making tradition of operating by consensus. Hardly ever has a vote been taken in the Governing Council; its sessions leave ample time for informal groups to meet and thrash out problems.

The Administrator of UNDP administers (assisted by more or less autonomous heads for each fund), and the UNDP Governing Council supervises a number of separate programs: the U.N. Fund for Population Activities, the U.N. Capital Development Fund, the U.N. Volunteers, the U.N. Revolving Fund for Natural Resources Exploitation, the U.N. Trust Fund for Colonial Territories, and the program of technical assistance financed from the U.N. regular budget.

Other important U.N. assistance programs are UNICEF and the joint UN/FAO World Food Program. Each of these have their own governing body.

Yet another important component within the United Nations system for financing development consists of the World Bank group. The World Bank, whose official name is the International Bank for Reconstruction and Development, finances country programs and projects submitted for each program or project separately. There is no question of country shares, by year or otherwise. Including its affiliates, the International Development Association (which provides assistance on "easy terms") and the International Finance Corporation (which invests in productive private enterprises), the World Bank's assistance has risen from $721,417,000 in 1958 to $8,749,000,000 in 1978. Although the World Bank has traditionally emphasized infrastructure projects such as roads, ports and power facilities, increasing emphasis is being placed on assisting the poorest in the developing countries through rural and urban development projects.

The main decision-making body of the World Bank is the Executive Board, which acts on recommendations of the President of the Bank, and normally takes decisions by consensus. The annual meeting of the Governors of the Bank (mostly finance ministers, and sometimes ministers for development) is essentially a rubber-stamping meeting, useful nonetheless as a place of contact and as a means of providing opportunities for policy speeches which may in some way influence the future decision-making process.

A similar set-up exists in the International Monetary Fund: the Board of Governors, meeting annually, as the highest decision-making organ, with day-to-day business in the hands of a Board of Executive Directors. However, the need to give special attention to the international monetary problems led to the establishment first of an Ad Hoc Committee (1972), transformed in 1974 into an Interim Committee of the Board of Governors on the International Monetary System, to be composed of ministers or "others of comparable rank". It was obvious that the principal governments did not want to leave delicate, partly political, matters of international monetary reform in the "technical" hands of the Executive Directors.

While the World Bank, with its affiliated organizations, the International Development Association and the International Finance Corporation, is channeling almost all of its resources to developing countries, the International Monetary Fund, by its nature, assists, within the limits of its Articles of Agreement and its procedures, any member country with balance of payments difficulties. "Nevertheless, the Fund has found it possible to adopt decisions that were intended to be of special benefit to developing members without confining the benefit of the decisions to them."[4] The Bank and the Fund have set up together a Joint Ministerial Committee of the Boards of Governors of the Bank and the Fund on the Transfer of Real Resources to Developing Countries, usually called the Development Committee.

In both the World Bank and the International Monetary Fund voting entitlements are based on the share of each country, the quota, in the capital of each organization. These quotas are revised from time to time. This feature does not exist in any other specialized agency, nor, of course, in the United Nations and its organs. Decision making in the World Bank and the IMF is based on consensus-seeking; the weighted-voting system has probably contributed to that.

There is one common characteristic to all operational activities: while general policy guidance can emanate from the supervisory policy bodies, the screening of projects to be assisted (or of balance of payments help to be given, in the case of the IMF) is very much in the hands of the staffs of the organizations. Such screening can simply not be done by intergovernmental bodies. The staffs of UNDP, UNICEF, other U.N. operational programs, the World Bank and the IMF are therefore in a position which is at the same time powerful and delicate.

3. Global Conferences

Because the United Nations system was essentially based on sector-oriented specialized agencies, the need for inter-disciplinary, cross-agency, multi-organizational forms of cooperation gradually became manifest. This first led to numerous inter-agency working groups. Later, as new problems, or newly discovered problems were identified, the technique of world conferences under U.N. auspices became popular.

The first in this recent series of world-wide conferences was the U.N. Conference on the Human Environment (Stockholm, 1972). It led to the establishment of the U.N. Environment Programme (UNEP), headquartered in Nairobi. The work of UNEP is showing concrete results, in particular those related to the "earth watch". This consists of several activities. One is an International Referral System which is designed to register all relevant information and make it available to governments and others. Another is an International Register of Potentially Toxic Chemicals. An interesting UNEP activity has been a conference of the coastal states of the Mediterranean aimed at a strategy which would prevent pollution and improve the status of this delicate eco-region; all governments around the Mediterranean, including the Arab countries and Israel, are cooperating in this effort. Measures to combat desertification constitute another major UNEP activity.

Other global United Nations or specialized agency conferences, past or planned, include the following:

1974—World Population Conference (Bucharest)
    —World Food Conference (Rome)
1975—International Women's Year Conference (Mexico City)
1976—HABITAT: United Nations Conference on Human Settlements (Vancouver)
    —World Employment Conference (Geneva) (sponsored by ILO)
1977—United Nations Water Conference (Mar del Plata)
    —United Nations Conference on Desertification (Nairobi)

1978—United Nations Conference on Technical Cooperation among Developing Countries (Buenos Aires)
1979—World Conference on Agrarian Reform and Rural Development (Rome) (sponsored by FAO)
— United Nations Conference on Science and Technology for Development (Vienna)
1980—World Conference of the United Nations Decade for Women (Copenhagen)
1981—United Nations Conference on New And Renewable Sources of Energy
— United Nations Conference on the Least Developed Countries
1982—Second U.N. Conference on the Exploration and Peaceful Uses of Outer Space

Each world conference is usually prepared by a preparatory committee and ends with the adoption of a "Plan of Action" which is subsequently discussed in the U.N. General Assembly and commended to member governments. Since the recommendations of the Plans of Action are not binding, it depends entirely on the real willingness of governments and others to follow them up.

The extent to which these world conferences have been a success is a matter of considerable debate. The first in the current series, the Stockholm Conference on the Environment in 1972, was generally applauded; it focussed attention on the "new" problems of the environment, and set up machinery which has turned out to be efficient. Other conferences, however, were criticized as either having turned "political" (e.g., the Women's Conference in Mexico City) or not having been able to come forward with really new proposals (e.g., the Habitat Conference in Vancouver).

Some of the world conferences have led to new intergovernmental machinery; for example, the World Food Conference recommended the establishment by the General Assembly of a World Food Council to act as coordinating mechanism for food policy and food aid by the agencies of the U.N. system; thus it duplicates to a certain extent what FAO is supposed to do (although it is serviced through the FAO Secretariat). The U.N. Environment Programme with its own Governing Council, resulted from the Environment Conference. Several of the world conferences have also resulted in new international funds for development assistance, independent from UNDP or the World Bank, such as the International Fund for Agricultural Development (IFAD), which subsequently became a specialized agency, the UNEP Fund, and the International HABITAT and Human Settlements Foundation.

The creation of so many new organs and funds reflects the state of the world, where nations obviously are reluctant to accept global guidance, much less world government. They prefer to operate in their own "clubs"; the world conferences are a device to have more and more functionally organized clubs. An additional reason for the proliferation of world conferences and of new funds is the demand by the developing countries for new funds and organs. The rationale is two-fold: to highlight the importance which they attach to those programs and the hope for an additional flow of development resources. Often there is not much enthusiasm on the part of the membership as a whole to accept new financial obligations; therefore, the line of least resistance is the creation of a new fund to which interested states may contribute, or refuse to contribute.

This is not the place to give any kind of preliminary or final judgment, but it is obvious that the present trend may encourage unbalanced approaches to world, regional and national problems, because fashionableness and sectoral lobbying may unduly influence the amount of attention and of financial resources given to a particular problem area, at the expense of other, perhaps more urgent issues.[5]

4. Special Sessions of the General Assembly: Decision Making for the New International Economic Order

Until 1974 special sessions of the General Assembly had only been held for urgent political problems. Early in 1974, after the "oil crisis" of the autumn of 1973, a group of developing countries led by Algeria which was then serving as the President of the group of Non-Aligned Countries, felt that the time was ripe to take drastic decisions regarding the international economic system; they therefore took the initiative in convening a special session of the General Assembly on "Raw Materials and Development" which met in April 1974.

This sixth special session of the General Assembly, which took place in an atmosphere of confrontation, produced a Declaration and a Programme of Action on the Establishment of a New International Economic Order (G.A. resolutions 3201 [S-VI] and 3202 [S-VI]). Although no vote took place, the situation was one of pseudo-consensus (see p. 128). Several countries, including the United States, were opposed to the essential parts of the Action Programme. The Programme for a New International Economic Order signalled, in essence, a strong request for various redistributions of a *quantitative* nature: a greater transfer of resources to developing countries, more voting rights, higher prices for their commodity exports in particular and for their other exports in general, improvement of other terms of trade, and even indexation: automatic improvement of certain or all commodity prices if inflation in the developed countries caused a rise in the prices of manufactured goods which would threaten the terms of trade of the developing countries.

The interval between the sixth and seventh special sessions had a sobering effect. Developing nations by and large realized that they could not "vote through" their wishes, but had to persuade the rich nations to share their points of view, that they had to negotiate, on the basis of strength or otherwise, to achieve concrete results.

In the autumn of 1975 another special session on "Development and International Economic Cooperation" took place and produced a real consensus decision, with a new program of work in the international economic field. At the closing meeting there were enthusiastic comments: "This system works" (D. Moynihan, U.S. permanent representative); "Things will never be the same again" (I. Richard, U.K. Permanent Representative).

The atmosphere and negotiations of the seventh session have been aptly characterized as follows:[6]

The atmosphere:

The Seventh Special Session of the United Nations General Assembly met, literally, at two levels. At the upper level, in the gold-domed grandeur of the Assembly Hall, delegates listened to the slow unfolding of the formal debate. The proceedings here went strictly by tradition and rule, with Algerian Foreign Minister Abdelaziz Bouteflika presiding from the green marble podium as representatives of 108 countries outlined their views and proposals on development and economic co-operation. Meanwhile, in the basement directly under the Assembly floor, work proceeded at a different pace. In small conference rooms blue with cigarette smoke, delegates met in closed sessions to haggle and argue over the issues dividing them. Here there was little formality to begin with and, as negotiations wore through long days and ever later into the nights, all unnecessary frills disappeared. Jackets were slung over the backs of chairs, shirt sleeves were rolled up, ties loosened, and voices rasped increasingly with fatigue and, occasionally, irritation.

The negotiations:

The negotiations in the basement conference rooms of the Assembly were between "contact groups". In main, they were between the 27-member contact group of the Group of 77 (developing countries) and the 12-member contact group of Western European and Other countries (WEO). This was as much because the socialist countries of Eastern Europe and China supported the position of the developing countries as it was because they did not play a major part in those aspects of the international economy which the developing countries want changed. As the Foreign Minister of the Federal Republic of Germany said: "Out of the total exports of the developing countries, 75% are absorbed by the Organization for Economic Co-operation and Development (OECD) countries alone, 20% constitute exchanges among the developing countries themselves, and 5% go to countries with centrally planned economies. This means the growth rates of the industrialized countries with free market economies and those of the developing countries are inseparably linked with each other."

Negotiations between the contact groups of the developing countries and the WEO countries were entirely in closed sessions. One set of negotiators met on the major problem areas of trade and transfer of resources; a second set worked on the other four items of the agenda, industrialization, science and technology, food and agriculture, and restructuring of the United Nations. The position of the European Community on major sections of the basic working paper tabled by the Group of 77 had already been subject to some negotiations during the preparatory phase of the Special Session. The United States' position, articulated as it was for the first time on the opening day of the conference, and containing as it did so many proposals, presented a major task for the negotiators.

As the first week passed and then the second, differences narrowed but not enough to warrant a full consensus. The scheduled end of the session came and went but the negotiations continued. They continued over the week-end of 13 September, continued all day and night on Monday. Finally, in the early dawn of Tuesday the bleary-eyed delegates reached agreement.

The resolution they agreed on consists of seven parts and covers all the major topics considered during the session. It was adopted without a vote in the closing plenary meeting on 16 September.

No doubt the success of the seventh special session must be sought in the existence of a real political will on all sides to come to a constructive result. The careful blend of public debate and private negotiations, with sufficient time and space available for both, helped in getting things done, in spite of the fact that only sixteen days were available.

A further special session of the General Assembly to consider progress in the establishment of a new international economic order and to adopt a new international development strategy for the decade of the 1980s has been scheduled for 1980. A committee of the whole of the Assembly has been established as an interim measure to serve as a forum for facilitating and expediting agreement on outstanding issues. The impetus for the creation of the committee of the whole as well as for the special session stems in part from the lack of substantial progress in the Conference on International Economic Cooperation (CIEC), a 27-nation group of developed and developing countries, which met from 1975 to 1977 outside the auspices of the United Nations. The participants in this conference agreed at its conclusion that the ongoing dialogue between developed and developing countries should be continued within the United Nations system.

5. Permanent or Quasi-permanent Ad Hoc Machinery

The General Assembly has frequently set up special machinery to deal with new issues. For instance, in 1959 the General Assembly Committee on the Peaceful Uses of Outer Space was established, the membership of which was gradually increased to 37.

Several treaties drafted by the Committee have come into force, including the 1967 Treaty on Principles Governing the Activities of States in the Exploration and Use of Outer Space, including the Moon and Other Celestial Bodies; the 1968 Agreement on the Rescue of Astronauts, the Return of Astronauts and the Return of Objects Launched into Outer Space; the 1972 Convention on International Liability for Damage Caused by Space Objects; and the 1976 Convention on Registration of Objects Launched into Outer Space. In 1978 the Committee finished drafting an agreement governing the activities of states on the moon and other celestial bodies, which was submitted for adoption to the General Assembly during its 1979 session. Another area where the Committee is working on draft principles is that of "remote sensing". Since the Committee functions on the basis of consensus, voting has almost never taken place. This work on outer space demonstrates that solid progress can be achieved even with limited but well-conceived institutional machinery to undertake such work. In other words, if there is a political will, progress can be made; if there is no political will, the finest institutions will not help. Of course, cooperation in the work on outer space benefits from the fact that outer space is still an area where no direct economic activity goes on.

The opposite is true for the oceans and the sea, because of the extensive economic uses of the oceans. While it is one thing for the General Assembly to proclaim that the sea bed and ocean floor beyond the limits of national jurisdiction, as well as the resources of the area, are the common heritage of mankind (G.A. resolution 2749 [XXV]), 17 December 1970), it is quite another thing to solve the problem of giving practical application to this principle. When the continuing meetings of the United Nations Conference on the Law of the Sea will have ended in general agreement, it will have been confirmed that a rational use of the seas is in the interest of all.

The rules of procedure of the Third United Nations Conference on the Law of the Sea, which started in 1974, stipulate that if at all possible decisions shall be made by consensus. The successive sessions of the Law of the Sea Conference have turned out to be real negotiating meetings, with no votes taken. Initially negotiations took place in three main committees and a number of working groups.

The First Committee dealt with all problems related to the international sea-bed area, the Second Committee with general aspects of the law of the sea, the Third Committee with a number of other problems, in particular marine environment, and research and technology. Certain common-interest groups emerged at an early stage, such as the Group of Coastal States, and the Group of Land-locked and Geographically Disadvantaged States (geographically disadvantaged states are countries with a sea-border but with an economic zone overlapping that of other countries). At the seventh session of the Third Conference (Geneva, spring 1978) seven negotiating groups of limited size, yet open-ended, were constituted to deal with certain hard-core issues:

Group No. 1: system of exploration and exploitation of the international sea-bed area; resource policy related to that area;
Group No. 2: financial arrangements between the International Sea-Bed Authority and sea-bed mining contractors;
Group No. 3: organs of the Sea-Bed Authority, their composition, powers, and functions;
Group No. 4: access of land-locked and certain other states to the living resources (fisheries) of the exclusive economic zone of coastal states;
Group No. 5: settlement of disputes relating to the exercise of the sovereign rights of coastal states in the exclusive economic zone;
Group No. 6: definition of the outer limits of the Continental Shelf and the question of payments and contributions with respect to the exploitation of the Continental Shelf beyond 200 miles;
Group No. 7: delimitation of maritime boundaries in the case of states with overlapping economic zones or continental shelves.

Other groups were the Drafting Committee and the Group of Legal Experts on the settlement of disputes relating to the sea-bed. Of crucial importance was the establishment, at the spring session of 1979, of a "Working Group of 21", composed almost equally of developed and developing countries, in order to obtain breakthroughs in crucial issues, in particular the regime for the sea-bed area. The actual country composition differed from subject to subject, and there were also "deputy members" for certain members, who could occupy the seat for an issue of particular interest to them.

There are other types of activity where the United Nations, through a pragmatic approach, has been able to set up appropriate machinery. Natural disasters, whether earthquakes, floods, or whatever, are being attended to by the Office of the U.N. Disaster Relief Coordinator (UNDRO), located in Geneva. For other situations analogous to disasters, ad hoc programs have been organized; one of these involved assistance to the Sahelian region which was afflicted by severe drought. Another was designed to assist a country such as Zambia which, because of the particular political situation in southern Africa, has been severely affected economically by its compliance with the embargo measures which the Security Council has imposed against Southern Rhodesia. Mozambique is in a similar situation.

The work of the U.N. High Commissioner for Refugees is a further example of how it is possible with a small organization to respond quickly to contemporary international problem situations: the needs of refugees unfortunately exist in many parts of the world. In 1951 the United Nations adopted a Convention relating to the Status of Refugees (General Assembly resolution 429 [V]), which was broadened to cover post-1951 refugees by a protocol which gave the U.N. High Commissioner for Refugees a permanent mandate (ECOSOC resolution 1186 [XLI] and General Assembly resolution 2198 [XXI]).

The U.N. Relief and Works Agency for Palestinian Refugees in the Near East (UNRWA) has been active since 1949, within the constraints imposed by a difficult political situation.

Another example of how the United Nations can meet a new challenge is provided by its work on transnational corporations. After a preparatory study by a "Group of Eminent Persons",[7] a Commission on Transnational Corporations has been created as a subsidiary body of the Economic and Social Council. On the Secretariat level there is a Centre for Transnational Corporations. In a very difficult field full of pitfalls, a useful start has been made with the cooperation of the private sector, in this case both the transnational corporations and the trade unions. The main elements of this work are the elaboration of a code of conduct (for governments and corporations) on transnational corporations, and the setting up of a comprehensive information system related to transnational corporations. The Commission on Transnational Corporations is assisted by a Group of Expert Advisers, composed of persons coming from transnational corporations, trade union organizations, and universities.

6. The Role of Groups

A bloc or group is composed of individual national delegations in pursuit of one or more common objectives. Special national interests are not submerged by participation in United Nations meetings. There are, at various times, divisions between the various regional areas, between developed and developing countries, between agricultural and industrial countries, between exporting and importing countries, between donors and recipients of economic aid, between totalitarian and democratic countries, between land-locked and coastal nations, as well as a whole range of other divisions. These divisions affect almost all the blocs. As a consequence, group solidarity is often somewhat artificial and occurs most frequently when an obvious but limited group interest is involved, e.g., in elections.

Some group division in the United Nations is undoubtedly necessary if the organization is to function at all efficiently. It may be even more important now in view of the growth in United Nations membership bringing the total over 150. As a point of comparison, the African group, for example, now numbers 49, only two less than the original United Nations membership, 51.

There would be much less stability or continuity to U.N. positions without some formal or informal groupings. The dangers of irresponsibility by individual delegations at the U.N. are great and represent the main basis for attacks on the U.N. as an institution. Groups tend to reduce these dangers and make isolated personal or national positions less frequent. To the extent that they unnecessarily exaggerate differences between groups of countries, they undo some of the value of the United Nations as an agency for the development of inter-regional understanding.

6.1. *Types of Groups*

Although the function of any group at a specific meeting is more important than its formal existence, a number of groups are so well known that they must be mentioned. They can be divided into:

a. regional groups;
b. political groups;
c. groups resulting from intergovernmental economic treaties;
d. groups based on a common level of economic development or some other common interest.

a. *Regional groups*
Some well-known examples are:

—African group[8]
—Asian group[8]
—ASEAN (Association of South East Asian Nations; Indonesia, Malaysia, Philippines, Singapore, Thailand)
—Latin American group[8]
—Nordic countries (Denmark, Finland, Iceland, Norway, Sweden)
—Socialist states[8] (Soviet Union and its allied Eastern European countries)
—Western European and others[8] (Canada, New Zealand, Australia). The United States, the Holy See and Switzerland participate as observers.

The formal geographical groups have two main reasons for existing: to exchange information and to agree on candidates for elections in cases where geographical criteria are relevant.

b. *Political groups*
Examples of political groups are:

—Commonwealth
—League of Arab States
—NATO
—Non-aligned Nations
—Organization of African Unity
—Organization of American States
—Warsaw Pact
—European Communities (European Political Cooperation)

The Commonwealth grouping has become, in most instances, a very loose one. It includes highly developed as well as developing countries in various stages of development. Politically, many of its members consider themselves "non-aligned". The non-aligned nations as a group develop and adopt common policy positions. These are usually adopted in communiqués at the end of ministerial or other meetings of the non-aligned countries, and then distributed to the General Assembly in a document listing all the agenda items covered by the communiqué. In the General Assembly, the non-aligned do a certain amount of caucusing, although less than the Group of 77. On the agenda item "Question of Cyprus", both in the Assembly and the Security Council, a small group of non-aligned nations, mainly India and Yugoslavia, is active in the resolution-drafting and negotiating process.

There are also even more informal political groups existing for specific purposes. Thus, in New York, the countries belonging to the Western European and others group (enlarged to include Japan) discuss political questions in the so-called Vinci Group, named after Ambassador Piero Vinci, the Italian permanent representative at the time of its founding. It usually meets at the Canadian Permanent Mission (which has one of the largest conference rooms available among the missions) and is co-chaired by the Canadian ambassador. The rationale for the existence of this group is that the formal WEO group strictly limits itself to electoral and related questions; it was founded in 1970 following the adoption of the Declaration on the Strengthening of International Security to provide these countries with a forum to discuss political questions. In recent years the Vinci Group has also become a consultative forum for the Western Europeans and others in dealing with economic questions in the Second Committee of the General Assembly; in effect, its function in that Committee is similar to that of Group B at UNCTAD in Geneva.

Another ad hoc political group is the Barton Group, which was named after Ambassador William Barton, Canadian permanent representative in Geneva (later in New York). In preparation of General Assembly sessions, this group discusses disarmament and arms control questions. Its members are the Member States of the European Communities, Australia, Canada, Greece, Japan, New Zealand, Norway, Portugal, Spain, Turkey, and the United States. Participation may differ from issue to issue. Occasionally other countries participate.

c. *Groups based on formal international economic agreements*

—BENELUX
—CMEA (Council for Mutual Economic Assistance)
—EEC (European Economic Community)
—EFTA (European Free Trade Association)
—OECD (Organization for Economic Cooperation and Development; includes all Western European countries, plus the United States, Canada, Japan, Australia, New Zealand; in addition, Yugoslavia has a special status).

The countries belonging to these groups try to coordinate their interests whenever this appears necessary. In the case of the EEC coordination on commercial and economic policy issues is obligatory under the Treaty of Rome establishing the EEC (see pp. 96-97).

d. *Groupings based on a common level of economic development or some·other common interest*

Prior to the first UNCTAD Conference (Geneva, 1964) the developing countries held consultations among themselves at conferences held in Cairo, which led to a joint declaration and common positions. At UNCTAD I these countries established a well-organized, streamlined set-up known at that time as the Group of 75, and later, with the addition of some more countries, as the Group of 77. During the conference the group held meetings, not only at head of delegation level, but also for each of the six commissions into which the conference had split up.

At the same UNCTAD Conference in 1964 the developed market economy countries also aimed at coordinating their positions. Their group, called Group B, consisted of the OECD countries as well as several smaller states (San Marino, Monaco, Liechtenstein, and the Holy See), all of which were represented at the UNCTAD Conference.

By and large the groupings emerging from the first UNCTAD Conference were the developing countries of the world on the one hand and the developed countries on the other, the latter being subdivided into a large number of market economy countries and a smaller number of state-trading countries.

The Group of 77 has become an important institutionalized group within the United Nations system and holds meetings in relation to many U.N. committees and bodies (see also pp. 99-100).

6.2. *Functions of Groups*

The functions performed by groups can be distinguished—in ascending order of commitment of the members—in the following way:

a. *To exchange information on all or part of the agenda of a conference, either in advance or during the conference*

b. *To develop common general positions on important agenda items, without definite voting commitment*

In this case, there is not only an exchange of information but also an effort to arrive at approximately identical positions for all delegations participating in group meetings. The OECD members, expanded by certain non-members, endeavor as the so-called Group B to coordinate their positions on various issues and agenda items in UNCTAD conferences.

Early in 1975 The Netherlands and Norway took the initiative to convene a consultation of a group of countries assumed to be "like-minded" on development issues, i.e., Denmark, Sweden, the United Kingdom and the two initiating countries. Meeting at the level of high officials the purpose was to arrive at common positions and if possible initiatives in the United Nations in general and ECOSOC in particular. The group met, also at the level of ministers responsible for development cooperation, at irregular intervals and with a composition changing at almost every meeting. Canada and Finland joined in 1975. Denmark, the U.K. and Canada left the group at the end of 1975, but Denmark and Canada came back in 1978. Belgium joined as from 1976, Austria in 1977. Ireland attended certain meetings of the group as from 1976. Throughout these years the core was constituted by the Nordic countries and The Netherlands. The group remained essentially consultative and did not aspire to formalize itself. It was occasionally successful in developing certain common concepts prior to important international conferences. At the fourth conference of UNCTAD (Nairobi 1976) the like-minded countries took the initiative regarding a statement on the question of the so-called "integrated commodities program". As mentioned before (p. 60), this statement, delivered on behalf of 20 developed countries, paved the way for subsequent negotiations leading, in 1979, to agreement "in principle", to establish a Common Fund to assist in financing the integrated commodities program. This was one case where a split in Group B came into the open.

Another informal grouping is the so-called Geneva Group, consisting of Australia, Belgium, Canada, the Federal Republic of Germany, France, Italy, Japan, The Netherlands, the United Kingdom and the United States, with Sweden and Switzerland as observers. It discusses principally administrative and budgetary matters, and meets in Geneva and other cities where the headquarters of specialized agencies are located.

c. *To develop common positions on certain agenda items or initiatives with agreement on how to vote*

Efforts to find not only common positions, but also agreements on how to vote, can and do occur in almost every group. They occur systematically in groups of nations bound together by a treaty requiring common points of view on certain questions as is the case for the member countries of the European Communities.

More and more in conferences of other U.N. meetings one can encounter examples of geographical, political or ad hoc groups deciding to vote in a certain way on draft proposals, on amendments, or on an expected procedural move. Explicit coordination of voting behavior is increasing, while in the past tacit or at most an improvised understanding arrived at just before voting led to voting alignments. Frequently, there is an explanation of the vote by one member of a group on behalf of that whole group.

d. *To agree on candidates to be put forward by the group or on a common vote for candidates outside the group*

This is one of the functions where development of a common point of view has meaning only if there is also agreement on how to vote. This may be for a single agreed slate of candidates of the grouping itself as well as for some combination out of a number of competing candidates of other groups. In connection with such election agreements there may be a joint plan of campaign for or against other candidates.

The formation of groups specifically designed to put forward candidates for certain positions has been motivated by the growing habit of taking a basic decision to allocate the number of seats going to certain groups. In chapter 2 (p. 29) we have indicated the arrangements regarding the election of the vice-presidents of the General Assembly and the chairmen of the seven Main Committees. The regional distribution of the non-permanent seats on the Security Council and of all seats on the Economic and Social Council was specified in those resolutions which the General Assembly adopted in calling for Charter amendments to enlarge the membership of those bodies.

e. *To agree on a common spokesman, and on the contents of the statement to be delivered*

A group of sponsors of a draft resolution usually agree on a common spokesman to introduce its text in the meetings. Furthermore, any of the groups which we have discussed above may, in a particular situation, decide on a common spokesman. The Group of 77 and the European Communities normally have their statements delivered by the delegation of the country which is the current chairman.

f. *To undertake joint action for or against a proposal*

Although linked to functions b. and c. such a ''lobbying'' function can be separate. A common position and an agreement on voting do not necessarily entail joint lobbying. Conversely, a joint lobbying campaign obviously requires an agreed position on the proposal or issue behind it.

92

7. Non-governmental Organizations (NGOs)

One of the potentially important innovations of the U.N. Charter was its Article 71, which gave the Economic and Social Council the right to make "suitable arrangements for consultation" with non-governmental organizations. As a result, as of January 1980, approximately 800 such organizations have a consultative status, divided into three categories:

Category I: Organizations which are concerned with most of the activities of the Council and can demonstrate to the satisfaction of the Council that they have marked and sustained contributions to make to the achievement of the objectives of the United Nations (with respect to international, economic, social, cultural, educational, health, scientific, technological and related matters and to questions of human rights), and are closely involved with the economic and social life of the peoples of the areas they represent and whose membership, which should be considerable, is broadly representative of major segments of population in a large number of countries.

Category II: Organizations which have a special competence in, and are concerned specifically with, only a few of the fields of activity covered by the Council, and which are known internationally within the fields for which they have or seek consultative status.

Roster: Other organizations which do not have general or special consultative status but which the Council, or the Secretary-General of the United Nations in consultation with the Council or its Committee on Non-Governmental Organizations, considers can make occasional and useful contributions to the work of the Council, or its subsidiary bodies or other United Nations bodies within their competence.

Granting consultative status entitles the organization to propose agenda items for consideration by the Council or its subsidiary bodies (category I), attend meetings (categories I and II and Roster), submit written statements (categories I and II and Roster) and be granted hearings (categories I and II).[9]

These arrangements have, however, had only limited effect. At Economic and Social Council sessions, papers submitted by non-governmental organizations, or speeches delivered by their representatives, with rare exceptions, receive scant attention.

However, there has been an increase in the role of non-governmental organizations in two specific ways—as advocates for human rights and as participants in the ad hoc world conferences organized under United Nations auspices.

Several international non-governmental organizations, such as Amnesty International and the International Commission of Jurists, have become well known, and indeed feared in certain quarters, for their relentless work on fact finding related to situations where human rights are suspected to have been violated. The work of NGOs in the area of human rights has done what the United Nations should have done, but was not permitted to do in most cases: ascertain the facts of human rights violations and make them public.

At the recent series of U.N.-sponsored world conferences, non-governmental organizations organized "parallel" conferences focusing attention on the issues involved and pushing for action. The first such parallel conference, called the Forum, was organized during the 1972 Stockholm Conference on the Environment.

The following description of the situation at the World Food Conference in Rome in 1974 shows how NGO representatives were able to participate in the actual decision-making process:

> While NGO's in consultative status with the Economic and Social Council have certain well-defined prerogatives, such as making written or oral statements, other lobbying activities depend more on luck, circumstances or just plain enterprise. Seldom have NGO's had such privileges as some made for themselves at Rome. The International Organization of Consumers Unions, for example, was one of several NGO's that spoke to one of the three Conference committees. Others, such as the Church World Service and World Conference on Religion and Peace, were made members of drafting committees. The traditional women's and population lobbies were also active at Rome and can take credit for tangible, if modest, successes.[10]

Other typical cases of parallel conferences were the Population Tribune held in connection with the World Population Conference in August, 1974, the International Women's Year Tribune which ran parallel to the International Women's Year Conference in Mexico City in June 1975, and the NGO Forum on the World Economic Order which took place simultaneously with the seventh special session of the U.N. General Assembly.

In addition, representatives of 25 NGOs and six research institutes were allowed to address the General Assembly, constituted as an ad hoc committee, during the tenth special session devoted to disarmament (1978). This was the first time that representatives of a broad section of such organizations addressed the Assembly on an issue of such world-wide importance as disarmament.

While the non-governmental organizations referred to so far have some special focus, there are a number of NGOs which support the United Nations generally, e.g., the United Nations associations in various countries, united in the World Federation of United Nations Associations (WFUNA). There are also certain national organizations, such as "U.N. We Believe" and the "Stanley Foundation" in the United States which engage in activities bringing the private sector and the United Nations closer together.

94

8. Liberation Movements

Liberation movements are certainly a new element in the United Nations. They consider themselves as the precursor of the government of the territory they have set out to liberate, and are recognized by (in some cases) large numbers of Member States of the United Nations.

We have seen (p. 32, p. 46), that certain liberation movements, such as the Palestine Liberation Organization (PLO), and the South West Africa People's Organization (SWAPO) have obtained a status within the United Nations. The PLO is recognized by the General Assembly as "the representative of the Palestinian people" (resolution 3236 [XXIX]), SWAPO as "the authentic representative of the Namibian people" (resolution 3399 [XXX]).

In the drafting of resolutions under the agenda item "Question of Palestine" the PLO is consulted, or it may prepare drafts itself. Similarly, the SWAPO gets involved in the drafting of resolutions on Namibia (South-West Africa).

Somewhere between governments and non-governmental organizations, liberation movements have become, in their own particular way, a participant in United Nations decision making.

9. Intergovernmental Organizations

In the early days of the United Nations, only the Organization of American States (OAS) had consultative status with the General Assembly. In recent years a number of other intergovernmental organizations have found it useful to acquire such status. The list of organizations having acquired permanent observer status with the General Assembly is as follows (September 1979):

—Agency for Cultural and Technical Cooperation (G.A. resolution 33/18)
—Commonwealth Secretariat (G.A. resolution 31/3)
—Council for Mutual Economic Assistance (G.A. resolution 3209 [XXIX])
—European Economic Community (G.A. resolution 3208 [XXIX])
—Islamic Conference (G.A. resolution 3369 [XXX])
—League of Arab States (G.A. resolution 477 [V])
—Organization of African Unity (G.A. resolution 2011 [XX])
—Organization of American States (G.A. resolution 253 [XIII])

Of these organizations, the European Economic Community, the League of Arab States, the Organization of African Unity, and the Organization of American States maintain permanent missions at United Nations headquarters.

The Group of 77 and the Non-Aligned Movement are not formally organized bodies, and therefore have no formal status in the General Assembly. Yet their influence is important, and, in the case of the Group of 77, often decisive.

9.1. *The European Communities (EC) and European Political Cooperation (EPC)*

The European Communities have become a lobbying and caucusing group of considerable importance, manifesting itself in two different incarnations. On economic matters, the nine member countries,[11] under the Treaty of Rome (25 March 1957, effective 1 January 1958) and subsequent decisions, are committed to operate as a unit on all matters coming under the Treaty of Rome, i.e., in principle, all economic matters. As a result, in the Economic and Social Council and in the Second Committee of the General Assembly, they make statements through a common spokesman—also as an "explanation of vote"— and cast their votes in pre-agreed identical ways.

The way that this group votes is a matter of interest to numerous other delegations; perhaps not only because of particular links which countries may have with the EC or its member countries, but also because it is known that on many matters the EC countries do not have identical positions to start with. Other delegations apparently reason that, if the EC countries have come to a common voting pattern, that position must be based on an "average" and perhaps consensus attitude. Of course, there are differences of opinion within the EC Member States on the extent of their commitment under the Treaty of Rome. For example, on matters concerning the restructuring of the United Nations economic and social sectors, The Netherlands and Denmark felt that any agreement on common positions of the nine was strictly voluntary.

A common statement of the EC in ECOSOC or the Second Committee is most often delivered by the representative of the country holding the EC presidency for the current semester (the EC chairmanship rotates every six months in alphabetical order). Occasionally it is delivered by the representative of the European Commission, in particular in matters where the EC Member States have delegated certain powers and functions to the Commission. This is particularly the case in all matters of commercial policy in the strict sense, in particular those related to tariff or trade negotiations.

The second, and essentially different method of EC coordination emanates from what is called "European Political Cooperation (EPC). This is an entirely voluntary effort, without an institutional basis, to:

a. consult each other and exchange information on current political issues of interest to all Member States of the EC;
b. establish coordinated policy positions; and
c. vote identically, on the basis of the positions referred to under b., in international organizations.

Among the EC Member States EPC operates in the form of monthly (more often if necessary) meetings of the political directors of the ministries of foreign affairs, of working parties which are more or less permanent (for example on certain regions) and of meetings of foreign ministers. The foreign ministers meet four times yearly (twice each half year in the capital of the government presiding the EC), with an additional informal meeting every six months, called "Gymnich type meetings" (after the German castle where the first such meeting took place). The foreign ministers also, if necessary, discuss EPC subjects when they meet in their capacity of members of the Council of Ministers of the European Communities (but strictly separated from these Council meetings).

At the United Nations EPC has over the years assumed elaborate forms. Once a week (less often outside the General Assembly period) the ambassadors meet to discuss current matters, and try to establish common positions, or discuss areas of disagreement.

For example, during the sessions of the General Assembly the EC representatives on the seven Main Committees meet at least once a week, usually more often. They compare instructions from their capitals; in case of conflicting instructions, the matter is referred to the meeting of ambassadors. If time presses, each delegation will report back to its capital, perhaps recommending a common line of action for the EC based on an emerging majority view. If there is a common position, the country occupying the chair of the EC for the current semester will deliver a statement or explanation of vote, or both, beginning with approximately the following words: "On behalf of the Member States of the European Communities I wish to state..."

Broad policy positions have been worked out by the EC on such issues as the Middle East problem, southern Africa issues (*apartheid;*

97

Southern Rhodesia, Namibia), and the Cyprus question. These positions are reflected in declarations emanating from ministerial meetings of the EC countries. Statements delivered on behalf of the EC have gradually been increasing in number, especially in the General Assembly. As for economic matters the views of the EC countries on political issues also are frequently solicited before a vote takes place: the EC is a nucleus of countries whose average position is seen as a mirror of a possible consensus world opinion.

A further interesting development has been that representatives of parties involved in some conflict may ask to be received and "heard" by the ambassadors of the EC countries. This has regularly happened during the past several years in the case of parties to the Middle East and Cyprus conflicts, whose representatives, occasionally ministers, requested to be heard by the ambassadors of the nine, in confidential, informal meetings.

In terms of voting the governments of the EC are gradually moving toward greater cohesion, as this statistic shows (in percentages):

	1976	1977	1978
common votes, including consensus decisions	82	83,5	84
divided votes	18	16,5	16

9.2. *The Group of 77*

The Group of 77 was created to prepare common positions on trade and aid issues for negotiations with developed nations. The success obtained at the first UNCTAD Conference, including the establishment of permanent UNCTAD machinery against the wishes of most developed countries—which instead wanted to give certain additional tasks to the Economic and Social Council—encouraged the 77 to continue. They now constitute a major decision-making element in the economic field, with (January 1980) 118 voting members.

The Group of 77 has no permanent secretariat. The chairmanship in New York rotates among regions about every twelve months; in Geneva, it rotates every four months so that each region chairs the

Group once during the year. The chairing countries provide minimal secretarial services. The working methods of the Group of 77 also differ between New York and Geneva. In Geneva, the three regional groups have separate positions and then try to harmonize them; they also sit by region in meetings of the Group of 77. In New York there is no seating by region and there are usually no separate regional positions on issues.

The Group of 77 often meets privately in relation to many U.N. committees dealing with issues of interest to the Group. Developed nations have become accustomed to wait for position papers or statements from the Group of 77 to be presented during almost every U.N. meeting. Draft resolutions are regularly submitted by a single developing country, usually the country holding the current chairmanship of the Group of 77, "in the name of the countries belonging to the Group of 77."

Since the Group of 77 constitutes a majority in both the General Assembly and the Economic and Social Council, as well as in most other U.N. bodies, it has been argued that it is undemocratic to submit a draft resolution in the name of a majority. In practice, however, the Group of 77 has gradually shown its awareness that it must aim at consensus decisions, and hence has been willing to negotiate towards that end.

On broad issues of development economics, the Group of 77 has held together. It works most effectively when it is dealing with principles or conceptual proposals. A further dimension has also been added in recent years with the increase in emphasis on economic and technical cooperation among the developing countries themselves. This was highlighted by the adoption of the Arusha Program for Collective Self-Reliance at the fourth ministerial meeting of the Group of 77 early 1979. Problems do arise, however, when negotiations take place on specific issues. There are increasing signs that the obviously great differences in economic levels and stages of development among developing countries as well as differences in concrete economic interests have led to varying viewpoints among them. As a result, in certain cases, common position papers have been arrived at only with great difficulty. For example, at the United Nations Conference on the Law of the Sea, developing countries are divided on many issues depending on whether they are land-locked or coastal states, producers or consumers of certain raw materials, and so forth.

While the original idea behind the creation of the Group of 77 was to prepare common positions on conceptual issues, the Group has become increasingly institutionalized to the point that it is expected to take a group position on many draft resolutions or candidatures.

However, there is not always automatic solidarity among the 77 in supporting a developing country against a developed country. For example, in 1977 a developing country (Mexico) competed with a developed country (Austria) in the Second Committee of the General Assembly for the site of the U.N. Conference on the Application of Science and Technology to Developing Countries (1979). The developing country tried to push through its candidature without being prepared to consult on the matter. This attitude caused unhappiness among its friends, and it did not win the endorsement of the Group of 77. When it came to the vote by secret ballot in plenary, it lost out decisively to the developed country.

On balance, though, there is no doubt that the ''countervailing power'' provided by the Group of 77 is of considerable importance.

Notes to chapter 5

1. International Foundation for Development Alternatives (IFDA) Dossier No. 11, Nyon, Switzerland, September 1979. The First U.N. Development Decade is enshrined in General Assembly resolution 1710 (XVI).

2. See chapter 10 for a case study on the setting up of the U.N. Special Fund.

3. R. Jackson, *A Study of the Capacity of the U.N. Development System,* 2 vols. (New York: United Nations, 1969). See also the review by Johan Kaufmann, ''The Capacity of the U.N. Development Programme: the Jackson Report,'' *International Organization,* vol. XXV, No. 4, 1971. Within the framework of UNDP the successful U.N. Fund for Population Activities exists. For its history see: Rafael M. Salas, *International Population Activities: The First Decade* (New York: Pergamon Press, 1979).

4. Joseph Gold, *The Second Amendment of the Fund's Articles of Agreement* (Washington, D.C.: International Monetary Fund, 1978, Pamphlet Series No. 25), p. 20. The decisions on both the Interim Committee of the IMF and on the Development Committee can be found in *Selected Decisions of the International Monetary Fund* (Washington, D.C.: International Monetary Fund, 10 May 1976), resolutions 29-8, 29-9.

5. On global conferences see: N. Graham and S. Haggard, ''Diplomacy in Global Conferences,'' in *UNITAR News,* vol. XI, 1979 (U.N. Institute for Training and Research, New York). Also: Thomas G. Weiss and Robert S. Jordan, *The World Food Conference and General Problem Solving* (New York: Praeger, 1976).

6. *The Seventh Special Session of the General Assembly, 1-16 September 1975, Round-up and Resolution* (New York: United Nations, 1975). A voluminous literature is forthcoming on the New International Economic Order. UNITAR is sponsoring a library of some 20 volumes on the NIEO. The initial volume is: E. Laszlo, R.M. Baker, E. Eisenberg, V. Raman, *The Objectives of the New International Economic Order* (Elmsford, N.Y.: Pergamon Press, 1978). On decision-making aspects see: Johan Kaufmann, ''Decision-Making for the New International Economic Order,'' in A.J. Dolman and

J. van Ettinger (ed.), *Partners in Tomorrow* (Essays for J. Tinbergen on his 75th birthday) (New York: E.P. Dutton, 1978); Robert W. Gregg (ed.), *An Institutional Framework for A New International Economic Order,* edited for UNITAR, 1980. Forceful and multi-facetted pleas in favor of the NIEO can be found in these two volumes: J. Tinbergen (coordinator), *Reshaping the International Order* (New York: E.P. Dutton, 1976); M. Nerfin (project director), *What Now,* The 1975 Dag Hammarskjöld Report, Development Dialogue (Uppsala: Dag Hammarskjöld Foundation, 1975). The activities around these two books led to the establishment of two foundations: the RIO (Reshaping the International Order) Foundation, Rotterdam, The Netherlands, and the International Foundation for Development Alternatives, Nyon, Switzerland.

7. *Report of the Group of Eminent Persons to Study the Impact of Multinational Corporations on Development and on International Relations,* doc. E/5500, rev. 1 (New York: United Nations, 1974).

8. These are the geographical groups referred to in certain General Assembly resolutions as being entitled to a specific number of seats or memberships (e.g., vice-presidencies of the General Assembly, number of seats on ECOSOC).

9. ECOSOC resolutions 288 (X) of 1950 and 1296 (XLIV) of 1968.

10. Homer A. Jack, "A persistent species at Rome: NGO's," *America,* 1 March 1975, as quoted in Berhanykun Andemicael (ed.), *Non-Governmental Organizations in International Cooperation for Development* (New York: UNITAR (paper no. 4 by A. Archer), 1978). On the role of NGO's in U.N. human rights activities see: Theo C. van Boven, "Partners in the Promotion and Protection of Human Rights," in H. Meyers and E.W. Vierdag, op. cit., pp. 55-71.

11. As of 1 January 1981 ten, with the accession of Greece to the Communities. For an analysis of European views on world problems, see: F.A.M. Alting von Geusau, *European Perspectives on World Order* (Leiden: A.W. Sijthoff, 1975).

Chapter 6

The People Who Do It:
Permanent Missions and Non-permanent Delegations, Their Organization and Methods

1. Missions and Delegations

A distinction must be made between a "mission" to the United Nations and a "delegation" to a particular meeting. Almost all members of the United Nations have in one form or another a "permanent mission to the U.N." located in New York. The permanent missions have the same continuing functions in relation to the U.N. and its headquarters as an embassy does in the national capital of a country. A permanent mission is headed by a permanent representative, generally with the rank and status of an ambassador, and has a varying complement of alternate or deputy permanent representatives, ministers, counsellors, first, second and third secretaries with supporting staffs. Most countries also find it necessary to maintain permanent missions at the United Nations office at Geneva, Switzerland, because so many U.N. meetings are held in the Palais des Nations and also because Geneva is the headquarters of a number of specialized agencies. These missions in New York or Geneva are staffed with officers as part of the usual tours abroad necessary in most foreign services. They maintain contact with the U.N. Secretariat on a continuous basis, report on previous meetings, anticipate coming meetings and act as a channel of communication and center of information for the relationships of their country with the U.N.

A "delegation" is established and accredited (usually by a formal note to the Secretary-General) for a particular meeting or series of meetings. Each year governments appoint a delegation to that particular session of the General Assembly or to a specific meeting of a U.N. body. Almost invariably such delegations include members of the permanent missions as advisers or as representatives. A member of a permanent mission appointed to a particular delegation therefore has two jobs for that period since he must keep up the continuing work in the mission for which he is responsible, in addition to participating in the work of the delegation.

While delegation working methods within the United Nations to some extent reflect the characteristics of their national governments, the structure and operations of the United Nations are such that most governments have been obliged to organize their representation at the U.N. on more or less the same pattern.

One of the most obvious problems facing missions at the United Nations is the wide variety of subjects which come before it. The scope of items dealt with by the Organization as reflected in the agendas of the various organs, especially the General Assembly, keeps increasing. Most missions have specialists in various fields: political, economic, legal, human rights, etc. Many items and issues recur year after year. The ease with which the larger delegations can communicate by telex with their capitals has the effect that often not even technical items are left to members of permanent missions to deal with.

2. Delegation Organization

Most delegations to the General Assembly are set up along roughly the lines described below, subject to individual variations depending on time and circumstances. The same general pattern, with changes in size and seniority, applies to delegations to certain other U.N. bodies, such as the Economic and Social Council.

The basis of any General Assembly delegation consists of one or more officials of the country's ministry of foreign affairs and the staff of the country's permanent mission to the United Nations. Governments tend to post experienced senior officials as the heads of the permanent missions in New York, both because of the importance of United Nations business and because the permanent representative in New York has a wide and significant representational function to fulfill. These missions are subject to pressure from other missions and to questioning by representatives of press and other communications media. Permanent representatives therefore are obliged to be well informed on government policy. Changes of national governments and of national policies are reflected almost immediately in the attitudes of the permanent missions to the U.N. To the extent that a country's foreign representation is determined on political grounds, the head and senior staff of a permanent mission may be changed soon after control in the national capital changes.

The head of a General Assembly delegation is often the foreign minister. The thirty-third session of the General Assembly saw this ministerial attendance: 4 heads of state, 6 heads of government, 118 ministers for foreign affairs, 7 other ministers. However, since the General Assembly generally meets for a period of approximately three months and sometimes longer, ministers seldom stay for the entire period.

In the absence of the foreign minister or the prime minister, the acting head of delegation is usually the permanent representative in New York. The first week of a General Assembly session is devoted to elections of officers and procedural questions, including the discussion of additionally proposed agenda items, first in the General Committee, then in plenary. The "General Debate" then follows (see p. 27).

It is customary for foreign ministers of Member States to congregate in large numbers at the United Nations in New York during the first weeks of each General Assembly session, which, in accordance with the Rules of Procedure, begins on the third Tuesday of September. Although each minister remains in New York only five days or so, he will try to meet a maximum number of other foreign ministers during his stay. These encounters may take place in the so-called Indonesian Lounge—named after sculptures donated by Indonesia—which is conveniently located directly in front of the General Assembly Hall, or another mutually agreeable place in the U.N. building such as a small meeting room obtained for this purpose through the Secretariat. If there is some more difficult business to be discussed, the encounter may well take place at the permanent mission offices or at the ambassador's residence of either country. In a five-day stay each minister may be able to see as many as thirty to forty colleagues, in a more relaxed atmosphere than is usually possible in formal bilateral visits to each other's capitals.

In some ways it is unfortunate that ministers often attend the least important part of a General Assembly session, since its final period requires more decisions to be made by the highest national authorities. However, the simultaneous attendance of many senior international figures, even if only at the beginning of a session, has great value in itself in facilitating informal discussions.

The political importance as well as the experience of individuals acting at the United Nations on behalf of governments have obvious significance since U.N. debates and decisions are affected considerably by the personalities of the representatives. The personality of the head of a country's delegation or permanent mission influences in many ways the composite personality of the delegation and even of the country concerned in the eyes of other delegates. An individual delegate can do much at the U.N. to improve or impair his country's reputation in international affairs. At the same time his own attitudes may be altered. Sometimes too long a period of service at the U.N. results in cynicism concerning the prospects for useful international cooperation. In other cases the result may be an unbalanced view of the importance of the institution.[1]

A Member State of the United Nations is authorized to send five delegates, whose travel expenses are reimbursed out of the U.N. budget, and five alternate delegates to each session of the General Assembly. These representatives are generally members of legislatures, senior officials of a government, or private individuals of national importance chosen by the government concerned. In addition, each delegation will have advisers, many of whom will be permanent mission members.

Occasionally there may be difficulties in relations between the official delegates, who are often very senior and experienced, and their advisers, who are usually younger but who are expected to be technical and tactical experts in U.N. matters. As a rule, however, there appears to be mutual benefit, the advisers gaining from the political experience of the delegate and the latter learning the "tricks of the trade" of the U.N. from his advisers. The delegate and adviser relationship depends largely on the establishment of a satisfactory personal understanding rather than precise regulations.[2]

Quite often a senior politician or national figure attached to a U.N. delegation may bring fresh insight to U.N. debates. Generally, however, the established instructions of the national government take precedence over a delegate's personal views. Only rarely, and then only when the representative is very senior or of an almost completely independent mind and position, will a delegate want to, or indeed be able to, change the basic instructions prepared by his government for a U.N. meeting. Such cases create great difficulty for the civil servant members of the delegations who must ensure that government instructions are carried out.

The practice of including members of parliament or other figures of national importance in a delegation is considered to have been salutary, because the inclusion of such people may later result in a better understanding of U.N. matters in the parliaments and elsewhere in the country. On occasion, however, a term as a U.N. delegate has served to exaggerate previously held prejudices against the U.N.[3]

The combination of the political element represented by members of parliament and the technical element represented by government officials will result in the more effective reflection of the national interests of the country concerned. Some governments designate parliamentarians as members of the official delegation whether they are supporters of or in opposition to the administration. Other governments make it their practice to appoint parliamentarians as delegates only if they are members of the party in power.

At this point one might note that women are playing an increasing role in United Nations affairs, not only in what are often considered traditional women's activities, such as the Commission on the Status of Women or the Third Committee (Social, Humanitarian and Cultural) of the General Assembly, but also as members of permanent missions and delegations of all kinds. When we use "he" or "his" in referring to a delegate, we really mean he or she and his or her. The problem may arise of whether one should address the chairman as "chairperson". Should one speak of "gentlepersonly" behavior? Should the chairman say, when giving the floor to a delegation without knowing who will actually address the meeting: "The next speaker on my list is the delegate of ..., and I give him or her the floor"? The author was possibly the first to have done so during a debate at the General Assembly in 1977, when, as vice-president, he substituted for the president at part of a meeting.[4]

Certain delegates to the General Assembly and to some of the other U.N. bodies tend to return to the meetings year after year. In many cases special relationships are established and the opening of a U.N. meeting of almost any kind is an occasion for a renewal of friendships. Shared experiences at U.N. meetings tend to allow representatives from countries which are frequently at odds elsewhere at least to make the acquaintance of one another. Conflicts between national policies debated in a public place tend to make all participants colleagues during a difficult session even though they are opponents. The club-like atmosphere of the United Nations also promotes this general friendliness. One may often find delegates, who have been opposing each other at a formal meeting, drinking coffee or cocktails together. These relationships tend to be superficial, however, since they are often the result of the unwritten code of pleasant behavior to which people adhere in the U.N. building.

For delegates to return year after year to the same U.N. meetings produces some disadvantages. Some build little empires which they guard jealously, at times without much regard for the coordination of government positions in their own national capital. They become much better informed than others in their governments about the subject in question. This situation may lead to excessive concern with relatively unimportant issues and slower U.N. debates than necessary.

Most delegations hold formal delegation meetings. Sometimes these take the form of regular sessions in which the events of the previous day and the possibilities for the future are reviewed in each of the fields for which the delegation members are responsible. The larger the delegation meeting the more formal and generally the less useful its proceedings. A very large delegation meeting is not suitable for taking all the major decisions of a delegation simply because there is no time to debate all the issues fully with all the members of a delegation whether they have any responsibility for the subject or not. Therefore, many major decisions are taken in smaller meetings of the head of delegation and advisers and delegates concerned with specific issues.

During the General Assembly many delegations will have their internal delegation meeting three times a week from 9:00 or 9:30 to 10:30. This permits both a review of major points in order to arrive at delegation positions not covered by the delegation's instructions and coordination where necessary of the views of delegates serving on different committees. However, all too frequent meetings sometimes adversely affect the ability of members of a delegation to do their work of drafting resolutions and discussing issues with other delegations early each morning. Much of the informal consultation at a U.N. meeting takes place just before the formal meetings begin. This is one reason why U.N. meetings almost always start late. It would be a poor chairman who started the meeting on time if this action deprived delegates of the time for consultation which would ensure the success of the meeting.

3. Coordination of Political and Financial Objectives

One of the important differences which affects many issues coming before the United Nations and which must be resolved within each delegation is the potential conflict between political or economic objectives on the one hand and their financial implications on the other. The freedom of action of representatives is greater when the question they are dealing with has no immediate financial implications. The financial influences within a delegation are primarily the expression of domestic economic influences and reflect both international and national budgetary limitations. In some delegations representatives with

108

budgetary responsibilities have a more direct line of authority to their superiors in the national capitals than the representatives with political responsibilities. The political lines of authority in a delegation run not only to the various sections in the ministry of foreign affairs, but also usually through that ministry, as part of its coordinating function, to other government departments and to political authorities in the country itself. In some delegations the finance ministry expert is completely absorbed into the delegation and, while a delegation member, he does not seek instructions directly from his own ministry. Much will depend on the position of the finance ministry in the government concerned and on whether it has general or limited responsibilities. Delegations which take a position on issues with financial implications without satisfying themselves that the financial authorities of their government will in fact support their position, are placing themselves and the U.N. in danger of irresponsible action. Conversely, a delegation which is able to back its position with financial resources is able to play a more effective role at the U.N. than might otherwise be the case.

Differences between political and economic objectives exist not only within delegations, but are also reflected in the General Assembly. The Fifth Committee and its organ, the Advisory Committee on Administrative and Budgetary Questions, have the responsibility of passing budgetary judgments on the proposals of other committees. There are two main concepts of the role of the Fifth Committee: one is that the governments which have taken a decision in another U.N. organ take their final decision in the Fifth Committee. From this standpoint it can "overrule" any other organ on financial grounds. The other view is, that once a substantive decision has been taken elsewhere, the Fifth Committee may examine its financial implications, but may not alter its essential features. Thus, sometimes delegations favor programs in one committee which they oppose later in the Fifth Committee. Usually governments endeavor to establish priorities for the different U.N. programs within the limits of the resources which they have available for U.N. purposes. In turn these resources are allocated within the limitations of national budgetary pressures. In general governments find it more difficult to obtain allocations for U.N. programs than for national programs. It is therefore necessary that each proposal for expenditure on behalf of U.N. programs is most carefully prepared. There are few votes to be gained by a national politician in supporting U.N. activities which involve major expenditures. In some cases, however, depending on local political factors, U.N. programs have had strong support. U.N. refugee programs have sometimes enjoyed this type of support as have U.N. programs for the economic development of developing countries, for example in The Netherlands, Norway, Sweden and Canada.

Related to the problem of coordination of policy within a delegation is, of course, that of coordinating policy in a national capital among the various authorities concerned. The importance of this problem was recognized early in the history of the United Nations by resolution 125 (II) of the General Assembly (1947) which urged governments to establish appropriate procedures.

If a government has a complicated or decentralized system which affects the authority and speed of the central authorities in issuing instructions, it may be at a disadvantage in the U.N. in comparison with those governments where the national decision-making process is concentrated and quick. The work of the Committee for Programme and Coordination (see p. 65) has had a useful effect in this respect, because it has clarified program issues.

4. Instructions

There are considerable differences in the amount and nature of instructions which delegations receive. Some are given lengthy and detailed instructions which severely limit their freedom of manoeuvre. Some governments instruct their delegation in terms of the position of other governments, i.e., "Vote more or less like ..." or "If ... votes 'no' you can abstain." Some governments provide no instructions at all, leaving matters to the discretion of the delegation. The ideal instructions would result from careful study by the officials of the interested departments in the national capital and subsequent approval by the highest political authorities of the general positions to be adopted. Such ideal instructions would be specific as to objectives and the degree of activity required but would leave considerable freedom of action to the delegation if events took an unexpected turn. The precise drafting of the language of a resolution cannot usually be done on the basis of instructions prepared in advance. Increasingly, instructions are the result of consultation or coordination within certain groupings, e.g., the European Communities, the Group of 77, or the Non-Aligned Movement.

No matter how close or how continuous contact may be between delegations in New York and the authorities in their national capitals, many decisions remain the responsibility of the local representatives.

110

At the U.N. events often move so quickly and their development is so complicated that it is virtually impossible to report all the relevant factors and have them taken into account before a decision is taken and instructions are despatched from headquarters. Of course, on decisions of great importance there is often a "strategic postponement" to give delegations time to obtain instructions from home. The distance from New York to the national capital and the efficiency of the confidential communications facilities available also influence the type of instructions possible for each delegation.

A difficult situation may arise when telephoned last-minute instructions are different from previous written instructions. I happen to know of one case which developed in the following unfortunate way: the permanent representative of a medium-sized country had been instructed by telegram to vote "no" on a certain, politically sensitive resolution (sensitive also in terms of domestic politics). On the day of the voting he received telephoned instructions from his foreign minister to align his vote to that of a certain friendly country, which might mean voting "abstention"; he was also requested to get in touch by telephone with his foreign minister just before voting, to get final instructions. However, at the crucial moment it was not possible to get through to the foreign minister. The permanent representative decided to vote "abstention", in agreement with the delegation of the friendly country to which he was supposed to align himself.

Finally, the instruction pattern of a government is influenced by domestic or other issues which may overshadow U.N. discussions. In such cases officials who should be involved in the preparation of instructions for a delegation to the U.N. may only be able to give little attention to U.N. matters.

5. Relations with Other Delegations

In New York delegations are generally free to interpret within certain limits the positions of their governments but cannot take major policy decisions on the spot unless the foreign minister or another competent authority is present and able to assume responsibility. Therefore, if a delegation wishes to influence the policy of another delegation on some major specific issue, it must generally do so through diplomatic channels. The first approach having been made through U.N. delegations, others may be made elsewhere. If the Blank delegation wishes to supplement its contacts at the U.N. with the delegation of Dot, there are a number of courses open. If there happens to be a meeting of foreign ministers or heads of government taking place concurrently, conversations could take place within that context. Whether the embassy of Dot in the Blank capital is approached by the Blank ministry of foreign affairs or whether the Blank ambassador in Dot is asked to speak to the appropriate authority in the Dot capital will depend on the subject matter, the personalities and timing. Sometimes all available points of official contact between Blank and Dot will be used if the issue is considered sufficiently important. It is not what you do, but the way you do it, which gets results.

As the time of discussion of an issue approaches, efforts can be made in New York to reconcile differing positions of delegations, perhaps by the use of semantics. A certain amount of pressure of various kinds is exercised at the United Nations, in particular as part of campaigns for election to some U.N. body. Yet there is less "arm twisting" and "log rolling" at the U.N. than is sometimes believed.

A certain amount of *do ut des*, "I will help you to achieve your objectives but you must help me to achieve mine," is to be expected. This process of mutual accomodation is generally implemented by gentlemen's agreements. Nothing is committed to writing. Naturally, agreements of mutual advantage occur not only between individual delegations, but also increasingly between groups.

Because of differences in language and in culture many consultations in New York take the form of an exchange of a "piece of paper". It is then possible, even for delegations speaking different languages and without bilingual personnel to help them, to cooperate quite closely provided each understands what the other intends to do. Most negotiations take place privately in order to protect national prestige and to give the participants greater freedom of manoeuvre. In such meetings personal relations are important. If a delegate is to be effective it is necessary for him to know and approach the right person in the right delegation at the right time. If this approach is made under conditions of pressure and decisions are urgent, close personal understanding between the individuals concerned is of special importance.

6. The Where and How of Delegation Contacts

6.1. *Negotiating: Physical Contacts*

Sometimes negotiation takes place by telephone. This is effective only when delegations understand each other's language perfectly and when security considerations do not interfere. If there is a possibility of misunderstanding, discussions are conducted face to face. This occurs to a large extent because the United Nations is a body in which national attitudes and political considerations not easily expressed verbally have considerable importance. At the U.N. "the why" and "the how" is often more important than "the what", and the atmosphere in which agreement is reached is frequently as significant as the nature of the agreement itself.

Most U.N. talks take place between small groups of delegations. Some of these negotiations take place outside the U.N. building at informal luncheons or at more formal meetings in delegation offices. There is a tendency for a greater part of these discussions to take place in the U.N. building itself, firstly because it is easier for all concerned to meet there in a non-partisan atmosphere, and secondly, because officials like to meet on the U.N. premises to save time, particularly during the General Assembly. The U.N. setting is also comfortable for those delegations who feel inhibited in other locations. In the U.N. building all delegations are on the same social and political level, and all are and feel they are part owners of the building.

The U.N. building in Geneva, the famous Palais des Nations is used as much as possible for meetings of organs other than the General Assembly, particularly in the summer when New York is unattractive. U.N. meetings are also held elsewhere than in New York or Geneva. The same pattern of behavior is followed wherever meetings are convened. A meeting in Latin America or Asia or Africa will have only a marginally different character from one held at the U.N. headquarters in New York or at the Geneva office.

Within the U.N. building delegates practise what has been called "the fine art of corridor sitting". Many delegates go to the United Nations, its lounges and its bars without any specific purpose in mind other than that of keeping in touch.

The various lounges of the U.N. headquarters in New York have been effectively designed for discussion. Not all conversations in the U.N. are about official business; many of them represent the development of personal friendships. However, since almost all who come to the building are international civil servants, government representatives or personnel of the information media, there is seldom a conversation at the U.N. without some professional significance.

Most of the important exchanges of view are those which are carried out in informal meetings in the small committee rooms at the U.N. headquarters. Delegations do not have office accomodation in the U.N. building itself, although the permanent members of the Security Council still have a small amount of office space in the building, which is occasionally used for small confidential meetings. If a group in the lounges begins to get too large or if it does not want to be noticed or have unwelcome delegates join it, some member of the group generally reserves one of the small conference rooms for its use. On occasion negotiating groups are organized during or after a formal U.N. meeting.

While the formal debate is proceeding in one of the main committee rooms, groups of delegates may be meeting in small rooms elsewhere in the U.N. building to try and work out decisions about the subject under discussion. Sometimes these meetings take place in the corridors and occasionally at the back of the committee chamber itself. A full committee seldom engages in the type of drafting and exchange of views which takes place in the background, although the Third Committee used to do so in regard to the Covenants on Human Rights, perhaps because agreement in small groups would not have been acceptable and the negotiations would have had to be repeated by the main body. When there is much detail or difficulty, a 152-member committee cannot engage in useful drafting. Even in smaller U.N. organs most of the drafting is done in small, informal groups.

There are many advantages to the main sites and buildings of the United Nations in New York and Geneva. To these has been added in 1979 the Vienna International Center, offered by the Austrian Government. Some Secretariat units from New York have been moved to Vienna, but most of the new buildings in Vienna will be used by the IAEA and UNIDO which were already headquartered there.

The U.N. facilities seem to be sufficiently imperfect to prevent the full application of Parkinson's Law, according to which an institution may be "choked by its own perfection."[5] The U.N. restaurant is mostly crowded, thus sometimes requiring delegates to take their meals in surrounding New York restaurants providing less noise and perhaps better fare. Even the disadvantages of the elevator service in the delegate's section of the U.N. building have had a useful effect. Many delegates who might otherwise become very heavy from the high New York caloric intake have been obliged to walk and occasion-nally even run up and down flights of stairs. The cordial atmosphere created when foreign ministers pile into small elevators may have facilitated accord on difficult issues when other conditions might have provided opportunities for the solitary accumulation of anger.

On the whole, then, the U.N. buildings are an asset, not a liability to the institution.

6.2. *Social Functions*

Eating and drinking have always played an important role in diplomacy. It has been said that the modern diplomatic method of "open agreements openly arrived at" has made the dinner table or bar stool superfluous. However, in the U.N. the "open" part of the proceedings is only the last phase of negotiations. As part of these negotiatons eating and drinking continue to be of considerable importance. At U.N. headquarters there are two bars, each strategically located near a lounge and near conference rooms. These bars are crowded and for this reason not particularly useful for important exchanges of opinion between delegations since such exchanges only function properly when there is at least relative privacy. The bar, however, provides a convenient and pleasant excuse for meeting, and delegates will sometimes be willing to have a drink together when they might not be willing to sit down "cold", as it were, side by side elsewhere in the building. Often preparations for further contacts are made at the bar. The bar near the so-called North Lounge in New York is the most frequented, especially shortly before or after meetings and at noon.

The business lunch, originally an Anglo-Saxon habit, has become customary for all delegates. The U.N. dining room is most frequently used if only because it is often impractical to leave the U.N. building in the relatively short interval between meetings. A meal is not the best place for actual drafting or negotiating, there being too many interruptions, and too little room for papers. Delegations to the General Assembly and other U.N. meetings frequently organize a series of goodwill luncheons. Part of the U.N. dining room consists of a number of smaller rooms where private luncheons can be held. If the intention is to conduct some specific piece of business, a member of a delegation may invite only one other delegate, and thus be able to engage in a more personal and confidential exchange of views. A less conspicuous or harried encounter is possible in the many restaurants in mid-town New York which offer a desirable background; or two delegates may "hide" themselves among the hundreds of U.N. Secretariat employees having lunch at the cafetaria in the Secretariat building. For U.N. meetings in Geneva, some work used to be done at the U.N. beach, "Plage ONU", during lunch hour. The many restaurants near the Palais des Nations provide negotiating opportunities in a leisurely atmosphere, affected in some way by the effects of wine usually accompanying the meal. The problems of distance and transportation in New York (those permanently stationed in New York often living an hour or more from the city) have meant that luncheon takes the place of dinner for most social purposes. Dinner parties are given, however, both of the formal black-tie variety (usually by heads of delegations or of permanent missions) or in a simpler, often buffet-style, manner.

The amount of business discussed at dinners is of course dependent on the composition of the group. Among close friends from friendly delegations discussion is easy. If the group is very mixed and formal, only general conversation may be possible. One delegate seldom has enough professional business with any one other delegate to spend the whole evening talking with him. Furthermore, since dinners are held in private circumstances it may be considered bad taste to promote too much discussion of specific political subjects. Events are sometimes arranged for delegates only, both men and women, if there is a professional objective. The old habit of segregating the men from the women during coffee-cognac time after the meal, supposed to facilitate professional conversation, has gone out of use under the combined effects of (a) larger numbers of female delegates, including in some cases (e.g., China, Sweden) wives who are permanent mission members, (b) smaller residences, and (c) the preference to bring specific persons together in a group much smaller than based on a division by sex.

The cocktail party, generally called a "reception", has made its own distinct inroads into other types of social diplomatic gatherings. It seems to have taken over the role of the 19th-century diplomatic salon or ball, since personal or national ostentation seem to be less fashionable than they once were. Recognition of the need to devote available financial resources to the constructive objectives of the U.N. appears to be mitigated, some would say damaged, by the desire to arrange functions which bring social credit to the host and his country. The cocktail party permits to canvass the views of a relatively large number of delegations in a short time, to try out new ideas, and to test the probable reaction to proposals. The sensible idea of replacing individual country receptions by receptions given by groups of countries is making only very slow progress.

No diplomat can or should expect immediate political returns for hospitality any more than a country should expect such returns for economic aid. Seldom are current delegation positions changed by personal relations, because individuals, unless very senior, have little influence on national policies. It is possible, however, to foster a better understanding and appreciation of national positions as a result of social contacts and sometimes to affect subsequent formal exchanges and long-term voting patterns.

In general U.N. social life is less formal than in the diplomatic circles in many national capitals because there is no special U.N. protocol to follow similar to that of most national capitals. Consequently there is a more relaxed social atmosphere than at perhaps any other diplomatic center.

One important factor which should be considered in connection with social functions is their debilitating effect. Because of the size of U.N. bodies and because of the distances between the homes of delegates in New York and to a lesser extent in Geneva, social events can involve a heavy expenditure of time and energy. No delegate can work well and intensively over a period of years, if he is obliged as frequently occurs to attend an almost continuous series of luncheons, dinners, and receptions. The pressure is particularly heavy on heads of delegations. "Digestive debilitation" also interferes with the ability to digest large amounts of information, especially during long-lasting meetings such as the General Assembly. Many a diplomat's service to his country has been shortened by the effect on his health of the social demands inherent in his work.

In the U.N. at least the word "diplomat" is rapidly losing its old time connotation of elegance and wealth. It has been said that it is difficult to tell the delegates from the visitors. Thus the U.N. has had an effect even on the appearance of U.N. delegates, and by its method of operation possibly on their characters. There is no doubt that the personal and parliamentary experiences which delegates acquire at the U.N. may have long-term consequences of value to the international community.

Notes to chapter 6

1. Several efforts have been made to analyze the attitudes of permanent mission members and other delegates: Chadwick Alger, "The United Nations Participation as a Learning Experience," *Public Opinion Quarterly*, Fall 1963; Chadwick F. Alger, "Personal Contact in Intergovernmental Organization," in Herbert C. Kelman (ed.), *International Behavior: A Social-Psychological Analysis* (New York: Holt Rinehart and Winston,

1965); Harold Jacobson, "Deriving Data from Delegates to International Assemblies," *International Organization,* Summer 1967, pp. 592-613; Manfred Ernst, "Attitudes of diplomats at the United Nations: the effects of organizational participation on the evaluation of the organization," *International Organization,* Autumn 1978, pp. 1037-1044.

2. Mrs. Eleanor Roosevelt described the importance of this aspect in *On My Own* (New York: Harper, 1958), pp. 48-49.

3. Such an example is provided in an amusing account as a one-term delegate by William F. Buckley, *United Nations' Delegate's Odyssey* (New York: Putnam's, 1974). See also Daniel P. Moynihan, *A Dangerous Place* (Little Brown and Company, Boston, 1978). On contacts with parliaments, see J. Goormaghtigh, *Parliaments and the United Nations: Dissemination of Information to Parliamentarians* (New York: UNITAR, U.N. Institute for Training and Research, 1979. Sales No. E.79.XV.ST/14).

4. On the role of women in the U.N., see Davidson Nicol and Margaret Croke (ed.), *The United Nations and Decision-Making: The Role of Women,* 2 vols. (New York: UNITAR, 1978). United Nations activities to improve the status of women have considerably grown during the tenure of office of Mrs. H. Sipila as Assistant Secretary-General for the Centre of Social Development and Humanitarian Affairs.

5. C. Northcote Parkinson, *Parkinson's Law and Other Studies in Administration* (Boston: Houghton Mifflin, 1957), p. 69.

Chapter 7

How To Get Results: Procedures and Tactics of United Nations Decision Making

1. Resolutions

Most U.N. decisions are in the form of resolutions. They generally consist of two parts, a preamble and an operative part. The preamble is designed both to explain the purpose of the resolution and to rally as much support as possible for the operative paragraphs which follow. The preamble often refers to earlier decisions, thus establishing some measure of continuity with previous U.N. action. If there are no previous U.N. decisions bearing directly on the subject, reference may be made to some appropriate article in the U.N. Charter. The operative part takes the form of a request for action, an endorsement of a situation or a statement of opinion.

Although few United Nations decisions are mandatory, the strenuous efforts delegations make in order to amend, defeat or avoid such draft resolutions, even when these contain very vague language, indicates the importance attached to these texts. The concern of a delegation may stem from direct instructions, or be dictated by what it believes, on the basis of general policy statements, its government's reaction might be. United Nations bodies come closest to mandatory decisions when requesting reports or studies to be undertaken by the U.N. Secretariat, when budget decisions are taken, or when the Security Council takes a binding decision.

Drafts of resolutions are usually prepared in New York on the basis of instructions from the national capitals, although from time to time on matters of great importance drafts of resolutions may be sent from the national capital concerned. If the draft originates in New York it generally takes the form of a preliminary working document, subject to correction from the national government to which the text will be referred. At any stage the Secretariat may be consulted on legal and other aspects of the text and on its drafting. A tentative draft resolution is sometimes called a ''working paper''.

Often an idea or proposal is highly tentative, mostly a trial balloon. In that case a delegate will produce a "non-paper", which may not even mention a delegation's name, although generally the authorship is known.

If the delegation intends to gain approval for a particular proposal, the first step must be to obtain the support of the delegation's close friends. At this stage perhaps not more than two or three other delegations are concerned. The proposal is presented in preliminary form and may frequently be altered to ensure the necessary basic support.

In the early days of the United Nations, among the first to be consulted on any draft resolution was, what was called a Great Power, by which was meant one of the permanent members of the Security Council. Most delegations would have considered it irresponsible to press a draft resolution without taking into account Great Power attitudes. Also, it was felt that without Great Power support a resolution had little chance of being implemented, financially or otherwise. With the advent of the group system, a delegation planning some initiative will seek support in the first place among its own group or from countries belonging to some other group. Western countries planning a draft resolution on an economic development issue, will consult at an early stage with members of the Group of 77, whose support will be vital for getting anything passed.

After these initial soundings, the next step, if there is time, is to approach either directly, or in cooperation with close friends, a larger representative group and then through this group as many delegations as possible from among potential supporters. There is not much point in these early discussions in approaching enemies or delegations which, for historical, personal or political reasons, will clearly oppose the proposal since it would serve no purpose to help the opposition prepare its tactics. However, it may sometimes be desirable—before formal presentation in committee—to explain to the opposition what a proposed text means so as to avoid unnecessary difficulties.

At the United Nations, as elsewhere, it is sometimes better to let others take the credit and to work behind the scenes rather than in the glare of the spotlights. No delegation can railroad anything through entirely on its own; it must work with others and sometimes a little modesty will yield good results. A delegation may therefore for tactical reasons sometimes let another delegation take or share the public credit for a resolution it originated (for an example see p. 153).

Eventually a text of a draft resolution is given to the Secretariat for translation, editing and official circulation. Before that time, of course,

120

a delegation will have endeavored to meet as many as possible of the points which have been made by those it has consulted so that the text submitted has the best possible chance of being adopted.

The sequence of steps involved in the handling of a draft resolution can be summarized as depicted in Chart 5.

Chart 5. Normal procedure for handling a draft resolution

1. Preparation of text (in capitals and at conference site)
↓
2. Informal circulation of text (among selected delegations or groups)
↓
3. Possible revision of draft text
↓
4. Constitution of group of sponsors
↓
5. Deposit of draft by sponsors with Secretariat
↓
6. Official circulation in working languages
↓
7. Oral introduction by one or more sponsors
↓
8. Debate (statements by other delegations); comments by sponsors
↓
9. Introduction of and debate on amendments
↓
10. Sponsors' comments on amendments
↓
11. Chairman may constitute negotiating group; negotiations
↓
12. Deposit of revised draft resolution
↓
13. Debate on revised draft and amendments
↓
14. Voting on sub-amendments and amendments
↓
15. Explanations of vote
↓
16. Voting on draft resolution
↓
17. Announcement by chairman of result of vote
↓
18. Additional explanations of vote

It is desirable to obtain a representative group of co-sponsors. The names of these countries are printed on draft resolutions. However, the names of the sponsors are not retained on the texts of the resolutions after adoption. If the delegations of a number of representative countries, for example, from Latin America, Europe, the Middle East, Africa, and Asia, agree to co-sponsor a draft resolution it has a better chance of easy adoption than a draft resolution sponsored only by countries from a single geographical area. On the other hand it is sometimes preferable for a delegation to submit a resolution without co-sponsors, which gives maximum freedom of manoeuvre. The delegation originally responsible for the basic text of a proposal is normally among the co-sponsors, but this is not an invariable rule. Sometimes a country does not sponsor a draft resolution which it favors, because to do so might arouse unnecessary opposition.

If a draft resolution has only a small number of co-sponsors, they will find it easier to take any necessary quick decisions on suggested modifications of the text and to coordinate tactics. If a draft resolution has a large number of co-sponsors, the difficulties involved in discussing and negotiating amendments are sometimes very great, although the committed support may be worth the trouble. Therefore, the list of co-sponsors on a draft resolution is usually long if it is non-controversial or if there has been fairly general advance agreement and the text is unlikely to be drastically amended. In some cases a long list of sponsors is used as a means of bringing pressure to bear on other delegations and to impress them with its probable support in the voting.

The practice of draft resolutions co-sponsored by or on behalf of the Group of 77 should be recalled. Perhaps the best group of co-sponsors for a difficult draft resolution would be five or six representative countries whose delegates are on friendly terms. However, opposition is sometimes created if too few delegations are included among the co-sponsors. Countries represented by ''difficult'' delegates are often sought as co-sponsors to prevent them, as much as possible, from proposing changes. Choosing and getting a good list of co-sponsors requires tact and diplomacy of a high order and a detailed knowledge of the current international political situation.

Once a draft resolution has been formally submitted to the Secretariat, it is circulated in the working languages (Arabic, Chinese, English, French, Russian and Spanish) to all participants. At this stage further co-sponsors may be added. When the subject is taken up on the agenda with or without (usually with) a formal presentation speech by one of the sponsors, oral and formal written amendments, also sponsored

122

by one or more delegations, may be introduced. The sponsors of the original text may accept some of these amendments, in which case a revised draft will be circulated before the actual vote.

Amendments are sometimes introduced to indicate that the decision the United Nations is taking is not exactly on the terms requested by the particular country which initiated the text. Of course, some individuals or delegations can be expected to introduce amendments of form if not of substance to almost any draft resolution, unless they are co-sponsors. Changes are also frequently required because of difficulty in translation. The text of a draft resolution may have to be changed even in its original language because some part cannot easily be translated into other languages. Similarly texts can offend the customs or concepts held by delegations or groups of countries. Thus amendments not only in language but also in substance may be required for cultural as well as technical reasons. The same words may have different political meanings in different parts of the world and quite often words have developed a meaning in U.N. circles which they do not have anywhere else.

When considering submitting an amendment it is important to bear in mind the provisions of rules 90 and 130 of the General Assembly Rules of Procedure (see Annex 2, p. 261). When there are several amendments, the one which is "furthest removed in substance from the original proposal" is first voted on, followed by the next furthest removed, and so on. If a delegation wants priority for its amendment, it will then consider submitting a rather drastic proposal, hoping thus to be "furthest removed". However, in so doing a delegation risks that, with reference to the last sentence of rules 90 and 130, the chairman will rule (or the meeting decide upon a procedural motion) that the amendment does not "merely adds to, deletes from or revises part of the proposal," and is therefore not an amendment. At the beginning of the thirty-fourth session of the General Assembly (1979) the Credentials Committee had recommended to recognize the delegation of the so-called Pol Pot regime of Cambodia rather than the delegation of the Heng Samrin regime. The delegation of India proposed as an amendment to leave the seat of Cambodia vacant. A procedural motion by Singapore and Malaysia held that the proposal of India was not an amendment, but a new and different proposal. This procedural motion was upheld in a vote by the General Assembly, after which the delegation of the Pol Pot regime was seated with a vote of 71 in favor, 35 against, 34 abstentions and 12 delegations "absent".

Sometimes a deadline is fixed for the submission of amendments. If a delegation aims at the deletion of some words or paragraphs, it can still ask, under rules 89 and 129, that the part of the draft resolution it wants deleted be voted on separately. The chairman will always permit such a request, but it is possible that some delegation will object, after which a vote on the motion for a vote "by division" takes place. The vote "by division" can also be requested in the case of voting on amendments.

2. Voting

The final stage in this process is that of voting. There are the following methods of voting:

1. *By a show of hands or non-recorded vote* (rules 87 and 127). This is the simplest method, and is used more frequently than any other. The alternative of standing up has not been used for a long time. When voting is by a show of hands, non-participation in the vote remains largely unnoticed. The show of hands is replaced in meeting rooms equipped with electronic voting machines by the non-recorded vote. During the voting period, the individual results show on the voting board; however, only the totals appear on the voting sheet which is produced by the voting machine.

2. *Roll-call or recorded vote* (rules 87 and 127). Under the roll-call method the names of countries are read out by the Secretary in alphabetical order, starting with a name which has been drawn by lot. Those who are relatively late in being called can benefit from the knowledge of how others have voted. It takes about twelve minutes for the roll-call to be completed. In the plenary hall of the General Assembly, and in several committee rooms in New York and Geneva, the roll-call is replaced by the electronically recorded vote: a button for yes, no, or abstention is pushed, and green, red or yellow lights are lit up opposite the countries' names on a large voting board. Within the voting period a delegation may change its vote by pushing the correct button. The recorded vote takes the same amount of time as the non-recorded vote; in the case of the recorded vote, however, the individual results appear on the voting sheet. The results of the vote are first printed on a sheet distributed very quickly after the vote, and then are inserted in full in the official record of the meeting.

124

3. *Secret ballot* (rules 93 and 103). A secret ballot is used in the case of elections of persons or Member States. This may be dispensed with in the committees, and it usually is. Even in the plenary, for the election of members of subsidiary organs, when the number of candidates endorsed by the regional groups corresponds to the number of seats to be filled, the secret ballot is dispensed with. For example, it is current practice at the start of sessions of the General Assembly, to elect the President and Vice-Presidents of the General Assembly without the secret ballot.

Required majority. Normally, a simple majority of those present and voting is all that is required. Under the rules of procedure of all U.N. bodies, abstentions, as well as invalid votes, do not count. Votes on "important questions" require a two-thirds majority in the plenary meetings. The Charter, and rule 83 of the Rules of Procedure of the General Assembly, spell out that the following votes are included in the "important questions" category: recommendations with respect to the maintenance of international peace and security, the election of the non-permanent members of the Security Council, the election of the members of the Economic and Social Council, the election of the members of the Trusteeship Council in accordance with paragraph 1c of Article 86 of the Charter, the admission of new members to the United Nations, the suspension of the rights and privileges of membership, the expulsion of members, questions relating to the trusteeship system, and budgetary questions.

Voting on amendments to texts of draft resolutions which come under the category of "important questions" also requires a two-thirds majority.

Occasionally a delegation or group of delegations endeavors to have some vote considered as dealing with an "important question". This is sometimes tried in the plenary if a text deemed unacceptable has been adopted in committee, since the two-thirds requirement does not apply in committee. A proposal to this effect is usually challenged by others. In practice this often means that the proposal for a two-thirds vote is defeated; the vote on the proposal to apply the two-thirds requirement is itself taken by a simple majority.

A statement by an influential delegation, made either in private or in public, of its intention to vote for or against a particular paragraph or text, will influence the vote of others. If the probable voting pattern is not clear, there may be hurried, and more or less obvious, consultations between possibly like-minded delegations. Efforts may also be made at this stage to persuade delegations to change their votes from a negative or positive vote to an abstention or vice-versa. In general it is hard to change voting patterns on a major issue at the last minute; therefore, efforts to do so are not usually worth the time and trouble. The voting reflects positions which have already been developed both in the debate and in informal discussions. However, there may be surprises and sometimes there are mistakes. For example, a delegate may have missed a key point in the debate or have failed to assess the situation correctly before the vote is taken.

A delegation will request the type of voting most favorable to its purposes. A roll-call vote will be sought if a detailed record showing each country's vote is required. This might embarrass some delegations, an effect which is sometimes sought.

There is no evidence of any malpractice in the voting procedures at the U.N., although mistakes in counting or voting are sometimes made. Obvious mistakes in the count are resolved by voting again. A delegation absent at the time of voting or having made a mistake cannot have the voting record altered but can make known its intentions as part of the record of the meeting. Sometimes a delegation which finds the situation acutely embarrassing or which considers the vote illegal or out of place will be deliberately absent when a vote is taken, and even indicate this by stating, in case of a roll-call: "not participating". If shouted with great emphasis, this causes hilarity.

There is a tendency for a resolution to be adopted on almost every issue at every meeting. The number of meetings and of members makes for a great many more or less non-controversial resolutions. Compromises tend, of course, to produce "neutral" texts. This tendency has debased the coinage of U.N. resolutions which frequently parrot previously agreed language or affirm the painfully obvious.

A distinction has been maintained between resolutions designed to establish and develop specific United Nations programs and resolutions intended to transmit general policy guidance to member governments. Resolutions concerning specific U.N. programs have had useful and constructive results while resolutions involving policy recommendations to governments have often been less effective.

Not all United Nations decisions are necessarily taken in the form of resolutions, although most decisions are expressed in some formal manner. For example, there have been a number of Security Council meetings which have ended by a summary from the Chair, or a "declaration" regarded as an agreed reflection of the consensus of the Council. The question of "consensus" will be discussed in the next section of this chapter. In other U.N. bodies, decisions have been taken by including certain agreed paragraphs in a committee's report rather than by passing a formal resolution. On certain occasions committees have been satisfied with statements reported in the summary records without the need for any formal action at all.

There are, of course, circumstances in which committees have decided to postpone or not to discuss items. On many occasions postponement represents an important action. Delay can indirectly "kill" a proposal, especially if the idea cannot be revived later or if the opposition to it meanwhile grows. On the other hand, postponement may also save a proposal that might have been defeated if put to an early vote, but which might be successful if presented at a later time. When a subject is regarded as of importance and a debate reveals either a consensus or substantial differences of opinion, there is generally a formal resolution before the United Nations body concerned. Such a resolution may propose little or no action, but can at least "note" and "consider" the matter.

Some resolutions are quoted long and frequently after they have been passed; others die immediately upon adoption, the process by which they were adopted being more important than their substance; and some gradually lose force and are eventually forgotten or ignored. However, any U.N. resolution can be useful if it represents internationally agreed language. If difficulties occur, these can usually be overcome by the use of sections or words from old resolutions to make up new ones. Delegations generally welcome the use of previously agreed language, since this means they are not called upon to negotiate new language and to take new decisions. The United Nations, like many parliaments, tends to reiterate old decisions unless fresh action is required by important new circumstances.

3. Consensus and Pseudo-consensus

Because voting is such a conspicuous element of conference diplomacy, it is sometimes condemned as an inferior method of decision making; this is especially so where large majorities, using the "voting machine", can push through resolutions which they insist on seeing adopted. This view neglects the fact that, in practice, a great many decisions are arrived at without any voting, through a process of consensus.

Consensus indicates that no vote was taken: the presiding officer, re-

ferring to a text either sponsored by delegations or occasionally presented anonymously, states that he understands that the draft decision
or resolution before the meeting commands general support, or words
to that effect. Alternatively, if such support does not in fact exist he will
simply state that he understands that it is the desire of the meeting to
adopt the text without a vote. In the first case one can speak of real
consensus, in the latter of a pseudo-consensus which takes the place of
what would have been a divided vote.

The Programme of Action for the Establishment of a New International Economic Order adopted at the sixth special session of the
General Assembly (New York, 1974) was a case of pseudo-consensus;
following its adoption a number of delegations, including the United
States and the nine countries of the European Communities, put on
record their reservations regarding several parts of the Programme of
Action. On the other hand, the resolution adopted at the end of the seventh special session (New York, 1975) can be called a real consensus.

Another example of pseudo-consensus on a proposal which had little
support occurred during the thirty-third session of the General Assembly: Costa Rica initially proposed in a speech by its president during
the general debate (which gave it maximum weight), and then in the
Second (Economic) Committee, the establishment of a "University for
Peace". Lofty as this idea may have been, it gained little support,
since a United Nations University as well as a United Nations Institute
for Training and Research already existed. Both were equipped to undertake whatever additional peace research which the international
community might deem necessary. After some informal consultations
the initial draft resolution presented by Costa Rica and others, providing for the establishment of this body, was changed: the Secretary-
General was asked to solicit the views of Member States on the possible
establishment of a University for Peace, while Costa Rica indicated
that the University for Peace was intended to be part of the U.N. University system. This proposal was adopted by "consensus", first in
committee, then in plenary meeting, although few countries saw the
need for a new and no doubt costly organ, in spite of the fact that Costa
Rica said it would donate land and buildings.

Most consensus decisions relate to some text of a draft resolution or
decision. A consensus procedure without a draft resolution is appropriate in the following situations:

a. The action to be taken follows directly and in a non-controversial
way from the debate. Many procedural decisions announced by the

chairman are in this category.

b. The action to be taken is more or less agreed, but the drafting of a specific text would cause insurmountable difficulties. Summing up by the chairman in sufficiently vague or general language is then the way out. In the U.N. Security Council this method of procedure is used repeatedly. It avoids sharp differences of views on drafting specific texts.

c. Decisions arrived at in negotiating conferences which are in fact the result of some sort of consensus.

d. Decisions to postpone an agenda item to a later session, or to refer it to another body.

It must be stressed that whether or not there is a draft resolution, all decisions taken without a vote require the careful judgment of the chairman. If he errs in his judgment, which must reflect what has been agreed privately, a procedural wrangle may well break out and the chairman's prestige will suffer.

4. What Does a Vote Mean?

In the old days a yes vote meant yes, a no was no, and abstentions were not too frequent. With the inflation in numbers of votes, and a frequent lessening of the significance of the contents of resolutions, countries often have a tendency to cast their votes in a way obscuring their real intentions: a yes vote can mean anything from enthusiastic support at one end of the range, to: I do not like this text at all, but find it inconvenient to distinguish myself by voting against it. An abstention can signal: yes, but..., or: no, but... Only a no vote has kept most of its unambiguity: it is rare for a country to vote no although it really likes the text. However, this may occur if a country aligns itself with a no vote of other members of its group.

It is sometimes said these days, with some exaggeration: if you are in favor of a proposal you can vote yes, no, or abstention; if you are against it, you can also vote yes, no, or abstention.

The uncertainty pertaining to the real significance of votes has also led to a considerable expansion of the number of "explanations of vote", which not only serve to qualify the yes or no vote cast, or to explain the reasons for an abstention, but also may take the place of a speech during the debate on the question or on the draft resolution.

5. Tactics

In the United Nations as in other organizations timing is of great importance. A resolution or suggestion which is presented too early during a session may arouse more opposition than need have been the case if it had been presented at a later stage. Similarly, a resolution presented too late may find delegates already otherwise committed or provoke resentment if delegates are not able to obtain fresh instructions and to study the text before the vote. In the United Nations it is generally impossible to get a decision on a matter if there has not been time to translate the relevant documents into working languages. Sometimes, under pressure of time, working papers may be distributed in one language only; however, if a representative of another language group requests a postponement until translations are ready, other language groups will generally support him.

Procedural motions are frequently used to delay or prevent a decision, often for political reasons. Most delegations at one time or another have had to request delays in U.N. proceedings to have time for the receipt of instructions and tend to sympathize with other delegations in similar trouble.

The Rules of Procedure of the General Assembly and those of certain specialized agencies based on it (for example of the World Health Assembly) make a distinction between procedural motions and points of order.

A procedural motion as provided for in the General Assembly Rules is related to the suspension or the adjournment of the meeting. Rule 77 of the General Assembly lays down the order in which procedural motions have precedence over all other proposals or motions before the meeting:

a. to suspend the meeting;
b. to adjourn the meeting;
c. to adjourn the debate on the item under discussion;
d. to close the debate on the item under discussion.

A point of order is

basically an intervention directed to the presiding officer, requesting him to make use of some power inherent in his office or specifically given him under the rules of procedure. It may, for example, relate to the manner in which the debate is conducted, to the maintenance of order, to the observance of the rules of procedure or to the way in which presiding officers exercise the powers conferred upon them by the rules. Under a point of order, a representative may request the presiding officer to apply a certain rule of procedure or he may question the way in which the officer applies the rule. Thus, within the scope of the rules of procedure, representatives are enabled to direct the attention of the presiding officer to violations or misapplications of the rules by other representatives or by the presiding officer himself. A point of order has precedence over any other matter, including procedural motions. [Rules of Procedure of the General Assembly, Annex V, para. 79]

For practical purposes the distinction between "points of order" and "procedural motions" has disappeared to the extent that a delegate will, lifting his hand or delegation-namecard in order to get the attention of the president, in both cases say or shout "point of order!" A procedural motion must immediately be put to the vote by the presiding officer. In practice, however, presiding officers often permit a series of conflicting procedural motions to be made: one delegate may move to adjourn debate and another delegate may move immediately thereafter for suspension of the meeting. A more or less confused procedural discussion will then result. Another deviation from the literal application of the rules of procedure is that under a "point of order" a delegate will not ask for a ruling from the presiding officer but either exercise his right of reply or make some remark on the way things are going without specifically asking for a presidential ruling. While such deviations may be regrettable, they are so frequent that conference diplomats have to take them into account as something normal.

"Procedure" and "substance" of a conference are supposed to be two separate things. In practice, however, procedural devices are used to obtain a substantive result and procedural debates often turn out to be debates on substance. The alert conference diplomat will see to it that his objectives are not thwarted by procedural moves by others, or as a minimum he will recognize such moves for what they really are.

In the United Nations a knowledge of the probable reaction of other delegations is necessary for the successful achievement of any objective. A delegation must know what can be sold and what cannot be sold. It is possible, for example, to estimate how many votes a particular proposal may receive by studying past voting records. Any delegation putting forward a proposal must expect opposition from some quarters. Few decisions are genuinely non-controversial, although many are claimed to be.

The entire process of negotiating a U.N. decision requires determination on the part of a delegation initiating a proposal. This determination must in general be based on clear authorization from its government and on agreement within the delegation. Any United Nations proposal may require a delegation to take positions not fully acceptable to its friends and may oblige it to anticipate a battle with its enemies. Therefore, in the negotiation of each decision there is usually a time, if a proposal has much substantive or political significance, when the delegation must decide whether to abandon the proposal, to agree to having it shelved for another year, or to push ahead with it. If a delegation is prepared to face the risks and difficulties involved and is determined to push ahead, it can often achieve its objectives. Self-confidence produces dividends at the U.N. as elsewhere. There have been many examples of delegations or of individual members of delegations securing acceptance of proposals to which almost everyone was opposed in private but against which no one was willing to fight in public.

The proposal of Costa Rica at the thirty-third session of the General Assembly (see p. 128) for the establishment of a University for Peace was probably one which a majority of the U.N. members did not support, but which nobody was willing to fight. This situation seems to confirm the fact that one cannot be against peace and a few other basic things. On the other hand the proposal of the Philippines at the thirty-second session of the General Assembly, to hold the next (1978) session of the Assembly, or at least its three-week general debate, in Manila, which was supported by an intensive and expensive campaign, including banquets addressed by the First Lady of the Philippines, had to be withdrawn: members realized that a session away from headquarters would be costly and inefficient, both for the Secretariat and for a majority of delegations.

Before a resolution is voted upon there is generally a moment of tension since it is seldom absolutely certain how the vote will go. Often an explanation before or after the vote is used to clear a delegate's conscience for a vote which did not accord entirely with his instructions or which went against the majority. Sometimes supporters and opponents of a resolution will give a different interpretation of it in their explanations of vote.

There is usually little real benefit to be gained by directly attacking any delegation, except on an issue of major substance or when some clear political difference is involved. While it is relatively easy to score debating points in the United Nations, such successes are of little practical significance and generally tend to make the final decision more difficult by exaggerating political differences. However, during the years of the intensive "cold war", political exchanges were the order of the day on almost every issue. Later, frequent political exchanges have occurred under many agenda items due to the Middle East situation and Soviet Union/China rivalry.

U.N. conference services provide for simultaneous interpretation of a statement into all the official languages at all formal meetings. Frequently, more important than the substance of a formal statement is its meaning and purpose. Although the good interpreter can make much clear by choice of words and intonation, a formal statement will frequently have to be expanded upon later by informal personal comment. After any major speech delegations will try to discuss what certain phrases mean in terms of proposals for decision by the U.N. body concerned. Comparisons may be made with statements of a particular delegation at previous sessions. Sometimes a statement is deliberately vague or confusing.

The excellent summary records and reports of proceedings of U.N. bodies are also of considerable importance. For example, a decision may be taken that the Secretariat should prepare a report "having in mind the discussions at the ...th session of the General Assembly" on such and such a subject. It would then be necessary for the Secretariat to review the debate and to be guided by any general directions or conclusions which emerged from that debate. In such a situation it may be good tactics to try to have as many delegations as possible make statements in support of the point of view one would like to see prevail.

Revisions to the summary records may be submitted within three days of their publication; delegations make use of this provision, sometimes with the advantage of hindsight. However, the Secretariat refuses any revision which would make the summary record an incorrect reflection of what has been said.

5.1. *Tactics to Have a Proposal Adopted and Tactics to Achieve Defeat or Delay*

I have discussed above (p. 123) the tactics involved in submitting an amendment. A delegation wishing to push a proposal has a relatively limited range of possibilities:

a. It must advance all possible arguments: intellectual, historic and other.

b. It can try to exercise some sort of pressure on other countries, in particular in fields not related to the United Nations setting, e.g., aid or trade matters. It is obvious that this sort of pressure, leaving alone its ethical undesirability, is not available to the vast majority of U.N. Member States.

c. It can propose a "deal", a log-trading transaction within the U.N. setting, e.g., support for some initiative or candidature of another delegation. This sort of leverage *is* available to many U.N. members.

d. It can and will organize an energetic campaign, in many cases weeks or months before the session where the initiative is to be launched, in favor of its proposal (this, however, may also alert opponents at an early date!).

On the other hand, a delegation opposing a proposal can avail itself of all four tactical moves mentioned above (in the case of d. this would be a sort of "counter-campaign"[1]), plus all the tricks permitted by the United Nations rules and practices of procedure, some of which are:

e. An opposing delegation can try to have an initiative referred to another body, whether inside or outside the U.N. I have called this kind of tactics "ping-pong"[2] because with skill it can be applied successively in a number of bodies.

f. An alternative draft resolution can be presented by opposing delegations prior to the tabling of the initiative itself. This is all the easier if the initiating delegation has given wide advance knowledge to its proposal, thus having forewarned its opponents. The alternative draft resolution will perhaps request a long-lasting inquiry by the Secretary-General among Member States, a well-known device to obtain a lengthy deferment. The inquiry would be the alternative to the action involved in the initiative.

g. The opposing delegation(s) can avail themselves of the procedural motions to adjourn a meeting, or adjourn the debate (see p. 130).

h. The opposing delegations(s) can engage in informal or formal consultations or negotiations and then enter into delaying tactics ("I have to get instructions from my government on this new text ...", etc.). If there is enough delay there may—in the rush of finishing a session—not be enough time to put the proposal of the initiating delegation to the vote.

6. U.N. Speeches

Formal speeches at the United Nations seem to have limited importance. A speech can be translated into action only through a resolution or other specific decision. Speeches will bear little relation to the actions of a U.N. body if they are made not as contributions to the debate, but as statements for domestic consumption or for general propaganda. Although speeches and statements are an important element in conference diplomacy communications, they are by no means the only form. Visual expressions, maintaining silence when challenged, informal conversations in lobbies, in delegation offices, at luncheons, dinners and cocktail parties, informal group meetings, delegation press releases, may all be as important a channel of communication as the conference statement, pronounced in plenary or committee meeting.

Effective communication means making one's thoughts understood by others and understanding oneself participants' thoughts and ideas. Three potential stumbling blocks for effective communication in conference diplomacy must be distinguished:

Linguistic difficulties: delegates and Secretariat members must not run into serious language difficulties in talking to each other. In formal meetings interpretation will remove many of these difficulties. However, since most of the decision-making process takes place in informal meetings, often without interpretation services, it is clear that a minimum of verbal understanding is indispensable to achieve communication in the linguistic sense.

Intellectual short-circuits: there must be an ability to grasp what the other is saying. Most arguments in international conferences center on the relative advantages or disadvantages of specific courses of action. Delegates will explain these advantages or disadvantages. It is necessary that their reasoning can be understood and followed by other delegates.

Conceptual roadblocks: in different parts of the world different value systems exist: basic standards and norms are not the same, so that a word may have a different significance for different people. For example, "to some compromise signifies a legitimate effort to reach an agreement by mutual concessions, to others it may imply an immoral or cynical sacrifice of principle."[3] In some conferences or negotiations the Latin tendency to define everything in considerable detail clashes with Anglo-Saxon pragmatism, with its preference for leaving things vague, for "muddling through". To establish communications in the conceptual sense, conference diplomats will see to it that their proposals, and the arguments to defend these proposals are presented in such a way that they are properly understood by those to whom they are addressed.

The timing of a statement, however brief, is essential, in the United Nations as elsewhere. Most U.N. speakers will try to place their statements in an advantageous position on the speakers list, i.e., not as the first speaker in the morning or afternoon when the room is half empty, and not immediately after an important speech. The chairman may announce the time (date and hour) when the speakers list will be closed; the alert delegate is of course aware of this.

In most U.N. meetings a delegation can choose from one or more of the following possibilities of making a statement:

a. A statement under the "general debate" on an agenda item. This gives the opportunity to explain the government's position and of announcing, perhaps tentatively as a trial balloon, an initiative which the delegation may take; it may also indicate support for an initiative taken by another delegation or by one of the groups.

b. Statement(s) when draft resolutions are discussed. If there are amendments proposed to a draft resolution, whether by the delegation itself or by others, additional statements can be made. If no speech has been made during the "general debate", or if no such debate has taken place, the speech or speeches on draft resolutions can incorporate general arguments. If, for some reason, a speech during the general debate drew little attention, the delegation may wish to repeat some arguments: "As I said before, and I quote...." The advantage of repeating arguments must be weighed against the possible irritation it may cause.

c. Explanation of vote. Although a favor granted by the presiding officer (under General Assembly rules 88 and 128), it is considered an acquired right; however, votes taken by secret ballot cannot be explained (cf. rule 88). Delegations can usually choose to explain their vote before the vote, with some potential influence on others, or after the vote. In the latter case, the explanation is merely for the record, although summary records, as distinguished from verbatim records, will sometimes only list the delegations that explained their votes without summarizing the contents of these statements. Often the presiding officer will appeal to delegations to limit explanations of vote to say 5 or 10 minutes.

d. In certain situations, the "right to reply" provides an additional opportunity. Rights of reply have become a standard feature of many U.N. debates. Rule 73 of the General Assembly provides that the President may accord the right of reply to any member if a speech delivered after the President has declared that the list of speakers is closed, makes this desirable. In practice, the right of reply may also be exercised before the list of speakers is closed. During the general debate in the General Assembly, it is the practice that all rights of reply are exercised at the end of the day, after the list of speakers of the day is exhausted. One reply often provokes a request for another reply, and so the weary President—or a vice-president substituting for him—finds himself forced to continue the meeting long after the official closing hour, unless, as often happened, the interpreters give notice that they will not go beyond a certain time limit. The President of the General Assembly requests that those who speak in right of reply limit themselves to ten minutes, and this prescription is usually adhered to. The grouping of the rights of reply at the end of the day is based on the recommendations of the Special Committee on the Rationalization of the Procedures and Organization of the General Assembly, which were approved at the twenty-sixth session of the General Assembly (G.A. resolution 2837 [XXVI]). The ten minute limitation was adopted later on the recommendation of the General Committee, and a decision to that effect is taken at the beginning of every session.

In general, one cannot say which option among the above possibilities for speech making will be preferred. The choice will depend on a number of factors, including the importance attached to the subject, the presence of some high-level personality to make a speech, the possible inclination not to ''stick one's neck out'' and, therefore, to speak at the latest possible moment or not at all. The tendency to have speakers take the floor on behalf of groups (e.g., the Group of 77, the European Communities, etc.) also provides the possibility of making one's opinion known through a group either instead of or in addition to a national statement. In the latter case, reference will then usually be made to the group statement. On certain more or less ceremonial occasions, such as the closing meeting of a General Assembly session, it has become a tradition for only the chairmen of the regional groups (who rotate in alphabetical order on a monthly basis) to take the floor and make a statement on behalf of their respective group.

The influential U.N. delegates are those, who, in addition to making good formal statements, can participate in informal debate. A rebuttal to the contentious statement of an opponent is best made immediately, not the next day, no matter how well it may be prepared by then. Although delegations will generally have had time to prepare written statements to read into the record, ad hoc statements at the right moment can have considerable effect. Experience with the subject, skill in presentation, fluency and timing are the tools required of the successful U.N. delegate.

7. Committee Officers

The importance of committee officers varies depending on the subject under discussion, the personality and nationality of the officer, the nature of any differences which may arise and the construction of each U.N. body. The officers are the chairman (in some organs called president), usually one or more vice-chairmen, often a rapporteur, all of whom are elected from among the representatives, and a secretary who is a member of the U.N. Secretariat.

A chairman or president is frequently able to use his position for the benefit of the committee by leading the debate into constructive channels. It is possible to do this by drawing attention to the nature and objectives of the discussion when it wanders, and by procedural suggestions designed to promote more effective consideration of individual issues. The chairman or the vice-chairman can be helpful in bringing opposing factions together. A chairman generally does not take initiatives on his own regarding matters of substance since this might involve him in controversy and affect his reputation for impartiality. However, in certain situations a chairman may have considerable influence in assisting in the settlement of disputes (see pp. 46-49, 66, 147-150 for examples).

A rapporteur, responsible, with the secretary, for the preparation of the committee's report, fulfills his function by submitting his report in terms acceptable to the committee; not always an easy task. Sometimes this officer will be asked by the committee to prepare a compromise draft or make suggestions to assist the committee's work.

The secretary of a committee is generally responsible for its organization and also acts as a channel through which communications pass on their way to the committee as a whole. He prepares working papers as required and arranges for other secretariat assistance to the committee. The secretary is by experience qualified to suggest informally improvements in the language of resolutions. At most U.N. meetings there is also present a representative of the Secretary-General who is frequently asked to advise on the substantive, legal or constitutional aspects of problems before a meeting. The Legal Counsel of the U.N. (an under-secretary-general), or his representative, is sometimes called upon to comment on the legal status of some proposal, or to interpret the rules of procedure. If the chairman makes the interpretation in place of the Legal Counsel, he may be challenged from the floor, and a vote will take place to decide the issue. There can be confusion if it is not clear whether the chairman puts to the vote his own ruling, or the motion to challenge it. If the vote is on his ruling, those who support it must vote yes; if the vote is on the motion challenging the ruling, those who support the chairman will vote no.

The officers and the secretariat of a U.N. body are empowered to assist greatly in promoting decisive and constructive action. In the final analysis, however, the secretariat is helpless without leadership from delegations. This in turn requires the interest and support of member governments.

8. Elections

It might be useful to describe in some detail how elections for General Assembly or other U.N. posts are conducted since the general procedure followed provides a good example of the way in which the various forces at the U.N. work.

Some weeks prior to the opening of the first meeting of the body in question, informal consultations begin.

There are generally accepted principles which govern the selection of officers, some of them being:

a. the need for a balance in the distribution of offices between different geographical areas;

b. the need for representation of particular interests (e.g., donors and receivers of economic aid);

c. the importance of finding a good and impartial chairman familiar with the subject matter;

d. the unwritten rule, that none of the permanent members of the Security Council present a candidate for President of the General Assembly or for chairman of an Assembly body.

Other things being equal, a good and experienced candidate will get the job as opposed to a poor and inexperienced candidate, but other things are seldom equal. In fact, however, most U.N. offices are distributed on a geographical or political basis without much regard for personal qualifications.

Once a rough distribution of officers between blocs and interests has been established, the interested delegations begin to consider possible candidatures among themselves. Some countries may put forward the names of their nationals whom they wish to see elected and when this is done such nominations must be carefully considered by all delegations concerned. In most cases, however, delegations hesitate to put forward a particular name until they have some idea whether their country is likely to be acceptable as the source of a candidate.

There is often more than one candidate for a position. If a delegation wants a U.N. position badly enough to embarrass its friends, exasperate its enemies and disregard the other possibly harmful consequences of a strong campaign, that delegation can often be successful in getting its candidate elected. Few candidates are prepared to create public personal embarrassment for their own and other delegations by forcing an election competition to the vote. Thus elections for the officers of U.N. bodies are seldom contested in public. Very strong pressure will be brought to bear on the rival candidates to settle the dispute between themselves if disagreement persists. A disputed election for a U.N. office will be considered to cause more bitterness than it is worth.

Sometimes à judiciously timed withdrawal just before an election (and on occasion even after it has begun), will settle the issue. For example, during the election for President of the twelfth session of the General Assembly (1957), Mr. Charles Malik (Lebanon) withdrew at the last moment in favor of Sir Leslie Munro (New Zealand), thus securing widespread support for a successful candidature at the thirteenth session of the General Assembly. Candidatures are often presented not so much in hope of being successful on the occasion in question but for the purpose of protecting a probable candidature in the future. Recently, though, candidates for the presidency of the General Assembly have been known as much as a year in advance partly because of the now established tradition that the presidency rotates regularly among the regional groups. However, there may be fierce competition within a group on the designation of the group candidate.

If there is serious difficulty in respect of a slate of officers, there will be informal meetings of delegations to discuss how these difficulties can be resolved. The Secretariat is often able to act as a clearing house for information on possible candidatures in order to avoid a division in public. The Secretariat also frequently acts as an agent for the proposers of the individual candidates. In the election of committee officers, rule 103 of the Rules of Procedure of the General Assembly specifies that "the nomination of each candidate shall be limited to one speaker." Traditions of reasonable behavior and the efficiency of the U.N. Secretariat have generally avoided major wounds as the result of the election of a slate of officers at the U.N.

The same procedure as that for elections to U.N. offices is followed in the election of countries to U.N. bodies with limited membership.

More is at stake in such elections since, instead of the predominantly honorific function of presiding officer, there is an active and direct part in the work of the body concerned. A permanent mission usually circulates a note on behalf of the candidature. Often permanent missions will support such formal letters by oral conversations. Furthermore, representations may also be made in national capitals in support of the candidature. In this kind of election personal considerations have little significance. However, the fact that a country has particularly able representatives in some special field or has a worldwide reputation for its national policies in a particular area may have some relevance in determining whether or not it is elected. For most U.N. bodies there are agreements, some of them formal and some of them informal, concerning the distribution of seats.

Usually it is left to the regional groups to determine what country should represent its area in a U.N. body; however, severe difficulties can arise if there is a dispute. At the 34th session of the General Assembly the Latin-American group was unable to agree on a candidate for the Latin-American seat on the Security Council becoming vacant 1 January 1980. Cuba and Columbia were candidates. A record 154 Assembly ballots failed to deliver the required two thirds majority, although Cuba was leading in all ballots, except one. The Assembly session had to be extended into 1980. Finally, both countries withdrew, and Mexico was elected to the vacant seat with an overwhelming majority. In the meantime, the Legal Counsel of the U.N., Mr. E. Suy, had given an interpretation that the Council, with one vacant seat, "may continue to function notwithstanding the fact that it is not legally constituted."4

One of the most difficult things to predict is the result of a contested election. Country X may well believe that it has 90 firm commitments for support, 35 promises of support "in principle", leaving only 25 undecided countries. The firm commitments probably came through formal diplomatic channels, in writing, or, in many cases, orally. However, in quite a few cases the delegation of a country supposed to have given firm support to country X will either not have sent any instructions at all, or have attached an "unbinding rider", i.e., any one of the following formulas:

—you vote for country X in the first ballot, but can switch on subsequent ballots to whichever candidate has the best chance of winning;
—you vote for country X provided most members of our (regional or political) group give similar support.

141

During the elections for the Security Council at the thirty-third session of the General Assembly (1978) Bangladesh and Japan were competing for the floating "Asian" seat on the Council. On the basis of indications of support Japan thought it would easily win, but after two ballots it was clear that Bangladesh was moving towards the required two-thirds majority, and Japan decided to withdraw from the race.

The regional groups meet prior to each session of the General Assembly, and after some deliberation usually manage to come up with "an agreed slate" for the President of the General Assembly, for its vice-presidents (see p. 29) and for each of the chairmen of the Main Committees. Such a slate is never challenged by another regional group. On one of the first days of the General Assembly session the plenary transforms itself successively into each of the seven Main Committees, exclusively to elect the chairman of each committee, who is nominated by a country belonging to another regional group than his own, usually by the delegation of the chairman of the previous year. Special sessions of the General Assembly are presided over by the President and Vice-Presidents of the previous Assembly session.

While the vice-presidents are countries, the chairmen of the seven Main Committees are individually elected persons. The regional distribution of these chairmanships has also been specified in G.A. resolution 33/138. However, except in the case of the First Committee (and the President), there is no automatic rotation among the five groups, although the same group would not hold the chairmanship of the same committee two years in a row. When a regional group cannot agree on its candidate, an open fight is inevitable.

Similarly, slates of countries to be elected from a regional group to be members of various U.N. bodies are put forward by each regional group. In some cases, especially for seats on the Security Council and the Economic and Social Council, voting by secret ballot must take place. An agreed slate from one group is traditionally accepted by other groups. Fairly frequently a group cannot agree on a slate, and an electoral fight ensues. Sometimes an unusual situation may arise. At the thirty-first session of the General Assembly (1976) all 25 members of the International Law Commission had to be elected. The various regional groups had informally agreed among themselves on the number of candidates each group was entitled to and requested the Secretariat to distribute lists of candidates on that basis. However, the President of the General Assembly (Ambassador Amerasinghe of Sri Lanka) felt that this procedure was illegal, and that the election, by secret ballot, should take place on the basis of a long list of all candidates in alphabetical order, their qualifications being the only element to be considered. The result was that Asia lost one member and the group of Western European and other states gained one member. When one of the Western European members died soon afterwards, the Western European group decided not to put up another candidate. Under a co-opting procedure laid down in its statute, the International Law Commission thereupon appointed a member from an Asian country, and the balance was thus restored.

At the time when the United Nations was established, it was intended that countries would be elected to U.N. bodies, firstly, because of their interest in and capacity for contributing to the work of these bodies, and only secondly because they belonged to certain regional or political blocs. Time has, however, reversed this order of priority and, some would say, virtually eliminated the functional basis for choosing members of U.N. bodies.

Observers have sometimes suggested that U.N. elections are "rigged". Often they are, but this rigging is the result of a prolonged process of negotiation. There have been few protests against the way in which U.N. elections are conducted. Governments may not always be elected at the time and to the bodies which they might prefer, but over a period of time the process seems to work. Certainly most delegations prefer discussion of an agreement on a slate before an election to avoid uncertainty and repeated balloting in which personal and national susceptibilities will possibly be hurt.

Notes to chapter 7

1. A well-known counter-argument is: "This proposal is interesting, but the time is not ripe: no financial resources would be available."
2. Johan Kaufmann, *Conference Diplomacy,* op. cit., p. 159.
3. UNESCO, *The Technique of International Conferences* (Paris: UNESCO, 1951), p. 28.
4. See GAOR, 34th session, 118th plenary meeting, 31 December 1979. Mr. Suy based his argument on the consideration that while on the one hand art. 23 of the Charter means that a Security Council of less than 15 members would not be legally constituted, on the other hand "the failure of the General Assembly to fulfil its constitutional obligations cannot be held to produce legal consequences so fundamental to the Organization as the paralysis of a principal organ" (ibidem).

Part Three

Case Studies of United Nations Decision Making

Chapter 8

How to Achieve Success: Six Examples

1. The Mediating Role of a Presiding Officer:[1]
U.N. Disarmament Commission

The tenth special session of the General Assembly (New York, 23 May
-1 July 1978) was entirely devoted to disarmament issues. It ended
with the adoption by consensus of a lengthy final document, consisting
of an Introduction, a Declaration, a Programme of Action, and recommendations concerning the machinery for international disarmament
negotiations (G.A. resolution S-10/2). In this latter field, the special
session took two important decisions. First, it decided to establish (as a
successor to an identically named commission which had not met for
many years, established at the sixth session of the General Assembly) a
Disarmament Commission composed of all members of the U.N., as

a deliberative body, a subsidiary organ of the General Assembly, the function of which
shall be to consider and make recommendations on various problems in the field of disarmament and to follow up the relevant decisions and recommendations of the Special
Session devoted to disarmament. The Disarmament Commission should, inter alia,
consider the elements of a comprehensive programme for disarmament to be submitted as recommendations to the General Assembly and, through it, to the negotiating
body, the Committee on Disarmament. [A/RES/S-10/2, para. 118a]

Secondly the special session recommended in the following terms the
establishment, as a successor body to the Conference of the Committee
on Disarmament (a non-U.N. body which, meeting in Geneva, had
been the principal multilateral negotiating organ on disarmament issues), of a new Committee on Disarmament:

The General Assembly is deeply aware of the continuing requirement for a single multilateral disarmament negotiating forum of limited size taking decisions on basis of
consensus. It attaches great importance to the participation of all the nuclear-weapon
States in an appropriately constituted negotiating body: the Committee on Disarmament.
    The General Assembly welcomes the agreement reached following appropriate con-

sultations among the Member States during the Special Session of the General Assembly Devoted to Disarmament that the Committee on Disarmament will be open to the nuclear-weapon States, and 32 to 35 other States to be chosen in consultation with the President of the 32nd session of the General Assembly. [para. 120]

The explicit separation in a General Assembly resolution of organs for "deliberation" and "negotiation" was probably unprecedented in United Nations history. In regard to the Committee on Disarmament it was explicitly stated in the Final Document that it would conduct its work by consensus (in conformity with the tradition of its predecessor); in regard to the Disarmament Commission the Final Document laid down that it "shall function under the rules of procedure relating to the committees of the General Assembly with such modifications as the Commission may deem necessary and shall make every effort to ensure that, in so far as possible, decisions on substantive issues be adopted by consensus." (para. 118b)

The first substantive session of the Disarmament Commission took place during May/June 1979.

There was a general debate followed by negotiations on a comprehensive omnibus draft resolution, proposed by a large group of countries, mainly the non-aligned nations, to "push ahead" with disarmament measures in comparison with the Final Document of the tenth special session and the resolutions of the thirty-third session of the General Assembly. This was opposed by a large group of other, mainly Western, nations. Thanks to the tireless efforts of the Chairman of the Committee, Mr. M.A. Vellodi (India, former Deputy Under-Secretary-General for Political and Security Council Affairs in the U.N. Secretariat) the proposed omnibus resolution was not put to the vote. The Committee session ended with the adoption by consensus of a series of recommendations on the elements for a comprehensive program of disarmament. However, it was a pseudo-consensus, because, as closing statements showed, many delegations were not satisfied. Yet, the deliberative character of the Commission had been upheld, and also the tenth special session's exhortation to aim at consensus.

This example is also a good illustration of the moderating influence an effective presiding officer can have. Had there been a vote, it would probably have destroyed the idea that the U.N. Disarmament Commission should mainly serve as a general deliberative organ and thereby would have wrecked the Commission's potential usefulness.

2. The mediating role of a presiding officer: Economic Commission for Europe

Another example of the moderating role of the chairman is provided by the following case. In 1971 the plenary session of the Economic Commission of Europe, one of the regional commissions of the United Nations, had before it the modalities and agenda of an ECE conference on problems relating to the environment, to be held in Prague in May 1971. The socialist countries of Eastern Europe pushed hard for participation by the German Democratic Republic, which, at that time, was not yet a member of the United Nations and therefore also not of the Economic Commission for Europe. This wish ran into fierce opposition by the Western members of the Commission. These had a majority (18 to 9) in the ECE, but wanted to stick to ECE's tradition of consensus decision making.

The Prague meeting was dubbed as a conference, to be attended by government representatives. Various precedents, advanced by the Eastern European countries, about German Democratic Republic experts having attended past expert meetings under the auspices of the ECE were therefore not relevant. In an objective legal opinion this fact was also pointed out by the Secretariat. A number of informal meetings were held under the chairmanship of the Executive Secretary of the Economic Commission for Europe, Mr. J. Stanovnik, to find a way out. Neither the Western European countries, nor those of Eastern Europe wanted this to become a major point of confrontation; the Western European countries did not want to impose their views by a vote. In the Economic Commission for Europe the consensus method had been a long-standing tradition, with votes highly exceptional. Various formulas for a compromise were advanced in the informal encounters, but none turned out to be acceptable to all concerned. During the plenary meeting, in which the matter was discussed, a stalemate seemed unavoidable, and the Prague conference, which all members of the ECE desired to be held (also because it had to recommend on future environment programs of the ECE), seemed to be in danger. During the debate in plenary, various delegates sent little pieces of paper to the Chairman (the author), suggesting new compromises. There seemed to be a last minute desire to find a consensus solution. The Chairman then decided to interrupt the meeting, and asked the delegates directly concerned to sit down with him around a small table in the middle of the conference room. After only half an hour of informal negotiations a simple compromise was found: the Prague conference would be split up into two parts, i.e.,

149

a. plenary sessions to be attended only by official government representatives and official observers, all representing Member States of the ECE, the U.N. or one of the specialized agencies, and
b. meetings of a technical committee of the whole, to be attended by experts. These experts would be included under a separate heading in the list of delegations. Among them would be experts from the German Democratic Republic.

The compromise was read out by the Chairman and rapidly adopted without a vote. This sequence shows that if governments are given time to reflect on a possible solution, an issue stalemated at time-point (a) can be solved at time-point (a + x). Of course governments have to be inclined, which they were in this case, to accept a certain amount of flexibility. However, if the Chairman had not provided time for the last-minute negotiation, the matter would no doubt have ended in a full stalemate, which, in this example, would have meant either no decision at all on the Prague conference (so that it could not have been held), or a vote imposed by the majority against participation by the German Democratic Republic. This probably would have provoked a withdrawal of the invitation of the Czechoslovak Government to act as host, and postponement of the conference.

3. An Initiative that Succeeded: The Question of Torture

For several years in the United Nations, both the General Assembly and the Commission on Human Rights had given attention to the inadmissibility of torture and similar practices applied to prisoners. However, there was no specific U.N. decision concerning this matter.

The scheduling of the Fifth U.N. Congress on the Prevention of Crime and the Treatment of Offenders (1-12 September 1975 in Geneva) provided an opportunity for The Netherlands and other countries which felt that the time was ripe for further action, to take certain initiatives.

Prior to the twenty-ninth session of the General Assembly (1974), The Netherlands, in close consultation with Austria, Ireland and Sweden, drafted a resolution, the intent of which was to request the above-mentioned U.N. congress and the governments represented there, to enlarge the existing Standard Minimum Rules for the Treatment of Prisoners with rules which would protect prisoners against torture and similar inhuman practices. The draft resolution was ready when the

150

twenty-ninth session started. The forum of action was the Third Committee. It was not difficult to form a group of sponsors: Austria, Bangladesh, Costa Rica, Ireland, Jordan, the Philippines, and Sweden. This was a balanced group of sponsors, except that it included no African country. The Dutch delegate introduced the draft resolution on behalf of the sponsors, drawing attention to Article 5 of the Universal Declaration of Human Rights which outlawed torture or cruel, inhuman or degrading treatment or punishment. This prohibition had been re-affirmed in resolution 3059 (XXVIII) of the General Assembly. After this speech, and no doubt because the resolution was likely to be acceptable to all or nearly all governments, Australia, Belgium, the Federal Republic of Germany, Colombia, Ecuador, France, Italy, Japan, New Zealand and the United States became co-sponsors of the draft (doc. A/C.3/L 2106). Under different circumstances such overwhelming enthusiasm could have become a source of difficulties, namely, if it had been necessary to obtain the agreement of all sponsors to important changes in the draft, in response to either criticisms or proposed amendments. As it was, after a speech by Iraq, which expressed some criticisms, only minor revision of the draft resolution was necessary. It was made clear, for example, that the resolution intended in no way to bypass the U.N. Commission on Human Rights. The revised draft was adopted in the Committee with 111 votes in favor, one against and 2 abstentions. The plenary meeting of the 1974 General Assembly delivered a vote of 125 votes in favor and a single abstention (G.A. resolution 3218 [XXIX]). This vote indicates that, between the Committee and the plenary, delegations occasionally change their minds, often to avoid isolating themselves from an overwhelming majority.

Beginning in 1975, The Netherlands and Sweden engaged in intensive consultations, mostly in the form of meetings of Dutch and Swedish officials dealing with human rights issues in Stockholm or The Hague. Also, in New York and Geneva the permanent missions of both countries, and of other countries desirous of making progress on the torture issue, were in touch constantly.

The double objective of all of these consultations was to prepare for the Fifth U.N. Congress on the Prevention of Crime, and to coordinate possible action at the 1975 General Assembly.

Another symptom of the fact that this issue was "alive" (and not, as happens with so many U.N. resolutions, forgotten shortly after adoption of a text) was the inquiry which the U.N. Secretary-General was to undertake among governments to solicit views on how to deal with the torture problem.

Also, the World Health Organization was, pursuant to G.A. resolution 3218 (XXIX), invited to draft an "outline of the principles of medical ethics which may be relevant to the protection of persons subjected to any form of detention or imprisonment against torture and other cruel, inhuman or degrading treatment or punishment." This draft was to go to the Fifth Congress.

Such a multi-polar attack on a problem is quite useful, provided there is an understanding as to "who does what".

The result of the Dutch-Swedish action, and of their consultations with other countries, was the deposit, by The Netherlands and Sweden, on 13 August 1975, of a draft recommendation for the Fifth Congress, of which the main element was a draft declaration against torture.

The adoption of this draft declaration at the Fifth Congress went smoothly. Some secondary difficulties were overcome. The Congress submitted the draft declaration for formal action to the thirtieth session of the General Assembly (1975).

There then followed intensive consultations, initiated by the delegations of The Netherlands and Sweden, on action in the Third Committee which was dealing with the matter. One tactical possibility was that of a short procedural resolution in which the General Assembly would generally express appreciation for the work of the Fifth Congress. However, this approach was rejected by the consulting countries, because while, on the one hand, it might have paved the way for formal adoption of the draft declaration on torture, it might, on the other hand, have strengthened the hands of those who did not want to see the declaration explicitly adopted. The argument would have been that the general endorsement of the work of the Congress was sufficient.

The conclusion which the consulting delegations reached was to have the declaration adopted by itself, and, moreover, to table a draft resolution deciding on further steps to implement the declaration. The draft declaration was before the General Assembly as a recommendation of the Fifth Congress. The report of the U.N. Secretariat on the work of the Fifth Congress (doc. A/10260) contained not only the draft declaration as adopted at the Congress without a vote (but with some reservations on specific parts of the text), but also some brief preambular paragraphs recommended for adoption by the General Assembly. The total text as recommended by the Fifth Congress (preamble plus draft declaration) was submitted by The Netherlands as a draft resolution to the Third Committee, and introduced by The Netherlands on 14 November 1975. The debate, in combination with that on additional measures against torture, showed that the draft declaration was generally acceptable. A minor drafting amendment proposed by the German Democratic Republic caused no difficulties. On 24 November 1975, the draft and thereby the declaration, was adopted "by acclamation". This full consensus was repeated in the plenary meeting of the General Assembly (resolution 3452 [XXX]): Declaration on Protection of all Persons from Being Subjected to Torture and Other Cruel, Inhuman or Degrading Treatment or Punishment.

The additional elaborating resolution was sponsored, apart from The Netherlands and Sweden, by Australia, Austria, Belgium, Canada, Costa Rica, Denmark, Ecuador, Germany (Federal Republic of), Greece, Ireland, Italy, Japan, Jordan, Mexico, New Zealand, Norway, the Philippines, Portugal and Venezuela. It is interesting to note that Africa and the socialist countries of Eastern Europe again did not co-sponsor the draft.

The additional resolution requested the Commission on Human Rights, inter alia, to ensure the effective observance of the declaration against torture and to formulate principles for the protection of all persons under any form of detention or imprisonment. The text also requested the Committee on Crime Prevention and Control to elaborate a Code of Conduct for Law Enforcement Officials. It requested the World Health Organization to give further attention to the elaboration of principles of medical ethics relevant to the protection of detained or imprisoned persons against torture.

The debate on the torture question was relatively brief; only 25 delegations participated. After this debate was concluded, the delegate of Greece introduced the draft resolution (doc. A/C.3/L.2187) on behalf of the group of 21 co-sponsors. Intentionally, neither Sweden nor The Netherlands, but Greece was chosen to undertake this somewhat delicate job; one of the reasons that Greece was selected was that it had recently emerged from the era of the "regime of the colonels" during which torture practices were deemed to have existed.

On the 21-nation draft resolution a long series of informal talks took place between the principal sponsors, and some other delegations, mainly from Eastern Europe. This resulted in the acceptance by the sponsors of several relatively minor changes. A revised draft (doc. A/C.3/L.2187/rev.1) was tabled on 27 November. A brief debate took place on 28 November, resulting in the acceptance by the sponsors of another (oral) amendment from the German Democratic Republic. After that, on 28 November 1975, the draft was adopted in the Third

153

Committee without a vote in what again was a real consensus. This performance was repeated in the plenary meeting of the General Assembly (resolution 3453 [XXX]).

The sequence of events which has just been described shows that in a delicate matter it is possible to adopt the right decisions in the United Nations. All the rules of the game were carefully observed: timely and continuous consultations were held, first among sympathetic governments, and later also with opponents; the cooperation of the Secretariat was obtained at an early stage; a homogeneous group of co-sponsors was formed; and sufficient time was available for informal consultations and negotiations.

4. Positive Action: Safety of International Civil Aviation

The question of taking hostages, like so many other practical international problems, had been of United Nations concern for some time. The General Assembly already had on its agenda two items with a direct bearing on hijacking, one being the report of the Ad Hoc Committee on International Terrorism, a committee in existence since 1972, which had not produced any concrete results, and the other being the report of the Ad Hoc Committee on the Drafting of an International Convention against the taking of hostages, established pursuant to a West German initiative at the General Assembly in 1976.

On 13 October 1977 a Lufthansa Boeing 737 was hijacked to Somalia. On 17 October the hijacking ended after the successful intervention of a West German government commando with the cooperation of the government of Somalia. However, before that the captain of the aircraft had been killed by the hijackers. The International Federation of Airline Pilots (IFALPA) called for immediate United Nations action against similar acts; its president flew to New York and urged Secretary-General Waldheim to take action. Certain national airline pilot associations similarly sent representatives to New York, where they consulted with the permanent missions of their countries.

It soon appeared that several delegations, mostly Western, had received instructions to find out what possibilities existed for rapid and efficient action, either under one of the existing agenda items, or under a new item. In one of those spontaneous moods which, fortunately, show that U.N. decision making does not always take place according to formalized patterns, an informal group of some 25 countries from all parts of the world met on 19 October to discuss possible options for action. Those attending were mostly Sixth (Legal) Committee delegates (including several ambassadors), since the two agenda items mentioned above on terrorism and hostages had been allocated to the Sixth Committee. It was soon apparent that a majority was favorable to the idea to request urgently the inscription of a new agenda item, under the procedure foreseen for such a situation.

The result of the meeting of 9 October, and of further meetings on 20 and 21 October, was, that during the afternoon of 21 October a table was arranged in one of the conference rooms, putting up for signatures the letter and explanatory memorandum (later circulated as doc. A/32/245) requesting, under rule 15 of the General Assembly Rules of Procedure, the inscription as an important and urgent item of "Safety of International Civil Aviation", and also requesting that the item be accorded "due priority". The words "due priority" were a compromise between those who felt that the high priority which the question had should be spelled out in the inscription request and those who felt that it was tactically wrong to stress too much the question of priority, in order not to antagonize certain countries which, it was known, might oppose the entire initiative. A total of 42 countries signed the letter on 21 and 22 October. At noon of that day the letter was given to the Secretary-General.

On 24 October the General Committee met—in record time after the request for inscription—to discuss the inclusion of the item in the agenda of the General Assembly and its allocation to a committee of the General Assembly. Only the delegate of Austria spoke on behalf of the countries which had requested the inscription of the item. The Austrian delegation had taken an active hand in the affair; astute knowledge of both the Rules of Procedure and of the tactical situation was of primary importance. The member of the Austrian delegation who specifically dealt with the affair had until recently been a member of the Secretariat, and was particularly well-versed to handle it, especially because he knew exactly whom to contact in the Secretariat in order to achieve fast action. The debate in the General Committee was quite brief. Only the delegate of Saudi Arabia spoke, pointing out that in his view it would have been better to widen the item to safety of all forms of transport and expressed his conviction that the saving of the lives of hostages was of paramount importance. In only an hour the Chairman of the General Committee (Mr. Mojsov of Yugoslavia, the President of the General Assembly) could declare the inscription of the item by acclamation, and also its allocation to the Special Political Committee. This latter decision was the result of consultations which had shown that most delegations did not wish the matter handled within the somewhat technical constraints of the Sixth (Legal) Committee; furthermore, the Special Policital Committee had a relatively light agenda. Only a day later, on 25 October, the plenary session confirmed the recommendations of the General Committee unanimously and without debate. The new item was number 129 on the agenda of the thirty-second session.

In the meantime continuous consultations had been taking place on the text of a draft resolution. The problem was whether to aim at precise and rather far-reaching recommendations, which would have endangered support for the text, or more "moderate" language, commending wide support, possibly a general consensus. The text as submitted by 46 countries (doc. A/SPC/32/L.2) was not very "strong", and concentrated on appeals to all countries to take steps for the improvement of security arrangements at airports and to ratify the three conventions relevant to civil aviation safety. This draft resolution read as follows:

The General Assembly,

Recognizing that the orderly functioning of international civil air travel under conditions guaranteeing the safety of its operations is in the interest of all peoples and promotes and preserves friendly relations among States,

Recalling its resolution 2645 (XXV) of 25 November 1970, in which it recognized that acts of aerial hijacking or other wrongful interference with civil air travel jeopardize the life and safety of passengers and crew and constitute a violation of their human rights,

Recalling also its earlier resolution 2551 (XXIV) of 12 December 1969 as well as Security Council resolution 286 (1970) of 9 September 1970 and the Security Council decision of 20 June 1972,

1. *Reiterates* and reaffirms its condemnation of acts of aerial hijacking or other interference with civil air travel through the threat or use of force, and all acts of violence which may be directed against passengers, crew and aircraft;

2. *Calls upon* all States to take all necessary steps, taking into account the relevant recommendations of the United Nations and the International Civil Aviation Organization, to prevent acts of the nature referred to in paragraph 1 above, including the improvement of security arrangements at airports or by airlines as well as the exchange of relevant information, and to this end to take joint and separate action, in accordance with the Charter, in co-operation with the United Nations and the International Civil Aviation Organization to ensure that passengers, crew and aircraft engaged in civil aviation are not used as a means of extorting advantage of any kind;

3. *Appeals to* all States, which have not yet become parties, to give urgent consideration to ratifying or acceding to the Convention on Offences and Certain Other Acts Committed on Board Aircraft signed at Tokyo on 14 September 1963, the Convention for the Suppression of Unlawful Seizure of Aircraft signed in The Hague on 16 December 1970, and the Convention for the Suppression of Unlawful Acts against the Safety of Civil Aviation signed at Montreal on 23 September 1971;

4. *Calls upon* the International Civil Aviation Organization to undertake urgently further efforts with a view to ensuring the security of air travel and preventing the recurrence of acts of the nature referred to in paragraph 1 above, including the reinforcement of Annex 17 to the Convention on International Civil Aviation.

The debate in the Special Political Committee opened on 26 October 1977, with statements by the President of the Council of the International Civil Aviation Organization, and by the President of IFALPA. There followed four more meetings in which item 129 was discussed. A sizeable number of delegations, i.e. 40, participated in the debate, most of them after the adoption by consensus of the resolution. A joint statement on behalf of the nine countries of the European Communities was made by its president at the time, the representative of Belgium. There was no serious criticism of the draft resolution. The representative of Saudi Arabia pursued his earlier approach and at one time submitted an alternative draft resolution (doc. A/SPC/32/L.4), according to which the saving of the lives of the hostages should remain the primary concern of the international community. In the end, however, he was willing to withdraw his draft resolution and settle for the acceptance of a relatively minor amendment to the draft resolution which the Committee was about to adopt.

A more serious problem was that certain delegations continued to have misgivings about the timeliness of the draft resolution; they felt that the question of safety of civil aviation could not be separated from certain political realities. The sponsors believed that tactically it was better to consult with Arab and other delegations in order to achieve a consensus. These delegations wished to add at the end of operative para. 1 the words "whether committed by individuals or states". The second amendment was to insert in operative para. 2, after the reference to "joint and separate action" which all states are called upon to take against hijacking etc., the words "without prejudice to the sovereignty or territorial integrity of any State". This was intended to be a reference to the desire not to infringe on the sovereignty of a state, in case a state was not willing to cooperate with another government to terminate a hijacking situation. The Israeli raid on Entebbe in 1974 to liberate a hijacked Air France plane was clearly meant. A third amendment led to the inclusion, in the second operative paragraph of the draft resolution, of a reference to the relevant United Nations resolutions. The African and Arab countries behind this idea had in mind resolutions affirming the right of oppressed peoples to struggle for their independence. After the draft resolution was adopted, the nine countries of the European Communities, as was stated by their spokesman, the Belgian representative, specified that they considered as relevant resolutions only those mentioned in the preamble of the resolution.

The sponsors had strong doubts whether these amendments should be accepted. Refusing them might have meant the submission of more, really crippling amendments, giving an even less desirable end result. In order to avoid giving the impression that the sponsors liked the two amendments just referred to, the cooperation of the Chairman of the Special Political Committee, Mr. Neugebauer (German Democratic Republic) was obtained in submitting a consensus text which, as he stated on 1 November, was the result of consultations between the sponsors and the various regional groups (in fact the Arab group and the African group). In essence the amendment to add to para. 1 "whether committed by individuals or States" had been accepted by the sponsors. The words "take joint and separate action" in para. 2 had been maintained, but mitigated by the words "subject to respect for the purposes and principles of the Charter of the United Nations and for the relevant United Nations declarations, covenants and resolutions and without prejudice to the sovereignty or territorial integrity of any State." After dealing with the relatively minor amendments proposed by Saudi Arabia already mentioned above, the resolution was adopted by consensus on 1 November. Adoption in plenary, also "without a vote", took place on 3 November 1977 (General Assembly resolution 32/8).

From the moment of dispatching the request for an additional agenda item to the adoption of a resolution in plenary session exactly twelve days had elapsed. The result was widely hailed as showing that the United Nations can act speedily. Of course, it remained to be seen what the real effect of the adopted resolution with its non-binding recommendations would be: in particular, whether it would lead to acceptance of the three covenants dealing with safety of civil aviation by governments who had not already done so. For many, the result was more than a pseudo-consensus (see pp. 127-129). Yet public opinion and world information media generally welcomed the swift United Nations action.

The sequence of events: consulting with a homogeneous group of delegations on the request for an additional agenda item, quickly submitting a draft resolution, engaging in negotiations with countries who desired changes in the text, enlisting the cooperation of the committee chairman who himself thereby demonstrated the useful role which a chairman can play in specific circumstances, was a good example of an optimalized case of United Nations decision making.

5. The Secretary-General Convenes an Urgently Necessary Informal Conference

While most United Nations meetings and conferences are convened according to rigidly determined rules and/or decisions by "higher organs", there are examples of remarkable speed and flexibility in convening a conference under United Nations auspices.

In the spring of 1979 the number of refugees from Viet Nam, mostly by way of the high seas ("the boat people"), took alarming proportions. The United Kingdom Government, supported by other governments, suggested that the problem should be discussed at a United Nations conference, to be organized by Secretary-General Waldheim. However, the Secretary-General did not have the legal possibility to convene a formal conference. Such a formal meeting would have had to be previously authorized by some competent U.N. organ, such as the General Assembly or the Economic and Social Council.

Mr. Waldheim found a way out by convening a "consultation", held in Geneva on 20 and 21 July 1979. He invited more than sixty countries which, for geographical or other reasons, were involved in the problem of Vietnamese refugees. There were no rules of procedure. It had, however, been agreed upon that the conference would concentrate on practical solutions and that there would be no "political cal" statements. This latter understanding was adhered to by all but a few of the participating governments, most of them represented on the ministerial level. The meeting became a kind of "pledging conference" where governments announced numbers of refugees they were willing to receive or financial contributions to the programs of the U.N. High Commissioner for Refugees, to alleviate the plight of Indochinese refugees. The meeting also led to a promise by Viet Nam, laid down in an agreement with the U.N. High Commissioner for Refugees, to put a temporary stop to the departure of refugees from Viet Nam. This promise, inspired by the wish to take care of large numbers of existing refugees, was controversial inasmuch as it was contrary to the right to emigrate, enshrined in the United Nations human rights documents.

Because there were no rules of procedure and because the meeting had been held outside the formal framework of U.N. conferences, governments did not feel constrained by the fear of being forced to accept an international commitment. They knew in advance that there would be no resolutions. The only government that accepted an international commitment was that of Viet Nam, which signed a memorandum of understanding between it and the Office of the U.N. High Commissioner for Refugees concerning the departure of persons from Viet Nam.

The meeting was considered a success by many. As Secretary-General Waldheim stated: "Offers of resettlement opportunities doubled from 125.000 to 260.000, and most substantial new pledges in cash and in kind, exceeding $160 million, were received. The participants were, I believe, as gratified as I was that so much could be accomplished in a two-day meeting of this kind."[2]

Without Secretariat action at the right time and without the courage to find a way to hold this "unauthorized" meeting, the conference would not have been possible.

6. The Usability of Contributions to the Special Fund— A Detailed Illustration of the U.N. Negotiating Process[3]

The currency issue is one of several problems which may confront U.N. development and other assistance activities. Governments contribute to programs for developing nations, including UNDP (and its predecessors the Special Fund and the Expanded Program of Technical Assistance), UNICEF, etc., according to their means and inclinations, not according to any fixed or assessed scales. The question has long existed: to what extent should these contributions be made in a convertible form? A more general concept of "usability" had been involved in lengthy discussions in the (no longer existing) Technical Assistance Committee of the Economic and Social Council. The Preparatory Committee of the Special Fund, ECOSOC and the General Assembly had all discussed this issue, sometimes with considerable acrimony. The results, as applied to the Special Fund, were incorporated in sections 47 to 50 of part B of General Assembly resolution 1240 (XIII). The essential provisions of those sections for the purpose of discussion in the meeting of May 1959 of the Special Fund Governing Council were the following:

Contributions shall be made by Governments in currency readily usable by the Special Fund consistent with the need for efficiency and economy of the Fund's operations, or shall be transferable to the greatest possible extent into currency readily usable by the Fund. To this end, Governments are urged to make available as large a percentage as they may find possible of their contributions in such currency or currencies as the Managing Director may indicate are required for the execution of the Fund's programme. The Managing Director should, consistent with the criteria set forth respect-ting the nature and utilization of contributions, endeavour to make the fullest possible use of available currencies.

Although general or partial convertibility of all contributions had been considered desirable by some delegations, there had been general agreement that all contributions must at least be in a form "readily usable" by the Fund.

In Ottawa an interdepartmental meeting was held, attended by officials of both the departments chiefly concerned, at which the reports from New York were discussed and a general policy for the delegation established. It was decided that no formal written instructions for this delegation were required because the earlier decisions of the government of Canada provided the necessary guidance. Furthermore it was not necessary, since the members of the delegation were familiar with the subject matter, to draft any speeches in advance. On Monday, 25 May, the Canadian representative on the Governing Council, an official of the Department of Finance, arrived. After a preliminary discussion in the Canadian mission in New York, the officers concerned had a meeting with officers of the United States delegation and later with a senior official of the Special Fund. At lunch time that day both members of the Canadian delegation to the meetings of the Governing Council came to the U.N. and had conversations with a number of other delegations.

The Managing Director had circulated a paper containing "Draft Provisional Financial Regulations" (doc. SF/L.9 of 24 April 1959). This paper, which would form the basis of the discussions in the Governing Council, had been studied both in Ottawa and in New York and appeared generally acceptable. It followed closely the language and intentions of General Assembly resolution 1240 (XIII) as quoted above. Article 6.2. of these proposed Financial Regulations read as follows:

Contributions shall be made in currency readily usable by the Special Fund consistent with the need for efficiency and economy of the Fund's operations, or transferable to the greatest possible extent into currency readily usable by the Fund, and shall be made without limitation as to use by a specific executing agency or in a specific recipient country or for a special project.

On the morning of the meeting on 26 May, the Indian, United Arab Republic and Yugoslav delegations circulated in document SF/L.14 a formal amendment to Article 6.2. which would, in the first line, after the word "currency" add the words: "as far as possible".

Observers often mock at the serious preoccupation of U.N. organs with what appear to be minor semantic points. Here, however, is a good example of "the importance of a few words."

In the first place the language of G.A. resolution 1240 (XIII) represented a carefully balanced compromise which had taken many weeks to negotiate. Many delegations continued to believe in the need for the maximum percentage of contributions being made in fully convertible currency. The compromise wording on currency of contributions was accepted partly because generally acceptable compromises were reached on other parts of the resolution. If to add "as far as possible" meant any substantial change in the basic legislation governing the program, the acceptability of the original resolution itself and of the program which developed from it might be affected with serious consequences for its financial support.

"Contributions shall be made in currency as far as possible readily usable"—this might mean that contributions could be made in *currency* as far as possible, and if this meaning were taken contributions might also be made in other forms, including goods and services. The result might be a situation in which the Fund would receive a wide variety of goods and services as contributions which could not be used to carry out the type of projects for which the Fund was established. The resolution of the General Assembly laid down that projects were to be requested by the developing countries, not proposed by the donors of the U.N. They were also to be "relatively large", for "one country, or a group of countries, or a region" and of a type which would be implemented over a period of years if necessary. If governments could contribute in forms other than currency and if many did so, where would the financial resources be found to transport the goods contributed, to pay the costs of the necessary headquarters staff and of the staff needed to execute the project? Was it not likely that the contributions in goods and services could not be used to carry out the projects requested? It also seemed undesirable that those countries which did contribute in a convertible form would in fact finance the use of the contributions of countries which did not.

"Contributions should be made in currency so far as possible readily usable" etc. could also mean, and might easily be taken to mean, that contributions could be made in currency which was not necessarily "readily usable". A government might state, for example, that its contribution could be used only within its own borders, thus providing no assistance in meeting the international costs of the program, or, that its contribution could be used only for the purchase of particular goods or services, which might not be wanted or needed for the program.

It was possible, however, that the proposed amendment arose from a previously expressed concern of the developing countries that they might be obliged under this provision to provide part or all of *their* contributions in convertible currency. Many developing countries could themselves be substantial contributors, in their own currencies, to the Special Fund. A good deal of their contributions would of course be spent on projects within their own territories but their participation would serve to broaden the base of the U.N. aid programs and increase the overall totals.

As soon as the amendment contained in SF/L.14 was circulated, the Canadian delegation spoke to all three of the sponsors indicating its difficulty with the proposal. At one point it was suggested by one of the sponsors that the Canadian delegation might propose some way of meeting the concern of the developing countries. These countries were (and many of them still are) experiencing serious foreign exchange difficulties. Since the program was designed to help them, it seemed contradictory at the same time to make their participation dependent on a form of contribution which might aggravate their financial difficulties.

At this point it became necessary to decide whether merely to ask for a vote on the Indian, U.A.R. and Yugoslav amendment in the expectation that it would be defeated. On the basis of previous votes within ECOSOC and the General Assembly by the delegations which were now on the Special Fund Governing Council, the proposal could probably have been defeated. However, such a debate would have been acrimonious and would have forced a vote in which the developed and developing members of the Council would have been divided. This would not have been a hopeful inauguration for a program whose purpose was the promotion of cooperative projects of economic development.

Since the Canadian delegation had been requested to suggest an alternative, discussions were held during the meeting (while other items were being considered in the Governing Council) with the sponsors of the amendment, the Special Fund staff and with representatives of the Secretary-General. At one point the Canadian delegation was asked by one of the sponsors of the amendment why the second sentence of paragraph 47 of General Assembly resolution 1240 had been dropped when Financial Regulations were drafted by the Managing Director. This sentence read:

To this end, Governments are urged to make available as large a percentage as they may find possible of their contributions in such currency or currencies as the Managing Director may indicate are required for the execution of the Fund's programme.

Under this provision the Managing Director was authorized to discuss with governments the need to make their currencies transferable and they were urged to cooperate "as they may find possible." This sentence protected what to the Canadian delegation was an important area of authority for the Managing Director; but it had also envisaged possible exceptions, which would have included the developing countries with foreign exchange difficulties. The developing countries had not been specifically exempted from any agreement to consider making all or part of their contributions transferable in resolution 1240 (XIII) because some developed countries argued that they, too, faced difficulties in their foreign exchange positions from time to time. It had also been noted that some developing countries were in strong financial positions—e.g., those producing oil—and might be able to contribute in a convertible form.

The Canadian delegation was informed by the Secretariat that the second sentence mentioned above had been omitted from the draft Financial Regulations largely because the text did not seem suitable for inclusion in basic financial regulations. Further discussion resulted, however, in acceptance by the Secretariat of the need to include such a provision if by doing so the re-opening of a difficult debate could be avoided. The Canadian delegation, after consultation with the three co-sponsors of the amendment, then gave to the Secretariat an additional amendment which read as follows (doc. SF/L.16):

Article 6.2.:
In the fourth line of the first sentence insert a full stop after the word "Fund". The text should then read as follows: "To this end, Governments are urged to make available as large a percentage as they may find possible of their contributions in such currency or currencies as the Managing Director may indicate are required for the execution of the Fund's programme. Contributions shall be made without limitation as to use by a specific executing agency or in a specific recipient country or for a special project.

About the same time the Soviet delegation submitted an amendment (doc. SF/L.17) which read as follows:

Article 6: Add the following sub-paragraph 5:
"Nevertheless, the provisions of this article shall not affect the right of Governments to make their contributions in the form of goods or services (expressed in appropriate monetary equivalents) which are compatible with the aims and purposes of the Fund".

Fortunately, from some points of view, luncheon intervened at this stage, after all the amendments were in, but before the section in question was reached in the Council's proceedings. During the lunch hour the Canadian delegation, and others of similar views, indicated to most other delegations why they were unable to accept either the Soviet or the three-power amendment. By this time the Indian, U.A.R. and Yugoslav delegations had more or less decided not to press their amendment to a vote since the Canadian amendment served to protect their views without creating a major division in the Council.

The Soviet amendment, however, would have created such a division. It is believed that in the lunch hour most representatives, including those of the developing countries, reached the conclusion that the Soviet amendment, if accepted by the Governing Council and then applied by many contributors, would mean that the projects of the Special Fund would have to be determined by the kind of contributions received. G.A. resolution 1240 (XIII) clearly meant that the choice of projects would be reached on the merits of requests originating in the developing countries.

The record of the 6th meeting of the Governing Council (SF/Min.6) reflects the public discussion of the issue. The report indicates that still other aspects of this question than those considered above had an important bearing on this particular decision. The minutes of that meeting read in part as follows:

The representative of the *Soviet Union* recalled that the purpose of his amendment (SF/L.17) was to provide the greatest possible flexibility with regard to contributions so that States wishing to participate in the Special Fund could do so within the limits of their abilities. The representative of the *United States of America* pointed out that the Council could not deviate from the terms of the General Assembly's resolution (1240 (XIII), para. 47) which provided that contributions should be made in currency readily usable by the Fund. The representative of the *United Kingdom* noted that it would be difficult to accept contributions in kind unless the Managing Director requested the donor to make such a contribution in lieu of currency pledged or agreed upon. However, he noted from the report of the Advisory Committee (A/4099, paragraph 8) that the Managing Director interpreted article 6 as not precluding altogether the acceptance, translated into the appropriate money equivalent, of contributions in such goods and services as were consistent with the needs, efficiency and economy of the Fund's operations. Consequently, goods would only be acceptable if they were needed from a particular country for a specific project. The *Managing Director* said that if the goods were needed for an approved project and could be provided at a cost and of a quality which compared favourably with other sources, the supplying country could make an equivalent contribution in its own currency which would be spent on those goods. In the light of those explanations, the representative of the *Soviet Union* withdrew his amendment (SF/L.17).

The representative of *Canada*, explaining his amendment (SF/L.16), noted that the Managing Director should be given full opportunity to use all contributions to the best advantage. His text reproduced the corresponding provision of resolution 1240 (XIII).

The amendment (of Canada) was adopted.

The three-power amendment never came to a vote. A relatively modest change in the draft proposed by the Managing Director had been made which helped to prevent more serious changes or at least fruitless acrimony. As a matter of fact the Governing Council was able to conclude its meeting by approving unanimously a series of specific projects. The Managing Director was thus placed in a much stronger position than if his instructions were based on a series of split votes.

This was a case study on a detailed issue. The activity of the Canadian delegation and that of other delegations which were conducting parallel discussions with the same or different objectives led to the result reported above. Similar processes were being followed for the large number of details which had to be settled at this meeting. The reason for giving this narrative is to illustrate how a middle power can take the lead and how informal contact takes place outside the meetings in nevertheless quite business-like ways. The casual visitor in the galleries would not have been able to appreciate what was involved in the relatively brief public exchange.

The problems related to non-convertibility of contributions continue to plague the United Nations. However, in the UNDP an acceptable solution was found in 1978 as a result of negotiations between the Administrator, Mr. Bradford Morse, and the Soviet Union.

Notes to chapter 8

1. The reader is also referred to other examples of the role of chairmen, e.g., the role of the President of the Security Council (chapter 3, especially pp. 45-50) and the role of the Chairman of the Ad Hoc Committee on the Restructuring of the Economic and Social Sectors (chapter 4, p. 66).

2. *Report of the Secretary-General on the work of the Organization,* GAOR, thirty-fourth session, Supplement No. 1 (A/34/1).

3. This case study, written in 1959 by John G. Hadwen, Canadian co-author of the 1960 edition of *How United Nations Decisions Are Made,* is still a good illustration of how a delegation can operate.

Chapter 9

Doing Your Best Does Not Always Work: Two Cases of Failure

1. Summitry at the First Part of the Fifteenth Session of the General Assembly (1960)

The first part of the fifteenth session was attended, mainly between the opening of the session on 20 September 1960 and the end of the general debate on 17 October, by 9 heads of state and 19 heads of government, in addition to 61 foreign ministers or other ministers.

The atmosphere of the fifteenth session in its early days was particularly tense. There are those who argue that its sensationalism was created and aggravated by attention from the press. The United Nations is in New York and thus at the center of an immense network of information media. It is doubtful if any previous international meeting had received so much coverage by television, by radio, by newspaper, through the thousands of individual channels which lead away from New York, as did the meetings of the U.N. in the fall of 1960. Certainly the general atmosphere was not conducive to diplomacy of the traditional kind.

Much of the tension at the meetings was caused by Chairman Khrushchev's interventions and his attacks on the Secretary-General. East-West relations had deteriorated following the collapse of the Summit Meeting in May 1960 between Kennedy and Khrushchev.

In many respects the services and facilities of the United Nations headquarters were seriously disrupted by the need to give full protection to the controversial world figures present. Meetings were delayed and took much longer than necessary. There was difficulty in establishing personal contacts with individual delegates. The social history of the U.N. in this period was marked by dinners, receptions and other social functions which were unavoidably cancelled or changed.

An added complication was the fact that some of the heads of state or heads of government had not previously been intimately associated with the United Nations or taken direct part in a meeting of the General Assembly of the United Nations.

When a head of state or head of government is present, the length of time involved in obtaining a decision on a U.N. problem in which he is directly involved could be shortened. In many respects this is an advantage. However, normally most U.N. problems are not of a kind which are capable of immediate and rapid decision. Many of them require the careful study by a series of government departments, or consultation through diplomatic channels with other governments.

It may seem a contradiction in terms for a head of state to be also a head of delegation. A delegation by definition is granted authority from a central government. It is not the government itself, it acts on instructions from the government. When a head of state or head of government is present, the delegation may assume some attributes of a government, depending on its structure. It would be unusual for a head of state or head of government to seek instructions from his government, while he is acting as the head of delegation. He must, and does assume reponsibility for the actions of the delegation in the name of the government, often of course after consultation with his colleagues in the national capital concerned. It was this atmosphere of total commitment on the part of delegations headed by heads of state or heads of government which produced much of the tension in the fifteenth session of the General Assembly.

The fifteenth session was dominated by the Congo dispute and also by one of the main consequences of that dispute, the attack by the Soviet Union on Secretary-General Hammarskjöld. The session also began at a time when relations between the Soviet Union and the United States were at a very low point. The political circumstances at the fifteenth session were definitely unfavorable for the attendance of heads of state and heads of government. It might well be that in other circumstances, the attendance of heads of state and heads of government at U.N. meetings might have had very different consequences.

The nature of the difficulties which arose from the attendance of heads of state at the fifteenth session of the General Assembly can best be illustrated by describing the fate of a resolution which has been called the "Five-Power Text". It is now generally recognized that this resolution was not handled in the best possible way by its sponsors, by its opponents, or even those not directly involved. In fact, there has been a tendency to forget this resolution by all concerned. Nevertheless, the experience contains some useful lessons.

In a letter dated 29 September 1960, the President of Ghana, the Prime Minister of India, the President of Indonesia, the President of the United Arab Republic, and the President of Yugoslavia submitted jointly the following resolution for adoption by the General Assembly (doc. A/4522 of 30 September 1960).

Ghana, India, Indonesia, United Arab Republic, and Yugoslavia: *draft resolution*
  The General Assembly,
  Deeply concerned with the recent deterioration in international relations which threatens the world with grave consequences,
  Aware of the great expectancy of the world that this Assembly will assist in helping to prepare the way for the easing of world tension,
  Conscious of the grave and urgent responsibility that rests on the United Nations to initiate helpful efforts,
  Requests, as a first urgent step, the President of the United States of America and the Chairman of the Council of Ministers of the Union of Soviet Socialist Republics to renew their contacts interrupted recently, so that their declared willingness to find solutions of the outstanding problems by negotiation may be progressively implemented.

There remains some uncertainty concerning exactly how and where the draft of this text originated. It was orally introduced by Prime Minister Nehru of India. Apparently it was developed as a result of high-level and confidential exchanges directly between the heads of government concerned. It will be noted that all of the five countries which submitted this resolution were members of what at that time was called the neutralist group. Their objective appeared to be that of using the session of the General Assembly for the purpose of reducing international tension particularly between the United States and the Soviet Union. It may well have seemed to the neutralist or uncommitted members of the United Nations that a meeting of the General Assembly at that particular juncture in world affairs would not have been complete without some effort on their part to reduce tensions between the two "Super Powers". The draft resolution was, however, presented to the General Assembly without the efforts to secure broad general support which would normally have preceded such a major effort.

The draft resolution circulated to the General Assembly on 5 October 1960, read in the last paragraph, instead of "Requests as a first urgent step...": "Express the hope that as a first urgent step..." This change was presumably made in response to the suggestion that it was wrong for individual members of the United Nations to be made the object of a specific and mandatory request from the General Assembly. The text, however, still referred to specific individuals, namely the President of the United States and the Chairman of the Council of Ministers of the U.S.S.R. The situation was further complicated by the fact that the United States was at that time in the midst of a presidential election involving, whatever its outcome, a change in the presidency of the United States of America.

Between the time when the five-power draft resolution was first circulated, and the time when it came up for consideration in the General Assembly, the Australian delegation submitted an amendment (doc. A/L.316) which would replace the last paragraph of the five-power text by the following:

Recalling that a Conference between the President of the United States of America, the Chairman of the Council of Ministers of the Union of Soviet Socialist Republics, the President of the French Republic and the Prime Minister of the United Kingdom of Great Britain and Northern Ireland was arranged to take place in Paris on 17 May 1960, in order that these four leaders should examine matters of particular and major concern for their four nations,

Recalling further that the Conference did not actually begin its work,

Noting that the President of the United States of America, the President of the French Republic and the Prime Minister of the United Kingdom of Great Britain and Northern Ireland thereupon made a public statement in the terms following:

They regret that these discussions, so important for world peace, could not take place. For their part, they remain unshaken in their conviction that all outstanding international questions should be settled not by the use or threat of force, but by peaceful means through negotiations. They themselves remain ready to take part in such negotiations at any suitable time in the future.

Believing that much benefit for the world could arise from a co-operative meeting of the Heads of Government of these four nations in relation to those problems which particularly concern them,

Believing further that progress towards the solution of those problems would be a material contribution to the general work for peace of the United Nations,

Urges that such a meeting should be held at the earliest practicable date.

The main difference between the five-power text and the text which was submitted by Australia was that the latter would have broadened the action of the General Assembly to apply not to two individuals but to a meeting of four heads of government of the United States, the Soviet Union, France and the United Kingdom. The text would then have urged a reconvening of the Summit Conference which had broken up earlier in the year.

It was quickly made plain that the five sponsors would not be prepared to accept the Australian amendment which some regarded as a new resolution and not as an amendment. On 5 October, the Soviet delegation circulated to all delegates a letter from Mr. Khrushchev, which had been sent earlier to each of the five initiators of the five-power resolution, containing the views of the Soviet Union on the failure of the Summit Conference (doc. A/4532). The Chairman of the delegation of the United States also circulated a letter dated 2 October 1960, addressed to the Secretary-General (doc. A/4529). Neither letter indicated that an early meeting between the President of the United States and the Chairman of the Council of Ministers of the Soviet Union was considered useful or likely.

Intense diplomatic activity surrounded these manoeuvres. A number of tentative efforts were made to produce some form of understanding which would have permitted the adoption of a text not necessarily in the precise form originally submitted by the five powers. The texts of the statements made in this connection can be found in the Official Records of the General Assembly (887th plenary meeting of 5 October 1960 and 889th plenary meeting of 5 October).

Consideration and voting on the five-power resolution by the General Assembly was pressed as a matter of urgency and, in fact, interrupted the general debate. The Australian amendment was defeated by 5 votes in favor, 45 against with 43 abstentions. The delegation of Argentina requested that a separate vote be taken on the phrases in the last paragraph of the five-power text which referred to the individuals of the governments of the United States and the U.S.S.R., namely the words "the President of" and "the Chairman of the Council of Ministers of". This suggestion was apparently designed to remove the objection, repeatedly made, that it would be improper for the General Assembly to address a resolution to two individuals rather than to two governments.

This request for a separate vote precipitated a lengthy procedural debate, which was further complicated by the fact that it took place early in the session of the General Assembly when a number of members were not fully familiar with the Rules of Procedure. The Argentinian request was disputed and put to the vote, being accepted by 37 in favor, 36 against and 22 abstentions.

It had been agreed that the five-power text was of a nature which would require a two-thirds majority in the Assembly, and therefore a two-thirds majority would be required to sustain any part of the text. When the vote which the Argentinian delegation had requested was taken, the result was 41 in favor of maintaining the text as it stood, 37 against and 17 abstentions. The words "the President of" and "the Chairman of the Council of Ministers of" had therefore failed to receive a two-thirds majority and were then considered as having been dropped from the text of the resolution. The President's ruling on this point was challenged but upheld: 43 in favor, with 37 against and 15 abstentions. The next step would have been to vote on the draft resolution without these words. However, at this stage the sponsors, considering that an essential part of their resolution had been eliminated, decided that, in the atmosphere then prevailing, the only action open to them was to withdraw the resolution. Mr. Nehru was their spokesman in so doing.

There is no doubt that one of the consequences of this debate was an atmosphere of bitterness which did not augur well for the work of that particular Assembly session. An idealistic initiative had been lost in a procedural morass. The importance attached to certain words is illustrated by this case, in which the United Nations as an institution was unable to provide a framework for securing agreement on an issue which was considered important and to which many delegations attached great urgency. In retrospect, the failure of the five-power resolution was not a disaster for the institution but an unusual opportunity which was missed.

2. An Initiative That Failed: Immediate Needs as a Result of Economic and Other Emergency Situations

From early 1975 on, through the General Assembly session of 1977, The Netherlands pursued the idea of setting up an improved United Nations effort to meet certain emergency needs. The idea had to be abandoned. This case illustrates how a constructive initiative could not succeed because of specific difficulties.

For many years the international community, through the United Nations system, had come to the assistance of countries which had been struck by natural or other disasters. In some cases special programs for particular countries were set up, e.g., Zambia, which suffered as a result of the economic sanctions against Rhodesia. In other cases, in particular earthquakes and similar disasters, assistance was channelled through UNDRO (Office of the U.N. Disaster Relief Coordinator), headquartered in Geneva. The Netherlands and some other countries felt that gradually the time had become right for a more systematic effort. A point of departure for such an effort may be found in the resolution adopted at the end of the seventh special session of the General Assembly (3362 [S-VII], 1-16 September 1975), which in chapter II, paragraph 14, requested the following:

Special attention should be given by the international community to the phenomena of natural disasters which frequently afflict many parts of the world, with far-reaching devastating economic, social and structural consequences, particularly in the least developed countries. To this end, the General Assembly at its thirtieth session, in considering this problem, should examine and adopt appropriate measures.

172

This paragraph reflected, to some extent, the concern of The Netherlands and certain other countries. The Netherlands had submitted a paper (conference room paper No. 8, 19 June 1975) to the Preparatory Committee for the Special Session, from which the following is quoted to indicate the extent of the idea:

9. *Natural* emergency situations could, for example, result from natural disasters including major crop failures. *Social* emergency situations include major population groups living at or under bare minimum subsistence levels or the plagues of social conflicts. *Economic* emergencies encompass things such as the impact of national or international business cycles, disruptions in terms of trade or sudden monetary fluctuations. Furthermore, the threat may be of a permanent, semi-permanent or temporary nature. Each threat requires its own set of remedies, to which the international community could contribute in various ways.

10. As far as the possible role of the United Nations is concerned, the following distinction seems appropriate:

(a) Permanent or semi-permanent emergency situations;

(b) Disaster-like economic emergency situations;

(c) Disaster situations.

11. *A permanent or semi-permanent emergency situation* is characterized by a structural threat to the (often already minimal) conditions or life of large population groups or even whole nations. In this connection, mass poverty in the slums of big cities and vast rural areas can be mentioned, as well as the structural difficulties in which the least developed countries find themselves. The need for relief in such situations has already been recognized in the new orientations of the World Bank programmes, such as for construction works in slums and more priority to small-scale agriculture.

12. *A disaster-like economic emergency situation* may result from social or economic dislocations, which create wide-spread disruptions, affecting all sectors of society. In contrast with the category mentioned earlier, a disaster-like emergency situation is expected to be limited in time, thus—in principle—only requiring temporary measures.

Examples: the m.s.a.- ["most seriously affected"] countries Bangladesh, Cyprus, Honduras, the Sahel zone, Zambia, Indo-China, colonies which have suddenly become independent, such as Guinea-Bissau etc.

So far, the Special Fund, the United Nations Relief Operation in Bangladesh (UNROB) and the Sahelian Office have been active to provide relief and reconstruction in this category of emergency situations.

Earlier, during the Economic and Social Council session of July 1974, the Dutch Minister for Development Cooperation had addressed himself to this problem in the following terms:

We should keep this in mind when tackling the present situation. We can carry out all sorts of emergency operations. We can relieve all kinds of suffering. But we cannot achieve anything fundamental, unless we bring about real changes in the distribution of power, income and property... We are beginning to see that we are not concerned with distributing wealth between rich and poor countries and between rich and poor individuals within countries, but also with distributing life and death between now and tomorrow... We, therefore, need to introduce a new component into development policy, a new component consisting of programmes and projects designed to tackle immediate needs directly. This is being brought up more and more in the developing countries themselves. The rich countries will have to respond. This means that they will have to make assistance available for immediate needs more systematically.

The President of the World Bank mentioned employment projects as a possible contribution. The World Food Programme has started to give emergency relief in addition to its projects in which food is used as wages. These are first steps and represent attempts to do something on the spot for people who are in urgent need now. I think we must go further and develop new concepts to cope with this issue within the U.N. system and formulate new plans of action. I see this as a challenge to the U.N. What we need is a policy and a plan of action how to deal with recurrent urgent situations.

What I have in mind is something similar to the U.N. Emergency Force in the political field: I am thinking of a U.N. economic emergency force capable to deal with all sorts of urgent and immediate needs. It might be based on the same sort of contingency planning that has given strength to U.N. peace-keeping operations...

The matter was taken up again at the thirtieth session of the General Assembly in 1975. A resolution was tabled by The Netherlands and 21 other countries (doc. A/C.2/L.1446). The main thrust of this resolution is apparent from the following quotation taken from the speech made by the Dutch delegate in introducing the draft resolution:

The international community is increasingly faced with responding to economic emergency situations creating widespread disruption in all sectors of society and calling for a response to the resulting immediate needs of the afflicted population particularly in the poorest countries in order to sustain the long-term development process. These economic emergency situations have in many instances endangered and indeed disrupted fundamentally the long term development process of the afflicted countries. It is therefore of enormous importance that the attention of the international community is focussed to meeting these immediate needs if the prospects for long term development are being kept up. Our work for the long term improvement of the standards of living of the developing countries is thus only to be strengthened by our concerns for the immediate needs in economic emergency situations.

The draft resolution was adopted without a vote; seemingly there was a real consensus, both in the Second Committee and in plenary meeting (G.A. resolution 3510 [XXX]). The essence of the resolution was a request to the Secretary-General, made in the following terms:

Requests the Secretary-General, in consultation with the appropriate organizations of the United Nations system and with a view to enabling the United Nations system to deal adequately with economic emergency situations and to respond more effectively to the resulting immediate needs of the affected populations in developing countries, to submit proposals to the Economic and Social Council at its sixty-first session, inter alia, on:

a. The elaboration of global criteria for identifying such economic emergency situations;

b. The possible establishment of procedures for periodically reporting relevant information through resident representatives of the United Nations Development Programme, in consultation with the Governments concerned, to a central focal point, to be established where appropriate, which will process such information;

c. The possible elaboration of procedures for submission, on the basis of such information, of proposals to the Economic and Social Council for the proclamation, where necessary, of a state of emergency with economic, social and structural consequences;

d. The strengthening of the co-ordinating mechanism of the United Nations system within its existing financial resources.

Things seemed to be going in the right direction! The Secretary-General did submit a report to the sixty-first session of ECOSOC in July 1976 (U.N. doc. E/5843). The report analyzed the situation with reference to the three situations originally indicated by The Netherlands: (a) disaster situations, (b) permanent or semi-permanent emergency situations, and (c) disaster-like economic emergency situations.

The following extract from the report reflects its main substantive points:

26. The capacity of the United Nations system for responding to disaster-like economic emergency situations in the developing countries and to the immediate needs of the affected populations could be rendered more effective if the Secretary-General had machinery at his disposal that would encompass, on an inter-agency basis, all appropriate elements of the United Nations system. This machinery might have the following principal functions:

a. to assess data referred to it by the system indicating the possibility or probability of disaster-like economic emergencies and to recommend, where necessary, measures for preventive action by the system;

b. to act, in the event of a disaster-like economic emergency, as the system's focal point for receiving data concerning the nature of the emergency and the impact on the affected populations;

c. on the basis of all available information received and assessed, to make recommendations to the Secretary-General for co-ordinated practical measures to respond to the requests of Governments;

d. to assist the Secretary-General in co-ordinating the implementation of such measures and to monitor their results; and

e. after the occurrence of a natural disaster, at the point where the Office of the United Nations Disaster Relief Co-ordinator begins to phase out its humanitarian relief operations, to co-ordinate the system's participation in the follow-up of the rehabilitation and reconstruction activities.

27. A small special unit might be established at United Nations Headquarters to report to the Secretary-General. Economic emergencies and disaster-like economic situations would be reported to this unit by the appropriate elements in the United Nations system which are in a position to monitor the economic situation in a particular country or region as well as by appropriate departments of the Government or Governments concerned. The unit would use the information communicated to it to make a rapid assessment of the situation, simultaneously apprising the Secretary-General of the situation to enable him to initiate whatever immediate action may be necessary and convene an appropriate inter-agency mechanism to advice him and assist him in dealing with the situation. The composition of this mechanism might vary on an *ad hoc*

basis according to the individual requirements of each particular potential emergency situation.

28. The assessment by the special unit would also normally involve the preparation of a preliminary report which would be submitted to the inter-agency mechanism and which would formulate specific recommendations for remedial action by the Secretary-General. The unit would then be responsible for co-ordinating any programme of assistance called for by the emergency until the situation either improved or became permanent or semi-permanent, in which case other arrangements would be made to relieve the unit of its responsibilities.

At the Council's sixty-first session no specific action was taken. The matter was carried over to the thirty-first session of the General Assembly (September-December 1976). During that session the Assembly requested the Secretary-General to submit further proposals (decision 31/422C). These were contained in a new report to the Economic and Social Council (doc. E/5989) which was taken up by the sixty-third session of the Council (July 1977). The report proposed again to set up a special unit at U.N. headquarters. It also proposed that a government should be able to request the Economic and Social Council to proclaim formally the existence of a disaster-like economic emergency situation. The report also proposed certain indicators which could be used in order to monitor disaster-like economic emergency situations.

The Netherlands consulted with other countries on further steps to take, particularly on a possible draft resolution to take up the proposals of the Secretary-General. It soon became obvious that a number of objections existed to the approach by the Secretary-General:

1. Many countries felt that it was not necessary to create a new unit in the Secretariat. They felt that there was a certain amount of "empire building" on the part of the U.N. Secretariat. This became especially apparent when the Secretariat submitted, in accordance with the Rules of Procedure, a statement of "program budget implications". Under this document a new post of Assistant-Secretary-General would be created. This post became the main focus of opposition.
2. Several delegations felt, that it would be very difficult to pinpoint exactly what was an economic emergency situation. They felt that the difference between a physical disaster and an economic emergency was not as clear cut as some people thought it was. They feared that certain developed countries with long-term structural economic problems could also qualify as coming under "economic emergency".
3. There was also latent and sometimes open opposition from some of the specialized agencies which felt that there was no need for an additional mechanism in the U.N. The FAO, for example, has a long-es-

tablished "early warning system" which deals with impending food crises.

Nevertheless, The Netherlands, together with Austria, Bangladesh, Kenya, Mauretania, New Zealand and the Philippines, submitted a draft resolution, the essence of which is as follows (doc. E/[LXIII]/L. 550):

4. *Requests* the Secretary-General to make, as necessary, administrative arrangements at United Nations Headquarters for the effective carrying out of the following functions:
a. the compilation and evaluation of data provided by the monitoring system referred to in paragraphs 2 and 3, the assessment of the assistance required in economic emergency situations in co-operation with the appropriate specialized agencies and the provision of advance warning of potential emergencies to the Government concerned;
b. the initiation of measures for the provision by the United Nations system of assistance to the Government concerned in an economic emergency situation in co-operation with the appropriate specialized agencies;
c. the establishment, through the designation of a lead agency or organization as appropriate in the circumstances, of flexible and effective *ad hoc* mechanisms for co-ordinating the measures of remedial action to be taken by the United Nations and the appropriate specialized agencies in consultation with the Government concerned in response to its request for emergency assistance;
d. providing assistance in the mobilization of voluntary contributions from potential donor countries and voluntary agencies and the co-ordination of such aid with that provided by the United Nations and its specialized agencies;
e. providing assistance, where necessary, in the co-ordination of the programmes of special emergency assistance which might be decided upon by the Economic and Social Council in the event of a proclamation of a state of emergency as envisaged in paragraph 5 below.

In order to meet some of the objections to this draft the sponsors decided to insert the words "within existing resources" in the first sentence of paragraph 4 after the word "arrangements". Thus the Secretary-General could not request additional funds from elsewhere. After this the sponsors made an "agonizing re-appraisal": they had to determine if the draft resolution would have sufficient support in the Economic and Social Council. They undertook what is usually called "a head count", and came to the conclusion that a majority probably could not be expected.

The sponsors then decided to try to have their initiative carried over to the thirty-second session of the General Assembly. Although there was some opposition, they managed to achieve a simple decision by ECOSOC which took note of the report of the Secretary-General and decided to transmit the report, with the text of the draft resolution, to the General Assembly. However, a vote had to be taken on this deci-

sion: it was adopted with 16 votes in favor, 5 against and 16 abstentions. This in itself was not a good omen; the total of no-votes and abstentions exceeded that of the votes in favor.

During the General Assembly session of 1977 things turned out to
be no better than during the session of ECOSOC. The same negative
arguments which prevailed during the Council's session were also
made at the General Assembly. An explanatory memorandum
distributed by The Netherlands when draft resolution L.550 was again
discussed did not make a significant impact, even though emphasis
was placed on (a) avoiding any duplication with other mechanisms in
the U.N. system, such as the Geneva-based UNDRO, and (b) the objective to have a more efficient overall operation. The resolution was
therefore not put to the vote in the General Assembly. This constituted
the end of a meritorious initiative.

The reasons for this failure can be analyzed as follows:

1. The distinction among three types of economic emergencies was too
subtle for most governments. In particular, there was a lack of confidence that the U.N. Secretariat would be able to apply these distinctions in practice in a way acceptable to the majority of Member States.
2. There was fear that the declarations of a state of economic emergency might also lead to strange consequences: e.g., presumably even
large developed countries with heavy balance of payment deficits
would qualify under the indicators which the Secretariat had proposed, among which were included balance of payments problems.
3. Not only were the distinctions between the various types of economic emergency situations insufficiently understood, there was also a feeling that the distinction between economic emergencies on the one
hand and physical disasters on the other hand was not sufficiently
clear.
4. The lack of confidence in the U.N. Secretariat was strengthened by
a feeling that things were not being handled as badly as The Netherlands and others thought they were. This again illustrates the frequently noted difference of views between governments who would like to
see the United Nations play a central coordinating role, and those
who, on the contrary, feel that a decentralized system where various
members of the "U.N. family" play their part is all that is needed.

Chapter 10

Turning Failure into Success: The Story of SUNFED, the U.N. Special Fund and the U.N. Capital Development Fund

1. The Long Agony of SUNFED

On 17 December 1957, the General Assembly of the United Nations adopted resolution 1219 (XII) deciding that "there shall be established as an expansion of the existing technical assistance and development activities of the United Nations and the Specialized Agencies a separate Special Fund which would provide systematic and sustained assistance in fields essential to the integrated technical, economic and social development of the less developed countries."

This resolution marked a turning point in a long U.N. debate on the question of the economic development of developing countries which, over the previous nine years, had been filled with frustrations and conflicts. The decision to establish the Special Fund[1] represented the beginning of a new approach to the provision of international economic aid.

The review which follows of action taken on this question by the Economic and Social Council and the General Assembly makes it clear that, while the principle of providing economic assistance through the U.N. was generally supported, there were wide differences of opinion on how much economic aid should be channeled through the U.N. and in particular on whether the U.N. should undertake a large-scale capital aid program in addition to technical assistance and other special programs (e.g., UNICEF).

The real question at issue was: How could the maximum amount of international economic aid be obtained and how could it be best used? There were many answers.

It was only natural that, armed with an impressive array of arguments, the developing countries would press for U.N. action in favor of large-scale international economic assistance and at the same time on various other fronts for both bilateral and multilateral action towards this end.

During the third session (1949) of the Economic and Social Council's Sub-commission on Economic Development, the chairman, Mr. V.K.R.V. Rao, submitted suggestions for the creation of a United

Nations Development Administration (UNEDA).[2] This was to be an overall organ, with

five fields of activity: technical assistance to under-developed countries, co-ordination of technical assistance as extended by the U.N. and the specialized agencies, assistance to under-developed countries in obtaining materials, equipment, personnel, etc. for economic development, financing or helping to finance schemes of economic development which cannot be financed from the country's own resources and for which loans cannot be asked on strict business principles, and the promotion, and, if necessary, the direction and financing of regional development projects.

This proposal did not get any further. The Economic and Social Council and the General Assembly concentrated their debates and decisions that year on the establishment of the Expanded Program of Technical Assistance. The Council did, however, adopt a resolution (222 [IX]D), which recognized that the economic development of developing areas required not only expanded efforts in technical assistance, but also assurances of an increased flow of international capital for the purpose of financing economic development.

On the initiative of the delegation of Chile, the fourth (1949) General Assembly session unanimously adopted resolution 306 (IV), which, inter alia, looked forward to ''receiving the Council's studies of and recommendations for international action concerning the urgent problems of financing, in all its aspects, economic development in underdeveloped countries.''

In 1950, at its eleventh session, the Economic and Social Council engaged in a more extensive debate on financing of economic development. It had before it not only some of the Secretariat studies requested by resolution 222 (IX) D, but also the report ''National and International Measures for Full Employment'', prepared by a group of experts. This report recommended a considerable expansion of the scope of activities of the International Bank for Reconstruction and Development and the International Monetary Fund, but did not go so far as to recommend an entirely new agency for the distribution of grant aid. Nevertheless, at this session of the Council, the delegations of India and Iran favored the establishment of such an agency. Others felt that the activities of the IBRD should be expanded, while some (including the United States and the United Kingdom) did not consider any change in the existing arrangements necessary at the time. The resolution adopted at that session (294[XI]) took no new concrete action. However, the distinction between self-liquidating and other types of projects came into the foreground, for the resolution recognized that ''economic development requires the execution not only of self-liquidating projects, but also of projects in such fields as transport, power, communications, public health, educational institutions and housing, which while not always fully self-liquidating, are justified by reason of their indirect effect on national productivity and national income.''

At its fifth session (1950) the General Assembly discussed the subject at length. The words "non-self-liquidating projects" had by now become generally accepted as describing the kind of projects for which new assistance was required. A draft resolution by a number of developing countries proposed that the Economic and Social Council should study "the extension of international machinery through which international public funds could be made available to accelerate economic development." Another draft submitted by Pakistan and the United Kingdom suggested further study by the Economic and Social Council of non-self-liquidating projects. This is what was essentially recommended by the resolution, unanimously adopted (400 [V]). Its wording went further than that of previously adopted resolutions: the General Assembly was "convinced that the volume of private capital which is currently flowing into under-developed countries cannot meet the financial needs of the economic development of the under-developed countries and that those needs cannot be met without an increased flow of international public funds.''

This General Assembly resolution called on the Economic and Social Council to submit recommendations to the sixth session of the General Assembly. Hence the Council received a new impetus to discuss the matter of financing economic development. There was also the report "Measures for the Economic Development of Under-Developed Countries", prepared by a group of experts in accordance with ECOSOC resolution 290 (XI). This group, in its recommendation 14, proposed that "the United Nations should establish an international development authority to assist the under-developed countries in preparing, co-ordinating and implementing their programmes of economic development; to distribute to under-developed countries grants-in-aid for specific purposes; to verify the proper utilization of such grants; and to study and report on the progress of development programmes." The group also recommended that the IBRD "should set for itself the objective, to be reached within the next five years, of lending $1 billion annually to under-developed countries." Before it was disbanded the Economic and Employment Commission devoted its sixth and last session to the problem of financing economic development without coming to any definite conclusions.

The thirteenth session of the Economic and Social Council (1951) had before it, besides the report "Measures for the Economic Development of Under-Developed Countries", a small number of government comments, including that of the United States, which had been submitted pursuant to General Assembly resolution 400 (V).

The discussion at the thirteenth session of the Council was lively. Chile, Pakistan, the Philippines and India favored the establishment of an International Development Authority. Others were more doubtful. A Chilean amendment which would have recommended to the General Assembly a decision to establish the International Development Authority was defeated by 10 votes to 1, with 7 abstentions. The resolution finally adopted by 14 votes to none, with 4 abstentions, dealt at length with various aspects of financing economic development. On the subject of grant aid the resolution states that ECOSOC neither accepts nor rejects the principle of the establishment of an international fund to assist in the financing of economic development. The Secretary-General was asked to formulate, in consultation with the IBRD and other appropriate specialized agencies, "a series of methods which he deems practicable for dealing with the problem of grant assistance." Member governments were asked to submit further comments, as they had been invited to do in resolution 400 (V) of the General Assembly.

The discussion at the sixth session of the General Assembly (1951/52) was along the same lines as that during the session of the Economic and Social Council. Again a number of developing countries urged the establishment of an International Development Authority and again the delegations of some developed countries used various arguments either against the establishment in general or at that specific time. Part A of the resolution adopted (520A [VI]) dealt with grant assistance and was adopted with 30 votes in favor, 16 against, and 11 abstentions. Most but not all of the developing countries voted in favor, most developed countries voted against and the Soviet group of countries plus a few developing countries (Brazil, Dominican Republic, Haiti, Nicaragua and Thailand) abstained. This text requested the Economic and Social Council "to submit to the General Assembly at its seventh regular session a detailed plan for establishing, as soon as circumstances permit, a special fund for grants-in-aid and for low-interest, long-term loans to under-developed countries for the purpose of helping them, at their request, to accelerate their economic development and to finance non-self-liquidating projects which are basic to their economic development." The Economic and Social Council, in executing this task, was to make recommendations concerning the size, composition and administration of the fund, the manner of collecting contributions, the policies as to the making of grants and loans, and the principles which the recipient countries should observe. It is interesting that, while previously the emphasis had been almost exclusively on grant aid, loans (long-term and low-interest) were now mentioned as being of equal importance.

The fourteenth session of the Economic and Social Council (1952) had before it a working paper of the Secretary-General and a small number of government comments. The debate repeated the by now familiar pattern. A group of delegations from developing countries submitted a resolution proposing the establishment of a committee of nine members to prepare "a detailed *scheme*" for a fund. The draft referred repeatedly to the establishment of a special fund. This went too far for a number of countries which could, however, accept reference to "a detailed *plan*", an example of subtle changes in words reflecting substantial differences of opinion. The Council's resolution (416A [XIV]) was in the end adopted with 15 votes in favor to none against, with three abstentions (Czechoslovakia, Poland and the U.S.S.R.). Thus "the Committee of Nine" was born to draft a "plan".

The seventh General Assembly session (1952) contented itself with adopting a resolution (622[VII]) which reiterated the request to the Economic and Social Council to submit to the General Assembly (at its eighth session) the "detailed plan" requested in G.A. resolution 520A (VI).

The Committee of nine distinguished persons submitted a unanimous report to the Secretary-General.[3] It proposed the establishment of a "Special United Nations Fund for Economic Development". The initials of this title, SUNFED, became widely used from this date onwards to describe the idea of a large-scale U.N. capital aid fund. Delegations henceforth were for or against SUNFED. As often happens with such abbreviated titles, the idea it conveyed was not very precise. Still the initials seemed to suggest the need to feed the developing countries or had some other appeal. The word SUNFED itself undoubtedly played a significant part in the debates which followed, and came to provoke—at times emotional—support or opposition.

The sixteenth session of the Economic and Social Council (1953) discussed the report extensively. For the first time disarmament as an issue affected the debates on this subject. The U.S.A. representative reminded the Council of a proposal by the President of the United States in a speech on 16 April 1953, to devote a substantial percentage of the savings achieved by internationally supervised disarmament to a fund for assistance to developing countries. The result was a recommendation by the Council to the General Assembly that an appropriate declaration be prepared. As to the establishment of the proposed fund, the Council limited itself to forwarding the expert committee's report to the General Assembly.

The eighth General Assembly session (1953) requested further studies. Resolution 724B (VIII) asked the member governments of the U.N. and the specialized agencies for comments and for an indication of "moral and material" support for the proposals of the Committee of Nine to establish SUNFED. This resolution also asked Mr. Raymond Scheyven (Belgium), then President of the Economic and Social Council, to examine the comments of governments, to consult with them, and to report[4] the results to the Council and the General Assembly, "with a view to assisting it [the General Assembly] to make such recommendations as it would find possible which would facilitate the establishment of such a fund as soon as circumstances permit." A declaration on the possibility of establishing an economic development fund in the U.N. with savings from disarmament was also adopted (G.A. resolution 724A [VIII]).

Mr. Scheyven's consultations confirmed the well-known divergence of views. The developing countries urged the rapid establishment of the fund; most of the developed countries expressed caution and warned against undue haste. But there were some significant shifts in attitude. Denmark, Norway and The Netherlands came out clearly in favor of the establishment of the fund without waiting for savings from internationally supervised disarmament. The sum required for the fund was considered insignificant compared with the amount spent on armaments. While Norway conditioned its willingness to contribute upon that of the great powers, Denmark and The Netherlands did not express any such reservation. The Council adopted a resolution (532A [XVIII]), which recommended that the General Assembly urge governments to review their positions with respect to supporting a U.N. fund. It also suggested that the General Assembly extend Mr. Scheyven's appointment.

The ninth General Assembly session (1954) adopted a resolution incorporating the recommendations of the Economic and Social Council, and further decided to ask for a new report from Mr. Scheyven, to be prepared with the assistance of an ad hoc group of experts (resolution 822 [IX]), "giving a full and precise picture of the form or forms, functions and responsibilities which such a Special United Nations Fund for Economic Development might have..." While the initials SUNFED were freely used as a name, at this stage they did not

184

stand for any specific agreed proposal.

In 1955 the Committee of Experts' report[5] came before the twentieth session of the Economic and Social Council and the tenth session of the General Assembly. The Committee's recommendations followed the general line of those of the Committee of Nine, with some important modifications. The experts expressed the view that the additional financing to be provided by the fund should be directed towards strenghthening the "economic and social infra-structure", which was defined as "the set of basic facilities needed for effective production, such as a minimum of roads, power stations, schools, hospitals, housing and government buildings. Experience has shown that it is only when this basis has been established that production can be developed smoothly and that private initiative can play its full part." This evaluation of the significance of infra-structure projects for economic development and the definition quoted above have come to be accepted within and outside the United Nations. The Council adopted a resolution asking governments to transmit before 31 March 1956 their comments on the report of the Committee of Experts to the Secretary-General and recommended to the General Assembly the establishment of an intergovernmental ad hoc committee to analyze the comments of governments as the basis for a report to the twenty-second session of the Council.

In 1955, when the tenth session of the General Assembly convened, the general atmosphere of optimism which existed regarding the imminence of international disarmament created powerful pressures towards "action". It was felt, among the proponents, that the drafting of "statutes" for a large scale U.N. capital aid fund should no longer be postponed. However, the resistance of some developed countries led to a compromise resolution (923 [X]), under which an ad hoc committee of government representatives was given the task of analyzing the replies which governments were to give to a specific questionnaire. The questions dealt with the type of activities of the proposed fund, the form of assistance (loans, grants) which it would give and the organizational arrangements which might be required.

The establishment of a governmental committee was considered by the proponents of the fund to be a big step forward in comparison with previous resolutions under which groups of experts had made reports. Although membership on this committee did not imply any commitment to contribute to a new U.N. capital aid fund, there can be little doubt that at least for certain governments the fact that their representatives sat on this committee exercised a certain degree of influence on

185

their attitude towards U.N. economic aid.

In the case of a U.N. capital development fund, the statute-drafting stage was considered a decisive step, a crossing of the borderline between analytical discussion of the merits or demerits of the fund and a decision to establish it. Some governments argued that to draft statutes implied no commitment and could be undertaken in a purely academic atmosphere. Other governments considered that only if they were prepared in principle to contribute to a U.N. capital aid fund, would they participate in preparing its legal outline.

The Ad Hoc Committee's task, under G.A. resolution 923 (X), was actually that of analyzing the written views of governments. The Committee had before it 46 written statements, later increased to 57. Some of the members tried to give to the task of "analyzing" the meaning that the Committee could select from among the many proposals those which it thought best. Others, including the representatives of the major potential contributors on the Committee, supported the preparation of a general analytical summary of the replies of governments, with some short "conclusions" which, without being "recommendations", would indicate the general pattern the fund might have in accordance with the majority opinion in the government replies.

When the Ad Hoc Committee's report[6] came before the twenty-second session of the Economic and Social Council (1956), the usual pressure for the drafting of statutes developed. Again a compromise was accepted in the form of a resolution which urged governments which had not submitted their written views in response to G.A. resolution 923 (X) to do so as soon as possible. The General Assembly was asked to consider further steps which might promote the early establishment of the fund. Of some interest is the fact that, at this session of the Council, for the first time the suggestion was made by Argentina that a start be made with some relatively small fund rather than with a large-scale fund. A special fund to finance regional training centers and natural resources surveys was sketched by the Argentinian representative but not presented as a formal proposal.

At the eleventh General Assembly session (1956) the pressure to draft statutes became almost irresistible. A group of 41 countries, a majority of the membership of the U.N. at that time, presented a resolution asking the Ad Hoc Committee to prepare a draft statute for the fund. Again, however, some developed countries vigorously opposed the move. The result was another compromise in the form of a resolution (1030 [XI]) which invented a new task for the Ad Hoc Committee, namely not to draft a statute, but to indicate "the different

186

forms of legal framework on which a Special United Nations Fund for Economic Development may be established and statutes drafted." The submission of new solutions to this issue was encouraged by a clause in the resolution which permitted the Committee to append to its report "any related suggestions or proposals for the provision of economic assistance to under-developed countries under the auspices of the United Nations which governments may wish to put forward."

At that session of the General Assembly Argentina renewed its suggestion for an intermediate solution, namely the establishment of a small U.N. organization which would study projects submitted by governments, and—once it had approved them—try to find from individual Member States the necessary financial resources. In this way bilateral aid programs would have been multilateralized (a horrible word) to some extent but the individual countries concerned would still have had direct control over specific projects. Again this idea was not formally proposed in view of the pressure from the majority of developing countries for SUNFED.

While the eleventh session of the General Assembly was in process, Mr. Paul G. Hoffman, at that time the United States representative on the Second Committee, published an article in which he suggested "a United Nations experimental fund of $100,000,000 (to which the United States would contribute in the usual proportion) to be used for surveys of mineral, water and soil resources, and for a limited number of pilot projects.[7] The article and Mr. Hoffman's presence in the Second Committee naturally provoked among delegates informal discussion of his proposal, although the idea had not been formally presented by the United States delegation.

When the Ad Hoc Committee started its work of drafting "legal frameworks", it encountered, as might have been expected, a divergence between those who thought the Committee could recommend a particular framework and those who considered that the Committee should present various alternatives. The latter view prevailed, but with some modification. The Committee's report[8] contained a section in which practically all alternative views were mentioned. These were derived not only from the government replies under G.A. resolution 923 (X), but also from the two previous expert committees' reports and from Mr. Scheyven's reports. It had been expected that some governments might put forward to the Ad Hoc Committee new suggestions not necessarily related to ideas previously discussed in the U.N., as the resolution had suggested, but this did not happen. Apparently the issue remained SUNFED or nothing.

The twenty-fourth session of the Economic and Social Council (1957) had the final and supplementary report of the Ad Hoc Committee before it. More than ever those members of the Council who had come out strongly for SUNFED in the past were in favor of rapid action towards establishment of such a fund. Again the major potential contributors opposed the immediate establishment of SUNFED. The United States representative on the Council put his views in the form of some critical questions which are quoted in extenso to give an idea of the nature of the debate which took place:

A majority of nations whose replies were analyzed in the reports of the Ad Hoc Committee support the establishment of SUNFED in principle. We have noted, however, extremely few promises of financial support. Of those that have been made, many are conditional upon the participation of the major industrial countries. Even if these promises of support were fulfilled, what would they amount to in the aggregate?...
The prospect is that assets of the Fund would consist of a few million dollars in the form of a heterogeneous assortment of currencies, and, possibly, some contributions in goods and services. Is it reasonable that a new international financing agency, charged with gigantic tasks, should be established with such pitifully meager resources? Can we pass lightly over all that is being done by private investors, by international lending agencies, and by the United States and other countries through bilateral programmes to direct billions of dollars into economic development? In view of the vast scale of present international development financing, how can it be maintained that the establishment of a Liliputian SUNFED is the nostrum which will obliterate poverty among millions of people in large parts of the world? So to believe, is surely to turn from reality to magic."[9]

Against these objections, the proponents of SUNFED argued that, once the decision in principle to establish the fund was taken, the various unresolved issues could then be settled as practical details.

Moving between these two positions, the delegation from Argentina revived its previous idea in a different form. The establishment of a small fund to carry out experimental projects was proposed. Under pressure from the SUNFED supporters, this proposal was not, however, put forward separately but was absorbed in the final resolution recommending the establishment of SUNFED. This resolution, urging the General Assembly to take steps leading to its "immediate" establishment, was then adopted by 15 votes in favor to 3 against, the United States, the United Kingdom and Canada being the dissenters. Neither the "victors" nor the "losers" were happy about the result. An open division had emerged on this subject, a situation that had been averted since the split vote at the sixth General Assembly session in 1951. A reconsideration of the issue was therefore required if similar divisions at the twelfth Assembly session were to be avoided.

2. Special Fund

Shortly before the twelfth session of the General Assembly (1957) it became known that the United States Government now favored the establishment of a small U.N. fund to undertake certain special projects which could not be financed from the existing Expanded Program of Technical Assistance (EPTA). Surveys of resources, and regional training and research institutes for agriculture, industry, statistics and public administration would be examples of the type of projects which this new fund would finance. The new fund would be part of the Expanded Program of Technical Assistance machinery, but certain changes would be made. Notably, the so-called "country programming" procedure would not apply to the new fund, nor would allocations be made to specialized agencies as under EPTA. The reason was that projects, each of them probably larger than the average project under EPTA, would be considered on their individual merits. The United States proposal was formally introduced in a draft resolution (A/C.2/L.354) of 18 November 1957. The proposed fund was called "Special Projects Fund". The United States delegation explained that the United States was thinking in terms of an increase up to a total of $100 million in the present resources of the Expanded Program, this total to be divided in some reasonable ratio between the two programs. In the meantime the proponents of SUNFED had not been idle. On 16 October, a month before the United States tabled its proposal, a group of 11 countries had tabled a draft resolution (A/C.2/L.331) which in several respects differed from the traditional SUNFED approach. It proposed not a new international agency, which since the days of the UNEDA had usually been associated with the SUNFED idea (both the Committee of Nine and the Scheyven Group of Experts had envisaged a completely separate body, with its own "General Council" as the supreme legislative body), but rather a "multilateral fund of the United Nations". The organization would be somewhat similar to that of the U.N. Children's Fund (UNICEF). There would be a small managing staff, headed by a director-general, and an executive board to approve or reject projects and establish specific policies. Otherwise the new fund would be under the general direction of the Economic and Social Council and the General Assembly. It would have no formal statute but a set of rules in the form of resolutions by the Assembly or the Council. This more modest suggestion was designed to meet the objections of those who had opposed the creation of "a new international bureaucracy".

Other efforts were made in draft resolution L.331 to meet previous objections by potential contributors to SUNFED. The draft resolution specified that contributions of both governments and others should be in, or transferable into, currency usable by the fund. Voting in the executive board would be by a qualified majority vote, i.e., two-thirds or three-quarters, and the membership of the board would be equally distributed between two groups, one consisting mainly of major contributing countries and the other consisting mainly of developing countries. This distribution, already suggested in the report of the Committee of Nine, was designed to meet the argument that in a U.N. body without such a provision, the developing countries would have a clear majority. The qualified majority vote was designed to prevent major contributing countries from being outvoted by the receiving countries, which, in case of a simple majority system, would only need the support of one country from the other group to enforce a decision. According to the draft resolution the recipient countries would also be expected to provide part of the funds needed for each project assisted by the fund. The name of the fund was changed too. Instead of SUNFED the simpler name Economic Development Fund (EDF) was suggested, thus avoiding the psychological attitudes which had come to be attached to the term SUNFED by both its supporters and its opponents over the years.

Difficult and protracted negotiations followed. These discussions took place within the framework of the arrangements described earlier and provided many classic examples of the use of small conference rooms and of the delegates' lounge, as well as the standard techniques for promoting compromise. Sunday morning and late night meetings and urgent telephonic or telegraphic exchanges of views between delegations and their governments in the capitals enlivened these negotiations. In their speeches the spokesmen for the 11-country group stressed that they would only support the United States proposal if it was not a "substitute" for their own proposal. The United States representative took pains to stress that the U.S. proposal was in no way a substitute for a larger capital development fund. The United States was not, however, prepared to accept a commitment that any fund now to be created along the lines of its proposal was in fact the first stage towards a much larger fund. To establish the two funds simultaneously was not considered a practical solution; financial support would then be scattered over the two and both would suffer. Among the EDF supporters few were prepared to insist on their proposal to the extent of refusing that sponsored by the United States, which promised at least some increase in the total volume of U.N. economic aid. For its part the United States was not prepared to accept implied commitments for which the delegation was not authorized to pledge financial support, but equally did not wish to see a further breakdown of the agreement which was traditionally forthcoming in the debate on the economic development of developing countries.

In the end a compromise was arrived at in the form of a resolution (1219 [XII]) consisting of two principal parts. In the first part the decision was taken to establish "as an expansion of the existing technical assistance and development activities of the United Nations and the specialized agencies, a separate Special Fund to provide a systematic and sustained assistance in fields essential to the integrated technical, economic and social development of the less developed countries." The word "expansion" was intended to denote not only a quantitative enlargement, but also the introduction of new fields of assistance. In the previous (revised) draft of the 11 countries' resolution on the EDF the phrase used to describe the new program had been "as part of the technical assistance and development programmes of the U.N. and the specialized agencies." However, the United States delegation could not accept this language in which "development" could be interpreted as "economic development", which then would have stood separate from "technical assistance" and implied some form of capital aid. Therefore the United States proposed a revision under which one would read: "as part of the programmes of technical assistance and development". The United States idea was that the adjective "technical" would then also relate to "development". This was in accord with the original United States proposal, according to which the new fund would promote "technical development". This United States draft was nevertheless rejected by the 11 countries for being too restrictive. Finally, however, agreement was reached on the language of the final resolution, which referred to "an expansion of the existing technical assistance and development activities." The compromise resolution, which was officially introduced by the 11 countries together with the United States, Canada and France, was, however, interpreted differently by the two groups in formal statements. The representative of India, reflecting the views of the SUNFED group, argued that the Special Fund was a step on the road to SUNFED, while the United States representative stated that the Special Fund stood entirely by itself.

This situation provides a good example of the way in which deep-rooted government positions may produce long wrangles over words which seem unimportant except to the participants charged with interpreting their governments' wishes. Sometimes it is not so much the language which is objectionable to a delegation as the intention behind the language and the manner in which it is presented or the quarters from which the idea originates.

The adopted resolution went on to state that, since the resources "prospectively available at this time were not likely to exceed $100 million," the fund would be used to enlarge the scope of U.N. programs of technical assistance by financing special projects, such as intensive surveys of resources, the establishing (including the equipping) of training institutes in public administration, statistics, technology and of agricultural and industrial research and productivity centers.

In the third part of the resolution the General Assembly decided that "as and when the resources prospectively available are considered by the Assembly to be sufficient to enter into the field of capital development, principally the development of the economic and social infrastructure of the less developed countries, the Assembly shall review the scope and future activities of the Fund and take such action as it may deem appropriate." By this phraseology an effort was made to indicate that, while the fund would not immediately enter into large-scale capital financing, the General Assembly might take further action towards that end in the future. Some countries considered that the activities of the Special Fund would in fact represent a form of capital assistance, although on a small scale. It will be noted that part of the compromise consisted in calling the new organ the Special Fund, rather than SUNFED (which it was not, being small), or EDF (which it was not, being limited to certain specific forms of assistance), or Special Projects Fund (which it was not, having been placed in a more general context than the original United States proposal for an expansion of the existing U.N. technical assistance programs).

The resolution established a Preparatory Committee of 16 countries to draft detailed rules governing the Special Fund. This Committee faced difficulties in giving substance to a finely balanced compromise but reported[10] unanimously to the twenty-sixth session of the Economic and Social Council and to the thirteenth session (1958) of the General Assembly. The result was G.A. resolution 1240 (XIII), which established the Special Fund, to commence operations on 1 January 1959.

Before this last decision was taken, however, there had been a lengthy debate on a separate paragraph which would have referred to the possible evolution of the Special Fund into a capital development fund. The United States and certain other delegations held that the future of the Special Fund was a separate matter which was to be discussed by the General Assembly at some later time in the light of available financial resources (in accordance with the terms of section III of G.A. resolution 1219 [XII]). It was felt that the resolution establishing the Special Fund should not anticipate future U.N. debates. This view prevailed, but later a separate draft resolution on capital development was presented, which after considerable debate was adopted in plenary session by 67 votes in favor (the developing countries and some developed ones), none against and 14 abstentions (most of the more developed countries including the largest potential contributors). The main clause of this latter resolution (1317 [XIII]) urged Member States "to continue working for the establishment of a United Nations capital development fund." Some countries, such as The Netherlands, a co-sponsor of this draft resolution, and Norway, had emphasized that in voting for this text they were not making any commitment concerning the organization of the proposed new fund. They considered, however, that it might prove possible to solve the organizational problems connected with the establishment of a large-scale U.N. capital development fund. The vital question of securing the necessary financial support would remain, but this might, they considered, turn out to be a little less difficult once a generally acceptable solution for the organizational problems had been found. Those delegations which abstained were not prepared to accept even an implied commitment for additional financial contributions to another aid agency under the U.N. at a time when the Special Fund had just been established, and consideration was being given to increasing the resources of the World Bank and the IMF. Such an increase took place in the course of 1959.

Most of the sponsors of resolution 1317 (XIII) did not want to leave the main organizational question in doubt and made it clear that a United Nations capital development fund meant for them a fund under the auspices of the United Nations General Assembly. An amendment submitted by the United Kingdom to have the words "United Nations capital development fund" replaced by the words "a capital development fund within the framework of the United Nations" was not adopted. Had this amendment been accepted, the organizational question would have been left open, and a solution along the lines of the proposed "International Development Association", for which the United States had indicated encouragement, could have been considered as one of the alternatives for the U.N. capital development fund.

United Nations consideration of a problem such as the promotion of the economic development of the developing countries had a beginning but not an ending. On the proposal of the United States, the Governors of the World Bank at their September 1959 session decided to establish the International Development Association. This decision was certainly influenced by the pressures in the U.N. for a capital development fund.

The establishment of the Special Fund has been presented as a case study of how United Nations decisions are made. Partly because of the decision to establish the Special Fund, 1958 has been described by the President of the Economic and Social Council at the time as "the year of the breakthrough."[11]

3. The Capital Development Fund

The question of the establishment of a U.N. capital development fund arose again at the fourteenth session (1959) of the General Assembly. With the decision to establish the International Development Association, taken only recently, there was at that time little support for the immediate establishment of a new capital development fund. The result was a moderate resolution, adopted by 67 votes in favor, with 15 abstentions, calling on Member States to re-appraise their positions on the early establishment of a United Nations capital development fund.

At the fifteenth session of the General Assembly, with the membership increased to 99 following the addition of 17 developing countries, the atmosphere was one of firm determination on the part of the developing countries to push ahead with a decision that could be regarded as establishing a U.N. capital development fund. A group of 45 countries, considered to be less developed submitted a draft resolution, of which the key phrase was: "The General Assembly decides to establish a U.N. Capital Development Fund." A committee of government representatives was to draft the statute of the new fund and the sixteenth session of the General Assembly was to take final action. In their statements the spokesmen for the developing countries made it clear, that what they wanted was a decision in principle, the details of the fund to be settled later, perhaps much later. They were aware that the largest potential contributors, particularly the United States and the United Kingdom, had not changed their positions and were therefore unable to support this resolution. As on previous occasions a group of countries tried to promote an alternative decision as a compromise. Initially this group consisted of Denmark, Greece, The Netherlands and Sweden. It proposed amendments, of which the principal one was that the General Assembly would "look forward to the earliest possible establishment of a U.N. Capital Development Fund." The proposed intergovernmental committee would be given the task of considering "the concrete possibilities for the establishment of a U.N. Capital Development Fund." While the drafting of statutes would be covered by the proposed new wording, it was expected to be more acceptable to the delegations in opposition since the drafting of statutes was not stated to be the only or main purpose of the committee.

The reaction of the 45 sponsors was not favorable. They felt that the proposed amendments would lead to undesirable delays. In the private conversations that followed the 45 sponsors agreed that the actual establishment of the fund would inevitably take place at a later date. They therefore offered a revised version of the resolution, with the crucial paragraph reading: "Decides that a U.N. Capital Development Fund shall be established." The word "shall" was inserted to indicate that the establishment would be in the future. However, the largest potential contributors did not like the word "shall" which was considered to have a mandatory connotation. Denmark, Greece, The Netherlands and Sweden then proposed: "Decides that a U.N. Capital Development Fund should be established." However, the forty-five sponsors, feeling that the desirability of this action was already beyond question and that this version therefore added nothing to the existing situation, rejected it. Finally, Denmark, Greece and The Netherlands offered as a last concession: "Decides in principle that a U.N. Capital Development Fund shall be established." This version was accepted by the forty-five sponsors.

Another amendment of Denmark, Greece and The Netherlands proposed certain guidelines to be taken into account by the governmental committee, namely:

a. the need to accelerate the economic and social development of the less developed countries by increased capital investments;
b. the necessity to have the fullest possible use of existing machinery for international assistance of the economic and social development of the less developed countries, especially the United Nations Special Fund;
c. the need for close working relationships and effective co-ordination between all organs active in the field of international financing of the economic and social development of the less developed countries.

Of these the second and third were the most important. The second guideline clearly held out the possibility (which ever since the adoption of G.A. resolution 1219 [XII] had been widely canvassed), that the Special Fund be transformed into a capital development fund. A number of developing countries, however, appeared to have decided that serious consideration should be given to setting up an entirely new organization. The third guideline emphasized that whatever action the intergovernmental committee recommended, attention should be given to the need for close cooperation and coordination of all organs providing international economic assistance. The phraseology of this third guideline was similar to that used in a resolution of the fourteenth session on cooperation between the new International Development Association and the U.N. (G.A. resolution 1420 [XIV]).

The 45 sponsors accepted the compromise language: "Decides in principle that a U.N. Capital Development Fund shall be established" on condition that the amendment containing the guidelines be withdrawn.

It was agreed between the 45 sponsors and the three countries sponsoring the amendment, that the report of the Second Committee to the plenary session would mention that the withdrawal of the guidelines was effected on the understanding that the 45 sponsors had no objections in principle to the paragraph containing them but that the draft was not comprehensive enough. It would take too long, they said, to draft a comprehensive text, acceptable to all. The intergovernmental committee would be expected, however, to take into consideration the suggested guidelines. The 45 sponsors and the three delegations had previously agreed that the committee would not be explicitly asked to draft statutes, but that it would "consider all concrete preparatory measures, including draft legislation," necessary to establish a capital development fund. The modified resolution (1521 [XV] [1960]) was adopted in the plenary session by 71 votes in favor (all the developing countries plus a number of developed European countries, such as Denmark, Norway, The Netherlands, Italy and Austria), 4 against (the United States, the United Kingdom, the Union of South Africa and Australia) and 10 abstentions (a number of developed countries, including Canada, France and Japan).

The debate which took place in the Second Committee prior to the adoption of this resolution, illustrated the way in which the developing countries at the fifteenth session of the General Assembly used their voting strength (four years before the establishment of the Group of 77!) to bring the utmost pressure to bear on those countries from which they hoped to receive additional economic aid. To a considerable extent the willingness of these developing countries to press this issue to a vote and to override the protests and opposition of the United States, the United Kingdom and other countries, was based on a belief that the new United States administration, which assumed office in January 1961, would take a different position on this matter than previous United States administrations. At no time were these delegations given any encouragement in this respect. However, during the resumed fifteenth sesion the United States indicated that it was willing to serve on the committee of 25 countries to be appointed pursuant to G.A. resolution 1521 (XV), provided that it was understood that this did not imply a change in the U.S. position on SUNFED and that the United States would retain complete freedom as to the attitude to be taken when the committee would meet.

For several years no progress was made. In 1966 a group of developing countries decided to table a resolution under which the Capital Development Fund (CDF) would be established as an autonomous organ of the General Assembly. The "autonomous organ" formula was borrowed from the examples of UNCTAD and UNIDO both of which had been accepted by the developed countries. Some Western nations, e.g., the United States and the United Kingdom, remained adamantly opposed, claiming that the proposed fund would duplicate the work of the World Bank and IDA. Others, notably the socialist countries of Eastern Europe, preferred to transform the UNDP (which had recently come into existence as the merger of the Expanded Program of Technical Assistance and the Special Fund) into a capital development fund. The Netherlands suggested, as a compromise and interim decision, a draft resolution under which the Governing Council of UNDP, in the light of the growth of UNDP's resources, should study, as a priority task, the possibilities for establishing the CDF. However, both the developing and most developed countries maintained their diametrically opposed views. The developing countries put their draft to the vote which was adopted with 59 in favor, 31 against (most Western nations) and 19 abstentions (including Greece and The Netherlands as the only Western states). Thus, with resolution 2186 (XXI) the General Assembly established the U.N. Capital Development Fund, as an autonomous organ of the General Assembly, with the objective "to assist developing countries in the development of their economies by supplementing existing sources of capital assistance by means of grants and loans."

The next year the General Assembly asked the Governing Council of UNDP and the Administrator of UNDP to assume provisionally the functions of Executive Board and of Managing Director of the Fund (resolution 2321 [XXI]). This provisional arrangement has continued.

From 1967 through 1972 there was practically no progress on the Capital Development Fund. Resolutions were regularly adopted in the General Assembly, reaffirming the structure of the CDF and calling on countries to contribute. Contributions, however, remained minimal, mostly token contributions from developing countries. The Administrator of UNDP continued to point out in his report that there was a useful role for the CDF to finance certain small projects. Gradually, governments started to see that there was truth in the Administrator's argumentation. At the fifty-fourth session of the Economic and Social Council (1973), the Dutch delegate, Mr. Gajentaan, was able to say: "... there exists a 'grey zone' of investment projects of particular value to least developed countries and, perhaps, the U.N. CDF will in due time, along the lines proposed by the administrator of UNDP step into this grey zone." The Administrator of UNDP had pointed out in his report that he felt that the CDF should be reoriented precisely towards this "grey zone" of pre-investment and other projects which other international aid organizations could not finance. The favorable atmosphere towards CDF was reflected in the Council's resolution (1753-LIV) of 1973. The key paragraphs on CDF were the paragraphs 2, 3 and 4. They appeared in the context of a resolution on least developed countries:

2. *Welcomes* the decision of the Governing Council of the United Nations Development Programme that the United Nations Capital Development Fund should be used to serve primarily the hard-core countries;

3. *Calls upon* the developed countries, in view of the new orientation of the United Nations Capital Development Fund, to reconsider their policy towards the Fund;

4. *Recommends* that the General Assembly, at its twenty-eighth session, should consider ways and means of further employing sizable sums of the resources of the United Nations Capital Development Fund, as well as other sources and arrangements, for the service of the least developed countries in solving their basic handicaps;

The twenty-eighth session of the General Assembly (1973) continued this positive consideration of CDF. G.A. resolution 3122 (XXVIII) deals extensively and specifically with CDF, expressing the hope that in the light of the new orientation of the Fund substantial voluntary contributions to the Fund will be forthcoming, in particular, from developed countries. Of interest is the following paragraph from the preamble of this resolution:

Considering that the United Nations Capital Development Fund could most effectively be used in complementing the technical assistance and pre-investment activities of the United Nations Development Programme, as well as the investment activities of existing international financial institutions, *inter alia*, in support of those development and investment activities that would build and strengthen the economic and social infrastructure of these countries, including in particular in the fields of integrated rural development and small-scale industries...

In 1974 there was further progress. The special session of the General Assembly in the spring of 1974 resulted in a program of action on the establishment of a new international economic order and a special program dealing with the least developed countries, for which a special aid program was set up. For this purpose a special fund was created; the idea of merging this special fund with the CDF was discussed, and this particular possibility was then referred to the ad hoc committee for this special program for the least developed countries in explicit terms. In the autumn of 1974 The Netherlands was the first of the developed countries to announce a sizeable contribution to CDF, with the understanding that the Fund would concentrate its assistance on the least developed countries and poorest population groups. This had a "triggering off" effect; later Norway followed the Dutch example, and gradually several developed countries followed suit. As from 1978 the United States started to contribute to CDF.

Thus the dogmatic differences of view on the usefulness of a Capital Development Fund have in fact been replaced by a largely pragmatic position, whereby the CDF found its own place in the constantly increasing family of multilateral financing institutions.

For 1979 a total of $25 million was pledged to CDF, modest, but reflecting the recognition that the Fund had found its own role. The philosophy of CDF is well reflected in the following paragraphs from the annual report of the Administrator of UNDP for 1977 on the U.N. Capital Development Fund (doc. DP/305, paras. 5, 6 and 7):

Project Development
5. The Fund's capital projects raise to minimal levels of acceptability the capacity of beneficiaries to acquire food, clothing, health services, education and decent working conditions. At times, however, such projects do not readily lend themselves to detailed identification in national development plans, particularly in those adapted from industrialized countries.
6. The Fund therefore assists the recipient Governments in preparing requests for suitable projects, based on the informal knowledge that may exist within governmental departments, UNDP field staff and project experts, bilateral programme personnel, nongovernmental organizations and in discussions with the prospective beneficiaries themselves. The UNDP field establishment, unique in its scope and experience has been a key supportive element in this activity.

7. The Fund's projects are geared to the needs, motivations and capabilities of the beneficiaries and involve appropriate technology as a matter of course. Such technology is used to improve traditional tools, materials, structures, physical fitness and working methods of the beneficiaries, and is not heavily dependent on traditional infrastructure. It makes labour more productive, but remains within the management capability, control, market accessibility and human satisfaction of the poor.

4. Difficulties which Confronted U.N. Action on a Capital Development Fund

A review of some of the arguments used in the course of the years in connection with the establishment of a U.N. fund for economic development financing shows the variety of factors influencing the decision-making process.

There was, as far as governmental expressions in the U.N. were concerned, no opposition to the principle of external assistance to meet certain financial needs which could not otherwise be met. Generally the developed countries had accepted in principle the need for international economic aid and had given substance to their principles by the establishment of bilateral aid and by supporting U.N. programs.

From 1950 to 1955 the developing countries as a group tried to influence the large potential contributors to support the establishment of a U.N. capital aid fund. The contributors were not enthusiastic. In 1951, considerable optimism concerning the prospective financial resources of the developing countries affected the debate. However, this optimistic view was not repeated as international economic conditions later changed.

An important argument in the debate on a U.N. capital aid fund was based on an assessment by those opposed to the immediate establishment of SUNFED that the resources required for large-scale financing of economic development by the U.N. were not available. The amount of $250 million, which was recommended as a starting point by the Committee of Nine and the Group of Experts headed by Mr. Scheyven, and lesser sums mentioned by later committees, were considered either unavailable, or even if available, insufficient in comparison to the objectives of the proposed fund. At that time an amount of at least some $400 or $500 million was sometimes mentioned as a minimum requirement. Those in favor of the fund argued that it was better to start with a small amount rather than to wait for larger sums. It was felt that, once started, the fund, if successful, would gain momentum and attract larger contributions. On the other hand, some countries argued that to start a fund for unlimited purposes with clearly insufficient resources would lead to disappointment and result in discredit for the United Nations.

The proposed organizational features of a U.N. capital aid fund also provoked disagreement. The opponents of the immediate establishment of a fund at times voiced doubts whether the organization proposed by, for example, the Committee of Nine or the Group of Experts under Mr. Scheyven, could be expected to give satisfactory results.

A "weighted-voting" arrangement, like that in the World Bank, where each country has a number of votes in proportion to its share in the capital subscribed, was considered necessary by the United States, the United Kingdom and some other governments. However, a majority of the U.N. membership, consisting chiefly of the developing countries, was in favor of equal voting rights for all members of a proposed fund organization, irrespective of the size of their contributions. This insistence contributed to the reluctance of many developed countries to support the immediate creation of a large-scale U.N. capital development fund.

A related question concerned the usability of contributions. Difficulties arose in finding uses for the contributions of some countries to the U.N. Expanded Program of Technical Assistance, because these contributions were made in inconvertible currency or qualified with difficult conditions as to their use. Major potential contributors were obviously unwilling to contribute the bulk of convertible currency to a large fund while others contributed inconvertible currency or imposed other restrictions. A similar difficulty did not appear to exist in respect of a small fund, i.e., the Capital Development Fund as actually established.

5. Disarmament and a Capital Development Fund

As early as 1951 the government of India had submitted to the General Assembly a draft resolution asking governments to state the principles and the scale on which they would be prepared progressively to reduce their armaments and to contribute to a U.N. fund for reconstruction and development. This draft resolution, which came before the First (Political) Committee, was withdrawn.

In 1953 President Eisenhower had stated that the United States was ready to ask the American people to join with all nations in devoting a substantial percentage of savings achieved by disarmament to a fund for world aid and reconstruction. Upon the initiative of the United States delegation, the Economic and Social Council and later the General Assembly unanimously adopted the following declaration (resolution 724A [VIII]):

We, the Governments of the Member States of the United Nations in order to promote higher standards of living and conditions of economic and social progress and development, stand ready to ask our peoples, when sufficient progress has been made in internationally supervised world-wide disarmament, to devote a portion of the savings achieved through such disarmament to an international fund, within the framework of the United Nations, to assist development and reconstruction in under-developed countries.

In the light of that 1953 declaration and in view of their estimate of the amounts needed for such a U.N. fund, a number of developed countries argued that the establishment of a large-scale U.N. capital development fund depended on sufficient progress being made in internationally supervised disarmament. The argument reached its peak in 1955, when, in the optimistic mood after the Summit Conference of that year, progress in disarmament seemed likely. Premier Faure of France had proposed that armaments budgets would be systematically reduced and the amounts saved used for the establishment of an international development fund.

These hopes were not fulfilled. On the contrary, the protracted unsuccessful negotiations suggested that the objective of early international disarmament lay farther and farther beyond the horizon of achievable goals. With those diminishing hopes, the "disarmament argument" to some extent lost its strength in *this* United Nations debate. It has not failed to come back in other forms later.

6. Merits of Bilateralism and Multilateralism

A more general issue which affected the entire debate was that of the merits of bilateralism versus multilateralism in the administration of international assistance. Some of the countries in favor of a U.N. capital aid fund argued that multilateral administration of foreign assistance had certain advantages. Specifically, multilateral assistance could avoid the charges of political or other interference which were made against bilateral assistance. Furthermore, multilateral aid agencies might have better opportunities than individual governments to suggest sound financial and economic policies to receiving governments. The International Monetary Fund successfully proposed needed anti-inflationary and other financial measures to member governments before giving assistance. A capital aid fund, therefore, might be a good influence in regard to domestic economic policies. The United Nations might be tough with developing countries without being accused of seeking political or commercial advantage. Equipment and services could be obtained by a U.N. agency from the cheapest sources of supply, while bilateral programs frequently had to use domestic sources which might not be competitive in price with world markets. Frequently a developing country will not need large amounts of capital immediately at the earliest stages of its economic development but assistance in building up its administrative service for using the available resources most effectively.

The U.N., by reason of its political neutrality in the eyes of most states and the widespread facilities on which it could call, was considered to be in a better position than bilateral programs to provide technical assistance experts who might be asked to work in politically sensitive but important areas of national administration (e.g., the civil service commission or a central electricity authority). For all these reasons many governments considered multilateral assistance superior to bilateral aid.

Other countries stressed, however, that bilateral assistance could be efficiently administered. The Colombo Plan was used as an example of bilateral assistance administered efficiently and without political overtones. Countries like the United States and the United Kingdom, with established programs of bilateral assistance to whose continuation they attached importance for a number of reasons, including national security, could not be expected to endorse a complete transfer to a multilateral system. Furthermore, among the recipient countries there were a number which were the beneficiaries of important bilateral programs; they did not want to see these sacrificed to an international program under which their share would be uncertain.

On the other hand, for donor countries with no or almost no bilateral aid program, channeling foreign assistance through multilateral channels promised to be the only efficient method available. Setting up their own machinery for administering foreign assistance would be cumbersome and costly.

Many developing countries argued that the amounts to be provided for multilateral assistance through the U.N. should be additional to and not replace bilateral aid. The U.N., they said, should not interfere with bilateral assistance programs in any way. Indeed, efforts were made at times to treat U.N. economic aid entirely separately from activities which countries might be undertaking outside the U.N. framework. What has been called a "U.N. umbrella over bilateral aid" is another way of dealing with the problem. The Lower Mekong Basin project, designed to benefit the four countries bordering on that great Asian river, provides an example. It was administered under U.N. auspices by a committee established jointly by the governments of Cambodia, Laos, Thailand and Viet Nam. The project was assisted not only by several U.N. programs and specialized agencies, but also by special contributions from a number of donor states.

There may be deeper reasons behind the motivations of those who are strongly in favor of either the multilateral or the bilateral method of providing international economic assistance. Those strongly in favor of multilateral assistance would probably say that they think more "internationally" than others. The bilateralists might consider themselves practical people who like the "do-it-yourself" approach.

7. Conclusion

Many years of lengthy debates resulted in the creation of both the Special Fund and the Capital Development Fund. The process of decision making in these cases took as long as it did because that was the length of time required to make any progress at all, in the light of other circumstances, other U.N. programs and the attitudes of member governments. Any attempt to reason away the causes of the delay would be unrealistic.

Of some importance was the fact that only five times in the innumerable debates on the question of the U.N. establishing a capital aid fund did major formal divisions between the less and the more developed countries occur (in 1951, 1957, 1958, 1960 and 1966). On other occasions the resolutions were adopted unanimously or with a few abstentions. The U.N. could be said to have provided a forum in which differences between donor and receiving countries were discussed during this period in such a way that a mutual understanding of some kind was reached. The developing countries always had a U.N. majority in favor of the immediate establishment of a large-scale capital aid fund. However, this majority was never used irresponsibly. No *final* action was taken which did not carry with it the countries from which the financial resources of any program would have to come. It is a tribute to the wisdom of governments and delegations from both sides during the period 1949 to 1959 that no definite split on this issue did develop. Had the issue been forced to a conclusion at any time in this period, a number of consequences would have followed. The analysis of these consequences depends to some extent on the side from which the issue is judged.

There were those who firmly believed that, had the U.N. established a large-scale capital aid fund, the potential donor countries would have had to support it because of the political loss they would face by failing to do so. There were also those who believed that there would soon be a change of government in some of the major potential donor countries which would bring to power parties more inclined to use the U.N. as a channel for giving aid. Domestic political differences thus had a direct bearing on the SUNFED debate.

On the other hand, many members of the U.N. seem to have come to the conclusion during the years in question that it was undesirable to force a decision down the throats of the few countries which would have to support it financially and that to do so might damage rather than assist U.N. objectives. SUNFED was opposed, therefore, on practical rather than substantive grounds. In the long run, and after great difficulty, U.N. organs took a pragmatic approach to the problem. One of the reasons for hesitation in taking a decision to establish a program in the hope that funds would be made available was the fear that if funds did not become available the idea of a large-scale U.N. capital aid fund would be dead once and for all. Delay from this point of view at least avoided a final negative decision.

There remained nevertheless a constant struggle between what might be called the idealists and the realists. Efforts towards middle courses of action developed as it became clearer that establishment of a large-scale capital aid fund under the General Assembly was impossible in the existing circumstances. It is interesting that the initial impetus towards these middle courses came from countries like Argentina and Canada, which had not been associated too much with the extreme view on either side. (A whole series of suggestions and proposals during this period for new approaches to international economic aid were made inside the U.N. in speeches, books, etc., for example, the Pineau Plan and the Pella Plan, but these did not specifically come before the U.N. for action.) Some of the European countries, especially the Scandinavian countries, and The Netherlands, also contributed to the forces of compromise. Among the developed countries The Netherlands was at times alone, at other times joined by the Scandinavian countries and France, in belonging to the group which supported immediate action to establish SUNFED.

From 1949 to 1957, when it was decided to establish the Special Fund, a series of techniques was used to "keep the idea of SUNFED alive." There were Secretariat studies, two expert group studies, one personal investigation by the President of the Economic and Social Council, several questionnaires submitted to and formal replies received from governments, and two reports of a special ad hoc committee to provide material for thought and discussion. In particular, the two ad hoc committee exercises, especially the last one, were largely to "fill time." This "keeping alive" activity must in itself be considered useful, although to many delegations it represented waste and delay. This record nevertheless compares favorably with other U.N. activities where, after one or more years of debate and a series of Secretariat reports, an idea "fades away" without any specific action.

The views of governments varied much during the development of this debate. It would be hard to determine what part U.N. discussions played in securing these changes. The fact that the issue was before the U.N. did, however, play a part, and perhaps a major part, in changing governmental attitudes. In the early debates there was a neat division between developing countries and industrialized countries. Soon some of the developed countries began to change their views. The first was The Netherlands, which changed its position during 1952 and voted as early as 1953 with developing countries on this issue. Some of the Scandinavian countries followed. In 1954 Mr. Scheyven was able to announce tentative contributions to SUNFED from The Netherlands, Denmark and Norway.

Without the U.N. there might well have been more dangerous divisions on this question between developing and developed countries. Some will argue that the U.N. needlessly aggravated the debate. However, the fundamental differences, both economic and political, between the developing and the developed countries on the subject of financing economic development programs would have been sharper and less productive in the immediate post-war period had there been no U.N. debate on the subject. The history of the establishment of the Special Fund demonstrates the impact of multilateral discussion of a subject by the U.N. on the policies of member governments. The public confrontation of positions for or against SUNFED tended to sharpen the positions of governments holding different views. In bilateral diplomacy the government of country X would have asked country Y for financial assistance and would have received it or not. In the U.N. a very large group of countries came back with a request year after year that "the United Nations" (more specifically those capable of contributing financially) should undertake an additional U.N. program for assistance to "the developing countries". The educational process on both sides undoubtedly had useful results.

While causal relationships of this kind are difficult to establish, it is possible that the persistent pressure for U.N. action to establish a capital aid program was responsible not only for the establishment of the Special Fund and the Capital Development Fund, but also, to some extent, for a number of related actions outside the United Nations. Within the U.N. framework the International Finance Corporation was established as an affiliate of the IBRD in July 1956 to aid private capital investment projects in the less developed countries. It was decided, in 1959, to establish the International Development Association. Also, member governments increased bilateral economic assistance programs and participated in regional multilateral programs. Assuming that donor countries are influenced to give economic aid as a result of pressure on them for such aid, the U.N. can claim a reasonably large share of the credit for the general atmosphere of increased international cooperation which resulted in specific action for increased aid.

Notes to chapter 10

1. The Special Fund dealt with in this chapter should not be confused with the U.N. Special Fund created as the follow-up to the program of emergency assistance to countries "most seriously affected" which had been set up at the sixth special session of the General Assembly (1974). The latter Special Fund has de facto ceased to operate.

2. Report of the third session of the Sub-commission on Economic Development (ECOSOC, Official Records, 9th session, Supplement No. 11B, E/CN.1/65, Annex). See also the U.N. Secretariat study, *Methods of Financing Economic Development in Underdeveloped Countries* (New York: United Nations, 1949).

3. *Report on a Special United Nations Fund for Economic Development* (doc. E/2381) (New York: United Nations, 1953) (Sales No. 1953.II.B.1).

4. *Special United Nations Fund for Economic Development,* Final Report by Raymond Scheyven, prepared in pursuance of G.A. resolution 724B(VIII), GAOR, Ninth Session, Supplement No. 19, New York, 1954. For an excellent description of the decision-making process preceding the adoption of resolution 724B, see R.E. Elder and F.D. Murden, *Economic Co-operation: Special U.N. Fund for Economic Development (SUNFED),* (New York: Woodrow Wilson Foundation, 1954).

5. *Special United Nations Fund for Economic Development,* Report prepared in pursuance of General Assembly Resolution 822 (IX), GAOR, Tenth Session, Supplement No. 17, New York, 1955.

6. *Final Report of the Ad Hoc Committee on the Question of the Establishment of a Special United Nations Fund for Economic Development,* GAOR, Twelfth Session, Annexes, Agenda Item 28, New York, 1957.

7. Paul G. Hoffman, "Blueprint for Foreign Aid," *New York Times Magazine,* 17 February 1957.

8. *Supplementary Report of the Ad Hoc Committee on the Question of the Establishment of a Special U.N. Fund for Economic Development,* GAOR, Twelfth Session, Annexes, Agenda item 28, New York, 1957.

9. Press release of 30 July 1957 of the United States delegation to the twenty-fourth session of the Economic and Social Council.

10. *Report and Recommendations of the Preparatory Committee for the Special Fund,* ECOSOC, Official Records, 26th Session, 1958.

11. George F. Davidson, "The Year of the Breakthrough," *United Nations Review,* New York, September 1958.

Chapter 11

The Future of U.N. Decision Making: Some Concluding Observations

1. The Evolution of Decision Making

The founding fathers of the United Nations had a fairly simple method of decision making in mind: one country/one vote, and let the majority, if need be in prescribed cases a qualified majority, decide. Let us summarize the principal possibilities for decision making as described in the previous chapters:

Voting
—simple or qualified majority;
—show of hands/non-recorded vote;
—roll-call/recorded vote;
—secret ballot.

Consensus/pseudo-consensus
—resolutions or decisions adopted by acclamation;
—texts of draft treaties or conventions arrived at by negotiation;
—negotiated declaration, read out for the record by presiding officer;
—agreed text to be included in report;
—agreement to postpone item or question to later session;
—agreement to refer item or question to higher or lower organ, or to another organization.

Gradually, perhaps too slowly, governments realize that decisions arrived at by consensus are more valuable—in most cases—than decisions arrived at by a vote. Hence most United Nations organs have a tendency to take decisions by one of the consensus methods, rather than by voting. The table on p. 210 reflects this trend.

	General Assembly 29th session (1974)		General Assembly 33rd session (1978)	
	number	%	number	%
Resolutions adopted by voting (in plenary)	92	51	145	46
Resolutions adopted without a vote	89	49	167	54

At this point I wish to emphasize the considerable difference between various categories of decisions. A distinction can be made between:[1]

1. decisions or resolutions on routine or secondary matters; for example the approval by the Economic and Social Council, after a non-controversial debate, of reports of subsidiary bodies such as the U.N. regional commissions;
2. decisions or resolutions on activities of the United Nations as an organization, i.e., of the Secretariat; the U.N. budget is the most important example;
3. recommendations dealing with fundamental political, economic, social, human rights or other policy issues, and draft treaties or international agreements on such matters.

It would obviously be useful if there could be some understanding, even if only informal, among governments, that decisions in the third category, and to the largest extent possible also those in the second category, should be arrived at by consensus, after adequate consultations and negotiations. Evidently, category 1 questions are the easiest to handle by the consensus method. Already there seems to be developing a habit to tackle category 3 by the negotiations-aimed-at-consensus method. The Law of the Sea Conference, with the consensus method written in its rules of procedure as the normal way of decision making, is an example.

In the Security Council there is a distinct trend towards consensus decision making. Although this cannot be formally proven, abstentions in the Security Council seem to be a way of going along with a consensus, much more so than in the General Assembly. In the Security Council the result of a vote is mostly known beforehand, either from the informal consultations or from statements prior to the vote. In the General Assembly, the result of a vote cannot usually be predicted with precision; in particular in votes requiring a two-thirds majority the number of abstentions may have a decisive influence, consciously exercised by those who vote "abstention".

The one country/one vote system has been criticized throughout the existence of the United Nations as undemocratic, giving the smallest and the biggest state equal power. The following table compares voting strength and population by region.

Voting strength and size of population
(compared for formal geographical groups under General Assembly resolutions)

U.N. electoral groups	Number of Member States and votes per group (based on U.N. membership as of 1 January 1980)		Population (mid-1978 or latest)* (in millions)	
	number	%	number	%
African group	50	33	434.78	10
Asian group	39	26	2326.90	56
Latin American group (including states of Caribbean area)	29	19	339.52	8
Socialist states of Eastern Europe	11	7	394.35	10
Western European and others (includes Australia, Canada, New Zealand, U.S.A.	23	15	642.82	16
Total	152	100	4138.37	100

* Source: *United Nations Monthly Bulletin of Statistics,* October 1979.

If voting strength per state were to be linked with population, as has been proposed by some, the result would be an overwhelming voting strength for Asia (even if one were not to count Japan with its 115 million people on the ground that it might often vote differently from the majority of Asian countries, especially on economic issues). It seems to be a foregone conclusion that any proposal suggesting to link voting power to population would have an extremely slim chance of being adopted, since it would be opposed by a large number of countries, certainly sufficient to constitute a "blocking third" in the inevitable situation of a two-thirds majority requirement, because such a proposal would be an "important question".

If voting is gradually receding compared to consensus decision making, it would become less and less necessary to modify the voting system. If, finally, one considers that the one country/one vote system is enshrined in the Charter (Article 18, para. 1) and that amendments of the Charter have to be approved by two-thirds of the Member States, it is obvious that changing the U.N. voting system is a theoretical issue.

Perhaps it is gradually realized that with the influx of newly independent nations into the United Nations, with social and historical traditions very different from the countries which founded the organization, decision-making methods are also changing.

Somehow, United Nations decision making appears to be moving from a Western concept of parliamentary democracy to a more complex system of decision making where traditional African, Asian and other methods of consensus building gain importance. Perhaps this new blend of forms of decision making is in itself symptomatic for the United Nations as it evolutes towards the twenty-first century. It has also the distinct advantage of moving away from the "I-win-you-lose" psychology which is so often inherent in United Nations decision making. Consensus decision making would also be symptomatic for the real result of effective international cooperation: everybody wins, nobody loses!

2. Does the Institutional Set-up Influence United Nations Decision Making?

There is little doubt that the answer to this question is: yes! As a rule of thumb one can say that for subjects in regard to which there are clear lines of responsibility, decision making is effected relatively smoothly, while for subjects on which there is divided responsibility the opposite is true.

The Security Council is, in the United Nations context, the best example of an established authority, in conformity with the U.N. Charter. This authority is not challenged by any other United Nations body. It is true that the General Assembly debates on practically every problem that is discussed in the Security Council, and, on occasion, has made recommendations on such a problem contrary to Article 12, para. 1 of the Charter. However, the Security Council has in every such case proceeded according to its own pace and procedures, without necessarily giving special attention to the recommendations of the General Assembly, for example regarding the Middle East issues and problems related to southern Africa.

In extreme contrast, in the other principal organ of the United Nations, i.e., the Economic and Social Council, as analyzed in chapter 4, decision making has continuously been made more difficult by the value attached by many countries to the Second Committee of the General Assembly, and by the successive establishment of other bodies with mandates overlapping that of ECOSOC. Is there a remedy for this situation?

It might help if, as many developing countries wish, membership of ECOSOC were to be thrown open, and become "open-ended". In the case of the Committee of the Whole for the Preparation of a New Development Strategy and in that of the UNCTAD Board, membership was thrown open to all interested members. The same was done in the case of the Ad Hoc Committee on the Restructuring of the Economic and Social Sectors of the U.N. System. In all these cases those who are really interested attend. If ECOSOC were to become open-ended, a salutary measure could be a de facto merger of ECOSOC meetings and those of the UNCTAD Board, which is already open-ended. This would produce a single large intergovernmental superior organ in the economic and social sectors, and thereby streamline, and presumably facilitate, decision making. Economic problems are by their very nature complex, in most cases probably more complex than most issues before the Security Council. Hence, trying to simplify institutional machinery in the economic area cannot have more than a relatively limited positive effect. Even with a merger of ECOSOC and the UNCTAD Board, meetings would remain too large to be an instrument for negotiation. The practice of the annual meetings of the contracting parties of GATT, i.e. of scheduling as much as possible public meetings only for half days, so that 50 percent of the time is available for informal negotiation or consultation, has much merit.

As recommended in para. 35 of the annex to resolution 32/197 on restructuring the economic and social sectors, a serious effort should be made to merge the governing bodies of various operational programs. In spite of the exemption granted by that resolution to UNICEF and the World Food Programme, it should be examined how to the benefit of all programs, there could be a single governing council for UNDP and all other U.N. funds giving technical and other assistance to developing countries. It is encouraging that the U.N. Conference on Science and Technology for Development decided to entrust, at least for the first two years, the management of a new interim fund for the transfer of science and technology to developing countries to the Administrator of the U.N. Development Program, implicitly putting the activities of the new fund under the general supervision of the Governing Council of UNDP.

3. Can the Methods of Decision Making in the United Nations Be Improved?

The answer is an unqualified yes. The present system has developed its own peculiar rationale. In spite of all the repetitive and lengthy rhetoric and the apparent or real loss of time by meetings starting late, the United Nations does produce opportunities for negotiations and can adapt to the requirements of particular situations. Thus, the lengthy and seemingly interminable meetings of the Conference on the Law of the Sea consist nearly entirely of informal negotiations aimed at consensus, with speech making virtually abandoned. In bodies like the General Assembly and the Economic and Social Council, a stricter conformity with the Rules of Procedure would result in more efficient decision making.[2] Yet, certain other tools for more efficient decision making could be considered:

3.1. An Ad Hoc Committee on Concepts and Definitions

A lot of time is lost on often unproductive debates on the definition of new concepts. The debate on "the" or "a" New International Economic Order was a good example of such wasted time. The choice between "the" and "a" opposed those who felt that the definition was

214

clearly spelled out in the resolutions of the sixth and seventh special sessions of the General Assembly and those who felt that a New International Economic Order was an evolving, as yet undefined concept. The debate lasted for a full two years, and came to a probably temporary end when those immediately concerned implicitly accepted the definition offered by the United States representative at the ECOSOC session of July 1977: "The international economic order is a system of relationships among all nations. The process of change, therefore, must be through an evolving consensus that takes into account the economic systems, the interests and the ideas of all countries. Thus we are talking about a process, or a broad framework for dialogue and progress, as much as an 'order'."3

Another example is the definition of agression which was worked out by a special committee of the General Assembly over a period of 22 years, and ended in a generally acceptable compromise. On the other hand, in its well-known controversial resolution 3379 (XXX) of 1975, which equates Zionism with racism, the General Assembly proceeded with a definition without thorough consideration.

My conclusion is that the United Nations might look at the pros and contras of establishing an ad hoc committee on concepts and definitions. Such a committee might be composed of scholars and practitioners, with the addition of experts on the specific questions discussed. Draft resolutions containing new definitions might be referred to the ad hoc committee.

Of course, such a committee should not become a mere drafting group. It should be instructed to report back to the next session of the General Assembly (or any other organ where the disagreement arose) and to make a real effort towards clarification and reconciliation of different concepts. Before a request for a definition would be submitted to it, opposing governments should formulate their definitions in the clearest possible way, with substantive arguments backing up a particular definition. The draft resolution containing a proposed definition would also be transmitted to the committee, as a background document. The Secretariat should give all possible assistance.

The proposed procedure will not overcome fundamental problems. It may, however, prevent sterile debate and produce a lowering of potentially inflammable tempers.

3.2. Cost/Benefit and Cost/Effectiveness Analysis

The current practice is that each new initiative, whether from a delegation or originating in the Secretariat, must be accompanied by a "statement of financial implications" submitted by the Secretariat. This statement indicates the costs of additional personnel, meetings, etc. which would result from the proposal, if adopted. The Committee on Programme and Coordination has undertaken a more systematic effort to analyze the costs and benefits of various activities.

We have seen (pp. 172-178) that the initiative regarding immediate needs resulting from economic and other emergencies failed, inter alia, because the potential benefits of the proposal were not clearly presented and understood.

It would seem beneficial if the current statement of financial implications were replaced by a "statement of costs and benefits". If the benefits cannot be quantified, the effectiveness of the proposed measure or activity should be indicated with as much precision as possible.

It might also be considered to make it a practice that a government or group of governments coming with a proposal for some new activity, should itself submit a cost/benefit estimate. A clearer insight into costs and benefits will obviously have a favorable effect on the decision-making process.

3.3. Speech Making versus Negotiations

In organs like the General Assembly and its committees, and the Economic and Social Council, a lot of time is spent on the delivery of statements, some of them quite lengthy. The general debate at each General Assembly session consumes a full three weeks. The thirty-third session of the General Assembly (1978) had to be continued into 1979 to finish its business.

It would make sense, even as a mere cost-cutting measure, to shorten statements in general and special debates to previously agreed limits, e.g., 30 and 15 minutes respectively. There might be a proviso that the remainder of a statement (up to an agreed maximum) can be entered in the official record. The main objective of such a perhaps not generally popular measure would be to make more time available for meaningful negotiations on difficult agenda items. The less delegates are preoccupied with preparing and delivering their own delegation's speeches and listening to those of others, the more time there is for informal or formal negotiations.[4] It would then also be easier to constitute contact groups mandated to search a compromise solution early in each session, instead of halfway or later as now often happens. Such an early start of the negotiations would also tend to prevent ''five-minutes-to-twelve'' negotiations which often fail because of lack of time.

As to the negotiations themselves, it is clear that the more flexible instructions are, the smoother negotiations can evolve. In particular, in the case of group-to-group negotiations, flexible mandates are required to avoid the ''maximum demand clashes with minimum offer'' phenomenon (see p. 62).

4. The U.N. Secretariat and the Future of U.N. Decision Making

The future of United Nations decision making will certainly be influenced considerably by the activities of, and the confidence in the Secretariat.[5] The personal role of the Secretary-General is particularly crucial, especially in the political field. Under the Charter (Article 99) the Secretary-General can bring matters to the attention of the Security Council if world peace is endangered. This authority has rarely been used. However, successive Secretaries-General have, without explicit reference to Article 99, written letters to the President of the Security Council expressing their concern about a given situation; Mr. Waldheim did so in respect of the civil war in Lebanon.

The Iran/United States crisis which had started with the taking of hostages at the U.S. Embassy in Teheran was put by Dr. Waldheim before the Security Council in the following terms:

I wish to refer to the grave situation which has arisen in the relations between the United States and Iran. The Government of the United States is deeply disturbed at the seizure of its Embassy in Teheran and the detention of its diplomatic personnel, in violation of the relevant international conventions. The Government of Iran seeks redress for injustices and abuse of human rights which, in its view, were committed by the previous régime. The international community is increasingly concerned that the dangerous level of tension between these two countries threatens peace and stability in the region and could have disastrous consequences for the entire world. In my opinion, therefore, the present crisis poses a serious threat to international peace and security. Accordingly, in the exercise of my responsibility under the Charter of the United Nations, I ask that the Security Council be convened urgently in an effort to seek a peaceful solution of the problem in conformity with the principles of justice and international law. [Letter dated 25 November 1979, from the Secretary-General addressed to the President of the Security Council, doc. S/13646].

The phraseology used is a clear reference to Article 99, even though it is not explicitly mentioned.

Behind the scenes the Secretary-General can play a role in helping to solve major or minor conflicts. During Dag Hammarskjöld's term of office the expression "leave it to Dag" came into current usage. Secretary-General Waldheim received an express mandate from the Security Council to mediate in the Cyprus conflict. In May 1979 Mr. Waldheim made a trip through Asia with the express objective to find out if his services could be useful in the conflict separating China and Viet Nam, and that between North and South Korea. On the question of China against Viet Nam, the Security Council had not been able to adopt a decision or resolution (owing to a veto by the Soviet Union). Mr. Waldheim indicated that he undertook his Asian trip to see what he could do to fill the gap left by the inability of the Security Council to pass resolutions.[6]

The significance of the Secretariat is potentially very large in the economic and social sectors in their broadest sense. The U.N. Department of International Economic and Social Affairs was very much shaped during the years that P. de Seynes headed the department, with courageous initiatives, e.g., the activity on transnational corporations, which started with the preparation of a report by a Group of Eminent Persons. The effort to involve non-governmental participants in this activity (see p. 86) was a Secretariat initiative. At UNCTAD, its dynamic start is intimately linked with the leadership of Raul Prebisch during its early years. The U.N. Environment Programme, now led by Mostafa K. Tolba, received a considerable push in its initial years from the leadership of Maurice Strong; the U.N. Centre on Transnational Corporations benefits from the impetus given by its first head, Klaus A. Sahlgren. Successive U.N. High Commissioners for Refugees have all been forceful managers of a by its nature politically delicate activity. UNDP and its precursors, the U.N. Special Fund and the Expanded Program of Technical Assistance, bear very much the imprint of such leaders as David Owen, Paul Hoffman and Bradford Morse, while in the case of UNICEF the names of Maurice Pate and Henry Labouisse (in 1980 succeeded by James Grant) are to be recalled as forceful and at the same time tactful leaders. I have already stressed (see p. 78) that in all operational programs the role of the Secretariat is especially important, because the job of preparing and screening concrete projects and programs cannot be done by intergovernmental organs.

The restructured set-up of the Secretariat's economic and social sectors offers great possibilities, but may turn out to be too heavy to perform optimally. On the political side, the continued presence since the

218

time of Secretary-General Lie of Under-Secretary-General Brian Urquhart, who was involved in all peace-keeping operations, has been a great asset.

The Secretary-General can only function efficiently, if he has the confidence of the overwhelming majority of the membership, including that of the Super Powers. The dilemma facing him is that, if he is too active in a conflict in which one of the Super Powers is involved, he risks its enmity, making his functioning more difficult, to say the least. Dag Hammarskjöld incurred the wrath of the Soviet Union when he became deeply involved in the Congo problem; U Thant alienated himself from the United States when he expressed his concern about United States action in Viet Nam. The wise Secretary-General will be aware of the outer limit to which he can throw his weight and prestige in the search for a solution of a conflict, and yet keep the support of the major powers.

5. U.N. Secretariat Recruitment Policies and the Confidence Factor

According to Article 101 of the Charter, "the paramount consideration in the employment of staff... shall be the necessity of securing the highest standards of efficiency, competence, and integrity," while also "due regard shall be paid to the importance of recruiting the staff on as wide a geographical basis as possible." In practice this last consideration has assumed an importance beyond what was in the minds of the drafters of the U.N. Charter. Each year the General Assembly is presented with elaborate statistics showing the geographical distribution of United Nations staff, with a so-called "desirable range" for each country, roughly based on the country's assessment percentage for the budget. The Secretariat, encouraged in this direction by General Assembly resolutions, endeavors to give priority, for any given position, to an "under-represented" country, provided of course the candidate is qualified (but perhaps not as qualified as a candidate from an "over-represented" country). Practically all governments, usually through their permanent missions in New York or Geneva (the higher posts in Geneva are also decided upon in New York) try to exercise pressure on the Secretariat to favor their candidate for a particular position. For the highest positions (director, assistant secretary-general, under-secretary-general and comparable posts) the Secretary-General is personally put under pressure. This practice is regrettable. If, as the result of such pressure, not the best persons are appointed, the blame rests primarily with the governments. It would be a good thing if governments could agree, and perhaps confirm this in a General Assembly resolution, that they would limit themselves to a role of "post office" in transmitting biographical and other details on any candidate and that the Secretary-General should automatically disqualify any candidate on whose behalf a government undertakes oral or written *démarches* to press his or her appointment.

If governments could, moreover, agree that, as follows from the U.N. Charter, they would leave their citizens alone once they have entered U.N. service, the independence of the Secretariat would benefit further.

Better recruitment policies will lead to a higher overall quality of United Nations staff. This will in turn favorably affect confidence enjoyed by the United Nations staff in general, and facilitate Secretariat participation in the decision-making processes.

6. By Way of Epilogue: Concluding Observation

When the United Nations was founded, immediately after the Second World War, there were, in many quarters, near limitless hopes for what it could do, and as a consequence there was much uncritical support. Criticism now often exceeds praise, the latter mostly reserved for the U.N. peace-keeping operations in the Middle East, Cyprus, and elsewhere, and for the U.N.'s technical assistance and related activities. This situation may be healthier than the earlier one, because uncritical support has no doubt led to disillusionment ("Why can't the United Nations do something about this problem?"). Still, it is better that the United Nations is the object of controversy than that it is ignored. The fear expressed at one time that the United Nations "would fade slowly away beyond thickening clouds of public boredom"[7] has not materialized.

One of the most encouraging signs of re-increasing interest in using the potential of the United Nations (and for that matter, of the United Nations system, i.e., including the specialized agencies) is, to me, not so much the ever-widening scope of its agenda, but the widening circle of participants in United Nations decision making. Individual governments and the Secretariat were the original participants. Additional actors now are: the various types of groups of governments, non-governmental organizations, and even, although this is still fairly exceptional, individual persons. Apart from the large number of persons serving in an individual capacity on groups of experts and U.N. committees, examples of the latter category are the experts assisting the Commission on Transnational Corporations and the persons who are heard by the Fourth Committee of the General Assembly and by other U.N. organs as informants on some question. Of course one must continue to distinguish between direct actors in the decision-making process (governments, the Secretariat, and presiding officers) and indirect participants. The latter do not cast votes, but their influence has been increasing. Is this caused by the fact that, in many countries the main thrusts towards innovation in many fields originate outside governments? In any case, it is a welcome development, which provides a broader base for the execution of decisions, most of which require the support of non-governmental sectors. It would therefore be useful if the General Assembly would give explicit encouragement to the participation of "indirect actors" in the work of the United Nations, including the preparation of decisions.

Of course, wider participation also has the inherent danger of a slowing down of the decision-making process, especially under consensus-seeking conditions. Yet there is no doubt that a consensus-type decision arrived at later, but with the full consent of all participants concerned, is distinctly superior to a hastily voted resolution which will meet with hard opposition.

The question is sometimes asked whether United Nations diplomacy, as practised anno 1980, is so much different from traditional diplomacy that the qualifications required of its participants are without precedent.[8] The answer, to me, is a qualified yes: the modern U.N. diplomat must be a "specialized generalist" or a "generalized specialist". He (or she) must know how to shift from one subject to another, to become not a full expert, but sufficiently familiar with the vocabulary and the problems related to a particular set of issues. Not only that, but the modern U.N. diplomat should also be a skillful negotiator. The more consensus decision making is going to prevail, the more there is a need for wise, experienced negotiators. Negotiating skills cannot be learned from a textbook. Yet, in the education of junior or candidate-diplomats, more time and attention could and should be devoted to negotiating techniques, especially also those applicable in conference diplomacy.

In his *In Praise of Folly*, the sixteenth century Dutch philosopher Erasmus raises the question whether those who dwell in Plato's famous cavern, seeing only the shadows of things in the real world, are perhaps happier than those who go outside in the real world. For the United Nations and for its Member States, whose wishes and limitations form the inner and outer limits of all United Nations activities, there is no choice: either the United Nations, and its decision-making processes conform to the "real world", or the U.N. is bound to perish in an ocean of words and irrelevant activity.

Notes to chapter 11

1. I put forward this differentiation in a speech during the twenty-ninth session of the General Assembly (GAOR, 11 December 1974) under the agenda item "Strengthening of the Role of the United Nations with regard to the Maintenance and Consolidation of International Peace and Security, the Development of Cooperation among all Nations and the Promotion of the Rules of International Law in Relations between States". This item was usually referred to as the "Romanian item", because Romania had first taken the initiative, in 1972, to have it included in the agenda of the General Assembly. The United States permanent representative at the time, Ambassador John Scali, used this agenda item to give a discourse on the "tyranny of the majority", stating that the new majority of the U.N. membership (mostly developing countries) did not take into account sufficiently the interests of the minority. The views of the United States representative were supported by certain developed countries, including France and the Federal Republic of Germany. The developing countries responded with a number of arguments, including the fact that when the new minority had had the majority of votes, it had not hesitated to impose its views on the minority at that time on a series of issues, e.g., the membership of the People's Republic of China.

2. This is also an essential part of the proposals of Secretary-General Waldheim in his report *Rationalization of the procedures and organization of the General Assembly*, GAOR, 34th Session, doc. A/34/320, with comments by the Latin American group in doc. A/34/365. An informal working group of ambassadors and permanent mission members, chaired by Ambassador W. Barton (Canada) and with Ambassador P. Marshall (U.K.) as rapporteur, made some sensible recommendations, such as the nomination of the president and chairmen of the Main Committees at the end of a General Assembly session in view of the coming session nine months later. The Stanley Foundation paid attention to improving U.N. procedures in two conferences and subsequent reports: *Decision-Making Processes of the United Nations* (conference held at Vail, Colorado, 1974), and *U.N. General Assembly Effectiveness* (Mohonk Mountain House, New Paltz, New York, 1979). When reading all these reports, the author is struck by the continuing importance and relevancy of the conclusions of the Special Committee on the Rationalization of the Procedures and Organization of the General Assembly, which were approved by General Assembly resolution 2837 (XXVI) of 17 December 1971.

3. Statement by Ambassador A. Young, ECOSOC, 63rd session, 8 July 1977.

4. The term "negotiations", as used here, is intended to cover all sorts of contacts, including consultations, talks, etc. The borderline between these concepts is, in any case, vague. Sometimes governments prefer a term such as "consultations" because they fear that using the term "negotiations" will give the meeting a formal character.

The most famous example of the use of an understatement to indicate negotiations is probably constituted by the use of the word talks in Strategic Arms Limitation Talks (SALT). For an insight into U.N. negotiations before the advert of the "group system", see: A.S. Lall, *Modern International Negotiation* (New York: Columbia University Press, 1966).

5. On the role of the Secretary-General and the Secretariat see: S.D. Bailey, *The Secretariat of the United Nations*. rev. ed. (New York: Frederick A. Praeger, 1964); Robert W. Cox, "The Executive Head: An Essay on Leadership in International Organizations," *International Organization* 23 (Spring 1969), pp. 205-230; L. Gordenker, *The United Nations Secretary-General and the Maintenance of Peace* (New York: Columbia University Press, 1967); Norman A. Graham and Robert S. Jordan, *The International Civil Service: Changing Role and Concepts,* published for UNITAR by Pergamon Press, New York, 1980.

6. Interview in *Newsweek,* 25 June 1979.

7. *The Economist* (London), 3 December 1955.

8. I have tried to give a systematic analysis of the requirements and characteristics of conference diplomats in my *Conference Diplomacy,* op. cit., pp. 130-140. See also Davidson Nicol, "The Diplomat today and tomorrow," in *UNITAR News,* vol. XI, 1979, UNITAR, United Nations, New York.

Annex 1

Charter of the United Nations

We the peoples of the united nations
  determined
to save succeeding generations from the scourge of war, which twice in our lifetime has brought untold sorrow to mankind, and to reaffirm faith in fundamental human rights, in the dignity and worth of the human person, in equal rights of men and women and of nations large and small, and
to establish conditions under which justice and respect for the obligations arising from treaties and other sources of international law can be maintained, and
to promote social progress and better standards of life in larger freedom,
  and for these ends
to practice tolerance and live together in peace with one another as good neighbours, and
to unite our strength to maintain international peace and security, and
to ensure, by the acceptance of principles and the institution of methods, that armed force shall not be used, save in the common interest, and
to employ international machinery for the promotion of the economic and social advancement of all peoples,
  have resolved to combine our efforts
  to accomplish these aims
Accordingly, our respective Governments, through representatives assembled in the city of San Francisco, who have exhibited their full powers found to be in good and due form, have agreed to the present Charter of the United Nations and do hereby establish an international organization to be known as the United Nations.

CHAPTER I. PURPOSES AND PRINCIPLES

Article 1

The Purposes of the United Nations are:

1. To maintain international peace and security, and to that end: to take effective collective measures for the prevention and removal of threats to the peace, and for the suppression of acts of aggression or other breaches of the peace, and to bring about by peaceful means, and in conformity with the principles of justice and international law, adjustment or settlement of international disputes or situations which might lead to a breach of the peace;

2. To develop friendly relations among nations based on respect for the principle of equal rights and self-determination of peoples, and to take other appropriate measures

to strengthen universal peace;

3. To achieve international co-operation in solving international problems of an economic, social, cultural, or humanitarian character, and in promoting and encouraging respect for human rights and for fundamental freedoms for all without distinction as to race, sex, language, or religion; and

4. To be a centre for harmonizing the actions of nations in the attainment of these common ends.

Article 2

The Organization and its Members, in pursuit of the Purposes stated in Article 1, shall act in accordance with the following Principles.

1. The Organization is based on the principle of the sovereign equality of all its Members.

2. All Members, in order to ensure to all of them the rights and benefits resulting from membership, shall fulfil in good faith the obligations assumed by them in accordance with the present Charter.

3. All Members shall settle their international disputes by peaceful means in such a manner that international peace and security, and justice, are not endangered.

4. All Members shall refrain in their international relations from the threat or use of force against the territorial integrity or political independence of any state, or in any other manner inconsistent with the Purposes of the United Nations.

5. All Members shall give the United Nations every assistance in any action it takes in accordance with the present Charter, and shall refrain from giving assistance to any state against which the United Nations is taking preventive or enforcement action.

6. The Organization shall ensure that states which are not Members of the United Nations act in accordance with these Principles so far as may be necessary for the maintenance of international peace and security.

7. Nothing contained in the present Charter shall authorize the United Nations to intervene in matters which are essentially within the domestic jurisdiction of any state or shall require the Members to submit such matters to settlement under the present Charter; but this principle shall not prejudice the application of enforcement measures under Chapter VII.

CHAPTER II. MEMBERSHIP

Article 3

The original Members of the United Nations shall be the states which, having participated in the United Nations Conference on International Organization at San Francisco, or having previously signed the Declaration by United Nations of 1 January 1942, sign the present Charter and ratify it in accordance with Article 110.

Article 4

1. Membership in the United Nations is open to all other peace-loving states which accept the obligations contained in the present Charter and, in the judgment of the Organization, are able and willing to carry out these obligations.

2. The admission of any such state to membership in the United Nations will be effected by a decision of the General Assembly upon the recommendation of the Security Council.

Article 5

A Member of the United Nations against which preventive or enforcement action has been taken by the Security Council may be suspended from the exercise of the rights and privileges of membership by the General Assembly upon the recommendation of the Security Council. The exercise of these rights and privileges may be restored by the Security Council.

Article 6

A Member of the United Nations which has persistently violated the Principles contained in the present Charter may be expelled from the Organization by the General Assembly upon the recommendation of the Security Council.

CHAPTER III. ORGANS

Article 7

1. There are established as the principal organs of the United Nations: a General Assembly, a Security Council, an Economic and Social Council, a Trusteeship Council, an International Court of Justice, and a Secretariat.

2. Such subsidiary organs as may be found necessary may be established in accordance with the present Charter.

Article 8

The United Nations shall place no restrictions on the eligibility of men and women to participate in any capacity and under conditions of equality in its principal and subsidiary organs.

CHAPTER IV. THE GENERAL ASSEMBLY

COMPOSITION
Article 9

1. The General Assembly shall consist of all the Members of the United Nations.

2. Each Member shall have not more than five representatives in the General Assembly.

FUNCTIONS AND POWERS
Article 10

The General Assembly may discuss any questions or any matters within the scope of the present Charter or relating to the powers and functions of any organs provided for in the present Charter, and, except as provided in Article 12, may make recommendations to the Security Council or to both on any such questions or matters.

Article 11

1. The General Assembly may consider the general principles of co-operation in the maintenance of international peace and security, including the principles governing disarmament and the regulation of armaments, and may make recommendations with regard to such principles to the Members or to the Security Council or to both.

2. The General Assembly may discuss any questions relating to the maintenance of

international peace and security brought before it by any Member of the United Nations, or by the Security Council, or by a state which is not a Member of the United Nations in accordance with Article 35, paragraph 2, and, except as provided in Article 12, may make recommendations with regard to any such questions to the state or states concerned or to the Security Council or to both. Any such question on which action is necessary shall be referred to the Security Council by the General Assembly either before or after discussion.

3. The General Assembly may call the attention of the Security Council to situations which are likely to endanger international peace and security.

4. The powers of the General Assembly set forth in this Article shall not limit the general scope of Article 10.

Article 12

1. While the Security Council is exercising in respect of any dispute or situation the functions assigned to it in the present Charter, the General Assembly shall not make any recommendations with regard to that dispute or situation unless the Security Council so requests.

2. The Secretary-General, with the consent of the Security Council, shall notify the General Assembly at each session of any matters relative to the maintenance of international peace and security which are being dealt with by the Security Council and shall similarly notify the General Assembly, or the Members of the United Nations if the General Assembly is not in session, immediately the Security Council ceases to deal with such matters.

Article 13

1. The General Assembly shall initiate studies and make recommendations for the purpose of:

a. promoting international co-operation in the political field and encouraging the progressive development of international law and its codification;

b. promoting international co-operation in the economic, social, cultural, educational, and health fields, and assisting in the realization of human rights and fundamental freedoms for all without distinction as to race, sex, language, or religion.

2. The further responsibilities, functions and powers of the General Assembly with respect to matters mentioned in paragraph 1(b) above are set forth in Chapters IX and X.

Article 14

Subject to the provisions of Article 12, the General Assembly may recommend measures for the peaceful adjustment of any situation, regardless of origin, which it deems likely to impair the general welfare or friendly relations among nations, including situations resulting from a violation of the provisions of the present Charter setting forth the Purposes and Principles of the United Nations.

Article 15

1. The General Assembly shall receive and consider annual and special reports from the Security Council; these reports shall include an account of the measures that the Security Council has decided upon or taken to maintain international peace and security.

2. The General Assembly shall receive and consider reports from the other organs of the United Nations.

Article 16

The General Assembly shall perform such functions with respect to the international trusteeship system as are assigned to it under Chapters XII and XIII, including the approval of the trusteeship agreements for areas not designated as strategic.

Article 17

1. The General Assembly shall consider and approve the budget of the Organization.

2. The expenses of the Organization shall be borne by the Members as apportioned by the General Assembly.

3. The General Assembly shall consider and approve any financial and budgetary arrangements with specialized agencies referred to in Article 57 and shall examine the administrative budgets of such specialized agencies with a view to making recommendations to the agencies concerned.

Voting
Article 18

1. Each member of the General Assembly shall have one vote.

2. Decisions of the General Assembly on important questions shall be made by a two-thirds majority of the members present and voting. These questions shall include: recommendations with respect to the maintenance of international peace and security, the election of the non-permanent members of the Security Council, the election of the members of the Economic and Social Council, the election of members of the Trusteeship Council in accordance with paragraph 1(c) of Article 86, the admission of new Members to the United Nations, the suspension of the rights and privileges of membership, the expulsion of Members, questions relating to the operation of the trusteeship system, and budgetary questions.

3. Decisions on other questions, including the determination of additional categories of questions to be decided by a two-thirds majority, shall be made by a majority of the members present and voting.

Article 19

A Member of the United Nations which is in arrears in the payment of its financial contributions to the Organization shall have no vote in the General Assembly if the amount of its arrears equals or exceeds the amount of the contributions due from it for the preceding two full years. The General Assembly may, nevertheless, permit such a Member to vote if it is satisfied that the failure to pay is due to conditions beyond the control of the Member.

Procedure
Article 20

The General Assembly shall meet in regular annual sessions and in such special sessions as occasion may require. Special sessions shall be convoked by the Secretary-General at the request of the Security Council or of a majority of the Members of the United Nations.

Article 21

The General Assembly shall adopt its own rules of procedure. It shall elect its President for each session.

Article 22

The General Assembly may establish such subsidiary organs as it deems necessary for the performance of its functions.

CHAPTER V. THE SECURITY COUNCIL

Composition
Article 23

1. The Security Council shall consist of fifteen Members of the United Nations. The Republic of China, France, the Union of Soviet Socialist Republics, the United Kingdom of Great Britain and Northern Ireland, and the United States of America shall be permanent members of the Security Council. The General Assembly shall elect ten other Members of the United Nations to be non-permanent members of the Security Council, due regard being specially paid, in the first instance to the contribution of Members of the United Nations to the maintenance of international peace and security and to the other purposes of the Organization, and also to equitable geographical distribution.

2. The non-permanent members of the Security Council shall be elected for a term of two years. In the first election of the non-permanent members after the increase of the membership of the Security Council from eleven to fifteen, two of the four additional members shall be chosen for a term of one year. A retiring member shall not be eligible for immediate re-election.

3. Each member of the Security Council shall have one representative.

Functions and powers
Article 24

1. In order to ensure prompt and effective action by the United Nations, its Members confer on the Security Council primary responsibility for the maintenance of international peace and security, and agree that in carrying out its duties under this responsibility the Security Council acts on their behalf.

2. In discharging these duties the Security Council shall act in accordance with the Purposes and Principles of the United Nations. The specific powers granted to the Security Council for the discharge of these duties are laid down in Chapters VI, VII, VIII and XII.

3. The Security Council shall submit annual and, when necessary, special reports to the General Assembly for its consideration.

Article 25

The Members of the United Nations agree to accept and carry out the decisions of the Security Council in accordance with the present Charter.

Article 26

In order to promote the establishment and maintenance of international peace and security with the least diversion for armaments of the world's human and economic resources, the Security Council shall be responsible for formulating, with the assistance of the Military Staff Committee referred to in Article 47, plans to be submitted to the Members of the United Nations for the establishment of a system for the regulation of armaments.

Article 27

1. Each member of the Security Council shall have one vote.

2. Decisions of the Security Council on procedural matters shall be made by an affirmative vote of nine members.

3. Decisions of the Security Council on all other matters shall be made by an affirmative vote of nine members including the concurring votes of the permanent members; provided that, in decisions under Chapter VI, and under paragraph 3 of Article 52, a party to a dispute shall abstain from voting.

Article 28

1. The Security Council shall be so organized as to be able to function continuously. Each member of the Security Council shall for this purpose be represented at all times at the seat of the Organization.

2. The Security Council shall hold periodic meetings at which each of its members may, if it so desires, be represented by a member of the government or by some other specially designated representative.

3. The Security Council may hold meetings at such places other than the seat of the Organization as in its judgment will best facilitate its work.

Article 29

The Security Council may establish such subsidiary organs as it deems necessary for the performance of its functions.

Article 30

The Security Council shall adopt its own rules of procedure, including the method of selecting its President.

Article 31

Any Member of the United Nations which is not a member of the Security Council may participate, without vote, in the discussion of any question brought before the Security Council whenever the latter considers that the interests of that Member are specially affected.

Article 32

Any Member of the United Nations which is not a member of the Security Council or any state which is not a Member of the United Nations, if it is a party to a dispute under consideration by the Security Council, shall be invited to participate, without vote, in the discussion relating to the dispute. The Security Council shall lay down such conditions as it deems just for the participation of a state which is not a Member of the United Nations.

CHAPTER VI. PACIFIC SETTLEMENT OF DISPUTES

Article 33

1. The parties to any dispute, the continuance of which is likely to endanger the maintenance of international peace and security, shall, first of all, seek a solution by

negotiation, enquiry, mediation, conciliation, arbitration, judicial settlement, resort to regional agencies or arrangements, or other peaceful means of their own choice.

2. The Security Council shall, when it deems necessary, call upon the parties to settle their dispute by such means.

Article 34

The Security Council may investigate any dispute, or any situation which might lead to international friction or give rise to a dispute, in order to determine whether the continuance of the dispute or situation is likely to endanger the maintenance of international peace and security.

Article 35

1. Any Member of the United Nations may bring any dispute, or any situation of the nature referred to in Article 34, to the attention of the Security Council or of the General Assembly.

2. A state which is not a Member of the United Nations may bring to the attention of the Security Council or of the General Assembly any dispute to which it is a party if it accepts in advance, for the purposes of the dispute, the obligations of pacific settlement provided in the present Charter.

3. The proceedings of the General Assembly in respect of matters brought to its attention under this Article will be subject to the provisions of Articles 11 and 12.

Article 36

1. The Security Council may, at any stage of a dispute of the nature referred to in Article 33 or of a situation of like nature, recommend appropriate procedures or methods of adjustment.

2. The Security Council should take into consideration any procedures for the settlement of the dispute which have already been adopted by the parties.

3. In making recommendations under this Article the Security Council should also take into consideration that legal disputes should as a general rule be referred by the parties to the International Court of Justice in accordance with the provisions of the Statute of the Court.

Article 37

1. Should the parties to a dispute of the nature referred to in Article 33 fail to settle it by the means indicated in that Article, they shall refer it to the Security Council.

2. If the Security Council deems that the continuance of the dispute is in fact likely to endanger the maintenance of international peace and security, it shall decide whether to take action under Article 36 or to recommend such terms of settlement as it may consider appropriate.

Article 38

Without prejudice to the provisions of Articles 33 to 37, the Security Council may, if all the parties to any dispute so request, make recommendations to the parties with a view to a pacific settlement of the dispute.

CHAPTER VII. ACTION WITH RESPECT TO THREATS TO THE PEACE, BREACHES OF THE PEACE, AND ACTS OF AGGRESSION

Article 39

The Security Council shall determine the existence of any threat to the peace, breach of the peace, or act of aggression and shall make recommendations, or decide what measures shall be taken in accordance with Articles 41 and 42, to maintain or restore international peace and security.

Article 40

In order to prevent an aggravation of the situation, the Security Council may, before making the recommendations or deciding upon the measures provided for in Article 39, call upon the parties concerned to comply with such provisional measures as it deems necessary or desirable. Such provisional measures shall be without prejudice to the rights, claims, or position of the parties concerned. The Security Council shall duly take account of failure to comply with such provisional measures.

Article 41

The Security Council may decide what measures not involving the use of armed force are to be employed to give effect to its decisions, and it may call upon the Members of the United Nations to apply such measures. These may include complete or partial interruption of economic relations and of rail, sea, air, postal, telegraphic, radio, and other means of communication, and the severance of diplomatic relations.

Article 42

Should the Security Council consider that measures provided for in Article 41 would be inadequate or have proved to be inadequate, it may take such action by air, sea, or land forces as may be necessary to maintain or restore international peace and security. Such action may include demonstrations, blockade, and other operations by air, sea, or land forces of Members of the United Nations.

Article 43

1. All Members of the United Nations, in order to contribute to the maintenance of international peace and security, undertake to make available to the Security Council, on its call and in accordance with a special agreement or agreements, armed forces, assistance, and facilities, including rights of passage, necessary for the purpose of maintaining international peace and security.

2. Such agreement or agreements shall govern the numbers and types of forces, their degree of readiness and general location, and the nature of the facilities and assistance to be provided.

3. The agreement or agreements shall be negotiated as soon as possible on the initiative of the Security Council. They shall be concluded between the Security Council and Members or between the Security Council and groups of Members and shall be subject to ratification by the signatory states in accordance with their respective constitutional processes.

Article 44

When the Security Council has decided to use force it shall, before calling upon a Member not represented on it to provide armed forces in fulfilment of the obligation assumed under Article 43, invite that Member, if the Member so desires, to participate in the decisions of the Security Council concerning the employment of contingents of that Member's armed forces.

Article 45

In order to enable the United Nations to take urgent military measures, Members shall hold immediately available national air-force contingents for combined international enforcement action. The strength and degree of readiness of these contingents and plans for their combined action shall be determined, within the limits laid down in the special agreement or agreements referred to in Article 43, by the Security Council with the assistance of the Military Staff Committee.

Article 46

Plans for the application of armed force shall be made by the Security Council with the assistance of the Military Staff Committee.

Article 47

1. There shall be established a Military Staff Committee to advise and assist the Security Council on all questions relating to the Security Council's military requirements for the maintenance of international peace and security, the employment and command of forces placed at its disposal, the regulation of armaments, and possible disarmament.

2. The Military Staff Committee shall consist of the Chiefs of Staff of the permanent members of the Security Council or their representatives. Any Member of the United Nations not permanently represented on the Committee shall be invited by the Committee to be associated with it when the efficient discharge of the Committee's responsibilities requires the participation of that Member in its work.

3. The Military Staff Committee shall be responsible under the Security Council for the strategic direction of any armed forces placed at the disposal of the Security Council. Questions relating to the command of such forces shall be worked out subsequently.

4. The Military Staff Committee, with the authorization of the Security Council and after consultation with appropriate regional agencies, may establish regional sub-committees.

Article 48

1. The action required to carry out the decisions of the Security Council for the maintenance of international peace and security shall be taken by all the Members of the United Nations or by some of them, as the Security Council may determine.

2. Such decisions shall be carried out by the Members of the United Nations directly and through their action in the appropriate international agencies of which they are members.

Article 49

The Members of the United Nations shall join in affording mutual assistance in carrying out the measures decided upon by the Security Council.

Article 50

If preventive or enforcement measures against any state are taken by the Security

234

Council, any other state, whether a Member of the United Nations or not, which finds itself confronted with special economic problems arising from the carrying out of those measures shall have the right to consult the Security Council with regard to a solution of those problems.

Article 51

Nothing in the present Charter shall impair the inherent right of individual or collective self-defence if an armed attack occurs against a Member of the United Nations, until the Security Council has taken measures necessary to maintain international peace and security. Measures taken by Members in the exercise of this right of self-defence shall be immediately reported to the Security Council and shall not in any way affect the authority and responsibility of the Security Council under the present Charter to take at any time such action as it deems necessary in order to maintain or restore international peace and security.

CHAPTER VIII. REGIONAL ARRANGEMENTS

Article 52

1. Nothing in the present Charter precludes the existence of regional arrangements or agencies for dealing with such matters relating to the maintenance of international peace and security as are appropriate for regional action, provided that such arrangements or agencies and their activities are consistent with the Purposes and Principles of the United Nations.

2. The Members of the United Nations entering into such arrangements or constituting such agencies shall make every effort to achieve pacific settlement of local disputes through such regional arrangements or by such regional agencies before referring them to the Security Council.

3. The Security Council shall encourage the development of pacific settlement of local disputes through such regional arrangements or by such regional agencies either on the initiative of the states concerned or by reference from the Security Council.

4. This Article in no way impairs the application of Articles 34 and 35.

Article 53

1. The Security Council shall, where appropriate, utilize such regional arrangements or agencies for enforcement action under its authority. But no enforcement action shall be taken under regional arrangements or by regional agencies without the authorization of the Security Council, with the exception of measures against any enemy state, as defined in paragraph 2 of this Article, provided for pursuant to Article 107 or in regional arrangements directed against renewal of aggressive policy on the part of any such state, until such time as the Organization may, on request of the Governments concerned, be charged with the responsibility for preventing further aggression by such a state.

2. The term enemy state as used in paragraph 1 of this Article applies to any state which during the Second World War has been an enemy of any signatory of the present Charter.

Article 54

The Security Council shall at all times be kept fully informed of activities undertaken or in contemplation under regional arrangements or by regional agencies for the maintenance of international peace and security.

CHAPTER IX. INTERNATIONAL ECONOMIC AND SOCIAL CO-OPERATION

Article 55

With a view to the creation of conditions of stability and well-being which are necessary for peaceful and friendly relations among nations based on respect for the principle of equal rights and self-determination of peoples, the United Nations shall promote:

a. higher standards of living, full employment, and conditions of economic and social progress and development;

b. solutions of international economic, social, health, and related problems; and international cultural and educational co-operation; and

c. universal respect for, and observance of, human rights and fundamental freedoms for all without distinction as to race, sex, language, or religion.

Article 56

All Members pledge themselves to take joint and separate action in co-operation with the Organization for the achievement of the purposes set forth in Article 55.

Article 57

1. The various specialized agencies, established by intergovernmental agreement and having wide international responsibilities, as defined in their basic instruments, in economic, social, cultural, educational, health, and related fields, shall be brought into relationship with the United Nations in accordance with the provisions of Article 63.

2. Such agencies thus brought into relationship with the United Nations are hereinafter referred to as specialized agencies.

Article 58

The Organization shall make recommendations for the co-ordination of the policies and activities of the specialized agencies.

Article 59

The Organization shall, where appropriate, initiate negotiations among the states concerned for the creation of any new specialized agencies required for the accomplishment of the purposes set forth in Article 55.

Article 60

Responsibility for the discharge of the functions of the Organization set forth in this Chapter shall be vested in the General Assembly and, under the authority of the General Assembly, in the Economic and Social Council, which shall have for this purpose the powers set forth in Chapter X.

CHAPTER X. THE ECONOMIC AND SOCIAL COUNCIL

Composition
Article 61

1. The Economic and Social Council shall consist of fifty-four Members of the United Nations elected by the General Assembly.

2. Subject to the provisions of paragraph 3, eighteen members of the Economic and Social Council shall be elected each year for a term of three years. A retiring member shall be eligible for immediate re-election.

3. At the first election after the increase in the membership of the Economic and Social Council from twenty-seven to fifty-four members, in addition to the members elected in place of the nine members whose term of office expires at the end of that year, twenty-seven additional members shall be elected. Of these twenty-seven additional members, the term of office of nine members so elected shall expire at the end of one year, and of nine other members at the end of two years, in accordance with arrangements made by the General Assembly.

4. Each member of the Economic and Social Council shall have one representative.

Functions and powers
Article 62

1. The Economic and Social Council may make or initiate studies and reports with respect to international economic, social, cultural, educational, health, and related matters and may make recommendations with respect to any such matters to the General Assembly, to the Members of the United Nations, and to the specialized agencies concerned.

2. It may make recommendations for the purpose of promoting respect for, and observance of, human rights and fundamental freedoms for all.

3. It may prepare draft conventions for submission to the General Assembly, with respect to matters falling within its competence.

4. It may call, in accordance with the rules prescribed by the United Nations, international conferences on matters falling within its competence.

Article 63

1. The Economic and Social Council may enter into agreements with any of the agencies referred to in Article 57, defining the terms on which the agency concerned shall be brought into relationship with the United Nations. Such agreements shall be subject to approval by the General Assembly.

2. It may co-ordinate the activities of the specialized agencies through consultation with and recommendations to such agencies and through recommendations to the General Assembly and to the Members of the United Nations.

Article 64

1. The Economic and Social Council may take appropriate steps to obtain regular reports from the specialized agencies. It may make arrangements with the Members of the United Nations and with the specialized agencies to obtain reports on the steps taken to give effect to its own recommendations and to recommendations on matters falling within its competence made by the General Assembly.

2. It may communicate its observations on these reports to the General Assembly.

Article 65

The Economic and Social Council may furnish information to the Security Council and shall assist the Security Council upon its request.

Article 66

1. The Economic and Social Council shall perform such functions as fall within its

237

competence in connexion with the carrying out of the recommendations of the General Assembly.

2. It may, with the approval of the General Assembly, perform services at the request of Members of the United Nations and at the request of specialized agencies.

3. It shall perform such other functions as are specified elsewhere in the present Charter or as may be assigned to it by the General Assembly.

VOTING
Article 67
1. Each member of the Economic and Social Council shall have one vote.

2. Decisions of the Economic and Social Council shall be made by a majority of the members present and voting.

PROCEDURE
Article 68
The Economic and Social Council shall set up commissions in economic and social fields and for the promotion of human rights, and such other commissions as may be required for the performance of its functions.

Article 69
The Economic and Social Council shall invite any Member of the United Nations to participate, without vote, in its deliberations on any matter of particular concern to that Member.

Article 70
The Economic and Social Council may make arrangements for representatives of the specialized agencies to participate, without vote, in its deliberations and in those of the commissions established by it, and for its representatives to participate in the deliberations of the specialized agencies.

Article 71
The Economic and Social Council may make suitable arrangements for consultation with non-governmental organizations which are concerned with matters within its competence. Such arrangements may be made with international organizations and, where appropriate, with national organizations after consultation with the Member of the United Nations concerned.

Article 72
1. The Economic and Social Council shall adopt its own rules of procedure, including the method of selecting its President.

2. The Economic and Social Council shall meet as required in accordance with its rules, which shall include provision for the convening of meetings on the request of a majority of its members.

238

CHAPTER XI. DECLARATION REGARDING
NON-SELF-GOVERNING TERRITORIES

Article 73

Members of the United Nations which have or assume responsibilities for the administration of territories whose peoples have not yet attained a full measure of self-government recognize the principle that the interests of the inhabitants of these territories are paramount, and accept as a sacred trust the obligation to promote to the utmost, within the system of international peace and security established by the present Charter, the well-being of the inhabitants of these territories, and, to this end:

a. to ensure, with due respect for the culture of the peoples concerned, their political, economic, social, and educational advancement, their just treatment, and their protection against abuses;

b. to develop self-government, to take due account of the political aspirations of the peoples, and to assist them in the progressive development of their free political institutions, according to the particular cirumstances of each territory and its peoples and their varying stages of advancement;

c. to further international peace and security;

d. to promote constructive measures of development, to encourage research, and to cooperate with one another and, when and where appropriate, with specialized international bodies with a view to the practical achievement of the social, economic, and scientific purposes set forth in this Article; and

e. to transmit regularly to the Secretary-General for information purposes, subject to such limitation as security and constitutional considerations may require, statistical and other information of a technical nature relating to economic, social, and educational conditions in the territories for which they are respectively responsible other than those territories to which Chapters XII and XIII apply.

Article 74

Members of the United Nations also agree that their policy in respect of the territories to which this Chapter applies, no less than in respect of their metropolitan areas, must be based on the general principle of good-neighbourliness, due account being taken of the interests and well-being of the rest of the world, in social, economic, and commercial matters.

CHAPTER XII. INTERNATIONAL TRUSTEESHIP SYSTEM

Article 75

The United Nations shall establish under its authority an international trusteeship system for the administration and supervision of such territories as may be placed thereunder by subsequent individual governments. These territories are hereinafter referred to as trust territories.

Article 76

The basic objectives of the trusteeship system, in accordance with the Purposes of the United Nations laid down in Article 1 of the present Charter, shall be:

a. to further international peace and security;

b. to promote the political, economic, social, and educational advancement of the inhabitants of the trust territories, and their progressive development towards self-government or independence as may be appropriate to the particular circumstances of each territory and its peoples and the freely expressed wishes of the peoples concerned, and as may be provided by the terms of each trusteeship agreement;

c. to encourage respect for human rights and for fundamental freedoms for all without distinction as to race, sex, language, or religion, and to encourage recognition of the interdependence of the peoples of the world; and

d. to ensure equal treatment in social, economic, and commercial matters for all Members of the United Nations and their nationals, and also equal treatment for the latter in the administration of justice, without prejudice to the attainment of the foregoing objectives and subject to the provisions of Article 80.

Article 77

1. The trusteeship system shall apply to such territories in the following categories as may be placed thereunder by means of trusteeship agreements:

a. territories now held under mandate;

b. territories which may be detached from enemy states as a result of the Second World War; and

c. territories voluntarily placed under the system by states responsible for their administration.

2. It will be a matter for subsequent agreement as to which territories in the foregoing categories will be brought under the trusteeship system and upon what terms.

Article 78

The trusteeship system shall not apply to territories which have become Members of the United Nations, relationship among which shall be based on respect for the principle of sovereign equality.

Article 79

The terms of trusteeship for each territory to be placed under the trusteeship system, including any alteration or amendment, shall be agreed upon by the states directly concerned, including the mandatory power in the case of territories held under mandate by a Member of the United Nations, and shall be approved as provided for in Articles 83 and 85.

Article 80

1. Except as may be agreed upon in individual trusteeship agreements, made under Articles 77, 79, and 81, placing each territory under the trusteeship system, and until such agreements have been concluded, nothing in this Chapter shall be construed in or of itself to alter in any manner the rights whatsoever of any states or any peoples or the terms of existing international instruments to which Members of the United Nations may respectively be parties.

2. Paragraph 1 of this Article shall not be interpreted as giving grounds for delay or postponement of the negotiation and conclusion of agreements for placing mandated and other territories under the trusteeship system as provided for in Article 77.

Article 81

The trusteeship agreement shall in each case include the terms under which the trust territory will be administered and designate the authority which will exercise the administration of the trust territory. Such authority, hereinafter called the administering authority, may be one or more states or the Organization itself.

Article 82

There may be designated, in any trusteeship agreement, a strategic area or areas which may include part or all of the trust territory to which the agreement applies, without prejudice to any special agreement or agreements made under Article 43.

Article 83

1. All functions of the United Nations relating to strategic areas, including the approval of the terms of the trusteeship agreements and of their alteration or amendment, shall be exercised by the Security Council.

2. The basic objectives set forth in Article 76 shall be applicable to the people of each strategic area.

3. The Security Council shall, subject to the provisions of the trusteeship agreements and without prejudice to security considerations, avail itself of the assistance of the Trusteeship Council to perform those functions of the United Nations under the trusteeship system relating to political, economic, social, and educational matters in the strategic areas.

Article 84

It shall be the duty of the administering authority to ensure that the trust territory shall play its part in the maintenance of international peace and security. To this end the administering authority may make use of volunteer forces, facilities, and assistance from the trust territory in carrying out the obligations towards the Security Council undertaken in this regard by the administering authority, as well as for local defence and the maintenance of law and order within the trust territory.

Article 85

1. The functions of the United Nations with regard to trusteeship agreements for all areas not designated as strategic, including the approval of the terms of the trusteeship agreements and of their alteration or amendment, shall be exercised by the General Assembly.

2. The Trusteeship Council, operating under the authority of the General Assembly, shall assist the General Assembly in carrying out these functions.

CHAPTER XIII. THE TRUSTEESHIP COUNCIL

Composition
Article 86

1. The Trusteeship Council shall consist of the following Members of the United Nations:

a. those Members administering trust territories;

b. such of those Members mentioned by name in Article 23 as are not administering trust territories; and

c. as many other Members elected for three-year terms by the General Assembly as may be necessary to ensure that the total number of members of the Trusteeship Council is equally divided between those Members of the United Nations which administer trust territories and those which do not.

2. Each member of the Trusteeship Council shall designate one specially qualified person to represent it therein.

Article 87

The General Assembly and, under its authority, the Trusteeship Council, in carrying out their functions, may:

a. consider reports submitted by the administering authority;

b. accept petitions and examine them in consultation with the administering authority;

c. provide for periodic visits to the respective trust territories at times agreed upon with the administering authority; and

d. take these and other actions in conformity with the terms of the trusteeship agreements.

Article 88

The Trusteeship Council shall formulate a questionnaire on the political, economic, social, and educational advancement of the inhabitants of each trust territory, and the administering authority for each trust territory within the competence of the General Assembly shall make an annual report to the General Assembly upon the basis of such questionnaire.

Article 89

1. Each member of the Trusteeship Council shall have one vote.

2. Decisions of the Trusteeship Council shall be made by a majority of the members present and voting.

Article 90

1. The Trusteeship Council shall adopt its own rules of procedure, including the method of selecting its President.

2. The Trusteeship Council shall meet as required in accordance with its rules, which shall include provision for the convening of meetings on the request of a majority of its members.

Article 91

The Trusteeship Council shall, when appropriate, avail itself of the assistance of the Economic and Social Council and of the specialized agencies in regard to matters with which they are respectively concerned.

CHAPTER XIV. THE INTERNATIONAL COURT OF JUSTICE

Article 92

The International Court of Justice shall be the principal judicial organ of the United Nations. It shall function in accordance with the annexed Statute, which is based upon the Statute of the Permanent Court of International Justice and forms an integral part of the present Charter.

242

Article 93

1. All Members of the United Nations are *ipso facto* parties to the Statute of the International Court of Justice.

2. A state which is not a Member of the United Nations may become a party to the Statute of the International Court of Justice on conditions to be determined in each case by the General Assembly upon the recommendation of the Security Council.

Article 94

1. Each Member of the United Nations undertakes to comply with the decision of the International Court of Justice in any case to which it is a party.

2. If any party to a case fails to perform the obligations incumbent upon it under a judgment rendered by the Court, the other party may have recourse to the Security Council, which may, if it deems necessary, make recommendations or decide upon measures to be taken to give effect to the judgment.

Article 95

Nothing in the present Charter shall prevent Members of the United Nations from entrusting the solution of their differences to other tribunals by virtue of agreements already in existence or which may be concluded in the future.

Article 96

1. The General Assembly or the Security Council may request the International Court of Justice to give an advisory opinion on any legal question.

2. Other organs of the United Nations and specialized agencies, which may at any time be so authorized by the General Assembly, may also request advisory opinions of the Court on legal questions arising within the scope of their activities.

CHAPTER XV. THE SECRETARIAT

Article 97

The Secretariat shall comprise a Secretary-General and such staff as the Organization may require. The Secretary-General shall be appointed by the General Assembly upon the recommendation of the Security Council. He shall be the chief administrative officer of the Organization.

Article 98

The Secretary-General shall act in that capacity in all meetings of the General Assembly, of the Security Council, of the Economic and Social Council, and of the Trusteeship Council, and shall perform such other functions as are entrusted to him by these organs. The Secretary-General shall make an annual report to the General Assembly on the work of the Organization.

Article 99

The Secretary-General may bring to the attention of the Security Council any matter which in his opinion may threaten the maintenance of international peace and security.

Article 100

1. In the performance of their duties the Secretary-General and the staff shall not seek or receive instructions from any government or from any other authority external to the Organization. They shall refrain from any action which might reflect on their position as international officials responsible only to the Organization.

2. Each Member of the United Nations undertakes to respect the exclusively international character of the responsibilities of the Secretary-General and the staff and not to seek to influence them in the discharge of their responsibilities.

Article 101

1. The staff shall be appointed by the Secretary-General under regulations established by the General Assembly.

2. Appropriate staffs shall be permanently assigned to the Economic and Social Council, the Trusteeship Council, and, as required, to other organs of the United Nations. These staffs shall form a part of the Secretariat.

3. The paramount consideration in the employment of the staff and in the determination of the conditions of service shall be the necessity of securing the highest standards of efficiency, competence, and integrity. Due regard shall be paid to the importance of recruiting the staff on as wide a geographical basis as possible.

CHAPTER XVI. MISCELLANEOUS PROVISIONS

Article 102

1. Every treaty and every international agreement entered into by any Member of the United Nations after the present Charter comes into force shall as soon as possible be registered with the Secretariat and published by it.

2. No party to any such treaty or international agreement which has not been registered in accordance with the provisions of paragraph 1 of this Article may invoke that treaty or agreement before any organ of the United Nations.

Article 103

In the event of a conflict between the obligations of the Members of the United Nations under the present Charter and their obligations under any other international agreement, their obligations under the present Charter shall prevail.

Article 104

The Organization shall enjoy in the territory of each of its Members such legal capacity as may be necessary for the exercise of its functions and the fulfilment of its purposes.

Article 105

1. The Organization shall enjoy in the territory of each of its Members such privileges and immunities as are necessary for the fulfilment of its purposes.

2. Representatives of the Members of the United Nations and officials of the Organization shall similarly enjoy such privileges and immunities as are necessary for the independent exercise of their functions in connexion with the Organization.

3. The General Assembly may make recommendations with a view to determining the details of the application of paragraphs 1 and 2 of this Article or may propose conventions to the Members of the United Nations for this purpose.

CHAPTER XVII. TRANSITIONAL SECURITY ARRANGEMENTS

Article 106

Pending the coming into force of such special agreements referred to in Article 43 as in the opinion of the Security Council enable it to begin the exercise of its responsibilities under Article 42, the parties to the Four-Nation Declaration, signed at Moscow, 30 October 1943, and France, shall, in accordance with the provisions of paragraph 5 of that Declaration, consult with one another and as occasion requires with other Members of the United Nations with a view to such joint action on behalf of the Organization as may be necessary for the purpose of maintaining international peace and security.

Article 107

Nothing in the present Charter shall invalidate or preclude action, in relation to any state which during the Second World War has been an enemy of any signatory to the present Charter, taken or authorized as a result of that war by the Governments having responsibility for such action.

CHAPTER XVIII. AMENDMENTS

Article 108

Amendments to the present Charter shall come into force for all Members of the United Nations when they have been adopted by a vote of two thirds of the members of the General Assembly and ratified in accordance with their respective constitutional processes by two thirds of the Members of the United Nations, including all the permanent members of the Security Council.

Article 109

1. A General Conference of the Members of the United Nations for the purpose of reviewing the present Charter may be held at a date and place to be fixed by a two-thirds vote of the members of the General Assembly and by a vote of any nine members of the Security Council. Each Member of the United Nations shall have one vote in the conference.

2. Any alteration of the present Charter recommended by a two-thirds vote of the conference shall take effect when ratified in accordance with their respective constitutional processes by two thirds of the Members of the United Nations including all the permanent members of the Security Council.

3. If such a conference has not been held before the tenth annual session of the General Assembly following the coming into force of the present Charter, the proposal to call such a conference shall be placed on the agenda of that session of the General Assembly, and the conference shall be held if so decided by a majority vote of the members of the General Assembly and by a vote of any seven members of the Security Council.

CHAPTER XIX. RATIFICATION AND SIGNATURE

Article 110

1. The present Charter shall be ratified by the signatory states in accordance with their respective constitutional processes.

2. The ratifications shall be deposited with the Government of the United States of America, which shall notify all the signatory states of each deposit as well as the Secretary-General of the Organization when he has been appointed.

3. The present Charter shall come into force upon the deposit of ratifications by the Republic of China, France, the Union of Soviet Socialist Republics, the United Kingdom of Great Britain and Northern Ireland, and the United States of America, and by a majority of the other signatory states. A protocol of the ratifications deposited shall thereupon be drawn up by the Government of the United States of America which shall communicate copies thereof to all the signatory states.

4. The states signatory to the present Charter which ratify it after it has come into force will become original Members of the United Nations on the date of the deposit of their respective ratifications.

Article 111

The present Charter, of which the Chinese, French, Russian, English, and Spanish texts are equally authentic, shall remain deposited in the archives of the Government of the United States of America. Duly certified copies thereof shall be transmitted by that Government to the Governments of the other signatory states.

IN FAITH WHEREOF the representatives of the Governments of the United Nations have signed the present Charter.

DONE at the city of San Francisco the twenty-sixth day of June, one thousand nine hundred and forty-five.

Annex II

Rules of Procedure of the General Assembly

(embodying amendments and additions adopted by the General Assembly up to 31 December 1978)

I. SESSIONS

Opening date

Rule 1

The General Assembly shall meet every year in regular session commencing on the third Tuesday in September.

Closing date

Rule 2

On the recommendation of the General Committee, the General Assembly shall, at the beginning of each session, fix a closing date for the session.

Place of meeting

Rule 3

The General Assembly shall meet at the Headquarters of the United Nations unless convened elsewhere in pursuance of a decision taken at a previous session or at the request of a majority of the Members of the United Nations.

Rule 4

Any Member of the United Nations may, at least one hundred and twenty days before the date fixed for the opening of a regular session, request that the session be held elsewhere than at the Headquarters of the United Nations. The Secretary-General shall immediately communicate the request, together with his recommendations, to the other Members of the United Nations. If within thirty days of the date of this communication a majority of the Members concur in the request, the session shall be held accordingly.

Notification of session

Rule 5

The Secretary-General shall notify the Members of the United Nations, at least sixty days in advance, of the opening of a regular session.

Temporary adjournment of session

Rule 6

The General Assembly may decide at any session to adjourn temporarily and resume its meetings at a later date.

Summoning by the General Assembly

Rule 7

The General Assembly may fix a date for a special session.

Summoning at the request of the Security Council or Members

Rule 8

(*a*) Special sessions of the General Assembly shall be convened within fifteen days of the receipt by the Secretary-General of a request for such a session from the Security Council or from a majority of the Members of the United Nations or of the concurrence of a majority of Members as provided in rule 9.

(*b*) Emergency special sessions pursuant to General Assembly resolution 377 A (V) shall be convened within twenty-four hours of the receipt by the Secretary-General of a request for such a session from the Security Council, on the vote of any nine members thereof, or of a request from a majority of the Members of the United Nations expressed by vote in the Interim Committee or otherwise, or of the concurrence of a majority of Members as provided in rule 9.

Request by Members

Rule 9

(*a*) Any Member of the United Nations may request the Secretary-General to convene a special session of the General Assembly. The Secretary-General shall immediately inform the other Members of the request and inquire whether they concur in it. If within thirty days of the date of the communication of the Secretary-General a majority of the Members concur in the request, a special session of the General Assembly shall be convened in accordance with rule 8.

(*b*) This rule shall apply also to a request by any Member of the United Nations for an emergency special session pursuant to resolution 377 A (V). In such a case, the Secretary-General shall communicate with the other Members by the most expeditious means of communication available.

Notification of session

Rule 10

The Secretary-General shall notify the Members of the United Nations, at least fourteen days in advance, of the opening of a special session convened at the request of the Security Council, and at least ten days in advance in the case of a session convened at the request of a majority of the Members or upon the concurrence of a majority in the request of any Member. In the case of an emergency special session convened pursuant to rule 8 (*b*), the Secretary-General shall notify Members at least twelve hours before the opening of the session.

Notification to other bodies

Rule 11

Copies of the notice convening each session of the General Assembly shall be addressed to all other principal organs of the United Nations and to the specialized agencies referred to in Article 57, paragraph 2, of the Charter.

II. AGENDA

REGULAR SESSIONS

Provisional agenda

Rule 12

The provisional agenda for a regular session shall be drawn up by the Secretary-General and communicated to the Members of the United Nations at least sixty days before the opening of the session.

Rule 13

The provisional agenda of a regular session shall include:

(*a*) The report of the Secretary-General on the work of the Organization;

(*b*) Reports from the Security Council, the Economic and Social Council, the Trusteeship Council, the International Court of Justice, the subsidiary organs of the General Assembly and the specialized agencies (where such reports are called for under agreements entered into);

(*c*) All items the inclusion of which has been ordered by the General Assembly at a previous session;

(*d*) All items proposed by the other principal organs of the United Nations;

(*e*) All items proposed by any Member of the United Nations;

(*f*) All items pertaining to the budget for the next financial year and the report on the accounts for the last financial year;

(*g*) All items which the Secretary-General deems it necessary to put before the General Assembly;

(*h*) All items proposed under Article 35, paragraph 2, of the Charter by States not Members of the United Nations.

Supplementary items

Rule 14

Any Member or principal organ of the United Nations or the Secretary-General may, at least thirty days before the date fixed for the opening of a regular session, request the inclusion of supplementary items in the agenda. Such items shall be placed on a supplementary list, which shall be communicated to Members at least twenty days before the opening of the session.

Additional items

Rule 15

Additional items of an important and urgent character, proposed for inclusion in the agenda less than thirty days before the opening of a regular session or during a regular session, may be placed on the agenda if the General Assembly so decides by a majority of the members present and voting. No additional item may, unless the General Assembly decides otherwise by a two-thirds majority of the members present and voting, be considered until seven days have elapsed since it was placed on the agenda and until a committee has reported upon the question concerned.

SPECIAL SESSIONS

Provisional agenda

Rule 16

The provisional agenda of a special session convened at the request of the Security

249

Council shall be communicated to the Members of the United Nations at least fourteen days before the opening of the session. The provisional agenda of a special session convened at the request of a majority of the Members, or upon the concurrence of a majority in the request of any Member, shall be communicated at least ten days before the opening of the session. The provisional agenda of an emergency special session shall be communicated to Members simultaneously with the communication convening the session.

Rule 17

The provisional agenda for a special session shall consist only of those items proposed for consideration in the request for the holding of the session.

Supplementary items

Rule 18

Any Member or principal organ of the United Nations or the Secretary-General may, at least four days before the date fixed for the opening of a special session, request the inclusion of supplementary items in the agenda. Such items shall be placed on a supplementary list, which shall be communicated to Members as soon as possible.

Additonal items

Rule 19

During a special session, items on the supplementary list and additional items may be added to the agenda by a two-thirds majority of the members present and voting. During an emergency special session, additional items concerning the matters dealt with in resolution 377 A (V) may be added to the agenda by a two-thirds majority of the members present and voting.

REGULAR AND SPECIAL SESSIONS

Explanatory memorandum

Rule 20

Any item proposed for inclusion in the agenda shall be accompanied by an explanatory memorandum and, if possible, by basic documents or by a draft resolution.

Adoption of the agenda

Rule 21

At each session the provisional agenda and the supplementary list, together with the report of the General Committee thereon, shall be submitted to the General Assembly for approval as soon as possible after the opening of the session.

Amendment and deletion of items

Rule 22

Items on the agenda may be amended or deleted by the General Assembly by a majority of the members present and voting.

Debate on inclusion of items

Rule 23

Debate on the inclusion of an item in the agenda, when that item has been recommended for inclusion by the General Committee, shall be limited to three speakers in favour of, and three against, the inclusion. The President may limit the time to be allowed to speakers under this rule.

Modification of the allocation of expenses
Rule 24
No proposal for a modification of the allocation of expenses for the time being in force shall be placed on the agenda unless it has been communicated to the Members of the United Nations at least ninety days before the opening of the session.

III. DELEGATIONS

Composition
Rule 25
The delegation of a Member shall consist of not more than five representatives and five alternate representatives and as many advisers, technical advisers, experts and persons of similar status as may be required by the delegation.

Alternates
Rule 26
An alternate representative may act as a representative upon designation by the chairman of the delegation.

IV. CREDENTIALS

Submission of credentials
Rule 27
The credentials of representatives and the names of members of a delegation shall be submitted to the Secretary-General if possible not less than one week before the opening of the session. The credentials shall be issued either by the Head of the State or Government or by the Minister of Foreign Affairs.

Credentials Committee
Rule 28
A Credentials Committee shall be appointed at the beginning of each session. It shall consist of nine members, who shall be appointed by the General Assembly on the proposal of the President. The Committee shall elect its own officers. It shall examine the credentials of representatives and report without delay.

Provisional admission to a session
Rule 29
Any representative to whose admission a Member has made objection shall be seated provisionally with the same rights as other representatives until the Credentials Committee has reported and the General Assembly has given its decision.

V. PRESIDENT AND VICE-PRESIDENTS

Temporary President

Rule 30

At the opening of each session of the General Assembly, the chairman of that delegation from which the President of the previous session was elected shall preside until the Assembly has elected a President for the session.

Elections

Rule 31

The General Assembly shall elect a President and twenty-one Vice-Presidents, who shall hold office until the close of the session at which they are elected. The Vice-Presidents shall be elected, after the election of the Chairmen of the seven Main Committees referred to in rule 98, in such a way as to ensure the representative character of the General Committee.

Acting President

Rule 32 [105]

If the President finds it necessary to be absent during a meeting or any part thereof, he shall designate one of the Vice-Presidents to take his place.

Rule 33 [105]

A Vice-President acting as President shall have the same powers and duties as the President.

Replacement of the President

Rule 34 [105]

If the President is unable to perform his functions, a new President shall be elected for the unexpired term.

General powers of the President

Rule 35 [106]

In addition to exercising the powers conferred upon him elsewhere by these rules, the President shall declare the opening and closing of each plenary meeting of the session, direct the discussions in plenary meeting, ensure observance of these rules, accord the right to speak, put questions and announce decisions. He shall rule on points of order and, subject to these rules, shall have complete control of the proceedings at any meeting and over the maintenance of order thereat. The President may, in the course of the discussion of an item, propose to the General Assembly the limitation of the time to be allowed to speakers, the limitation of the number of times each representative may speak, the closure of the list of speakers or the closure of the debate. He may also propose the suspension or the adjournment of the meeting or the adjournment of the debate on the item under discussion.

Rule 36 [107]

The President, in the exercise of his functions, remains under the authority of the General Assembly.

Rule 37 [104]
The President, or a Vice-President acting as President, shall not vote but shall designate another member of his delegation to vote in his place.

VI. GENERAL COMMITTEE

Composition
Rule 38
The General Committee shall comprise the President of the General Assembly, who shall preside, the twenty-one Vice-Presidents and the Chairmen of the seven Main Committees. No two members of the General Committee shall be members of the same delegation, and it shall be so constituted as to ensure its representative character. Chairmen of other committees upon which all Members have the right to be represented and which are established by the General Assembly to meet during the session shall be entitled to attend meetings of the General Committee and may participate without vote in the discussions.

Substitute members
Rule 39
If a Vice-President of the General Assembly finds it necessary to be absent during a meeting of the General Committee, he may designate a member of his delegation to take his place. The Chairman of a Main Committee shall, in case of absence, designate one of the Vice-Chairmen of the Committee to take his place. A Vice-Chairman shall not have the right to vote if he is of the same delegation as another member of the General Committee.

Functions
Rule 40
The General Committee shall, at the beginning of each session, consider the provisional agenda, together with the supplementary list, and shall make recommendations to the General Assembly, with regard to each item proposed, concerning its inclusion in the agenda, the rejection of the request for inclusion or the inclusion of the item in the provisional agenda of a future session. It shall, in the same manner, examine requests for the inclusion of additional items in the agenda and shall make recommendations thereon to the General Assembly. In considering matters relating to the agenda of the General Assembly, the General Committee shall not discuss the substance of any item except in so far as this bears upon the question whether the General Committee should recommend the inclusion of the item in the agenda, the rejection of the request for inclusion or the inclusion of the item in the provisional agenda of a future session, and what priority should be accorded to an item the inclusion of which has been recommended.

Rule 41
The General Committee shall make recommendations to the General Assembly concerning the closing date of the session. It shall assist the President and the General Assembly in drawing up the agenda for each plenary meeting, in determining the priority of its items and in co-ordinating the proceedings of all committees of the Assembly. It

shall assist the President in the general conduct of the work of the General Assembly which falls within the competence of the President. It shall not, however, decide any political question.

Rule 42

The General Committee shall meet periodically throughout each session to review the progress of the General Assembly and its committees and to make recommendations for furthering such progress. It shall also meet at such other times as the President deems necessary or upon the request of any other of its members.

Participation by members requesting the inclusion of items in the agenda
Rule 43

A member of the General Assembly which has no representative on the General Committee and which has requested the inclusion of an item in the agenda shall be entitled to attend any meeting of the General Committee at which its request is discussed and may participate, without vote, in the discussion of that item.

Revision of the form of resolutions
Rule 44

The General Committee may revise the resolutions adopted by the General Assembly, changing their form but not their substance. Any such changes shall be reported to the General Assembly for its consideration.

VII. SECRETARIAT

Duties of the Secretary-General
Rule 45

The Secretary-General shall act in that capacity in all meetings of the General Assembly, its committees and its subcommittees. He may designate a member of the Secretariat to act in his place at these meetings.

Rule 46

The Secretary-General shall provide and direct the staff required by the General Assembly and any committees or subsidiary organs which it may establish.

Duties of the Secretariat
Rule 47

The Secretariat shall receive, translate, print and distribute documents, reports and resolutions of the General Assembly, its committees and its organs; interpret speeches made at the meetings; prepare, print and circulate the records of the session; have the custody and proper preservation of the documents in the archives of the General Assembly; distribute all documents of the Assembly to the Members of the United Nations, and, generally, perform all other work which the Assembly may require.

Report of the Secretary-General on the work of the Organization
Rule 48

The Secretary-General shall make an annual report, and such supplementary reports as are required, to the General Assembly on the work of the Organization. He shall communicate the annual report to the Members of the United Nations at least forty-five days before the opening of the session.

Notification under Article 12 of the Charter
Rule 49
The Secretary-General, with the consent of the Security Council, shall notify the General Assembly at each session of any matters relative to the maintenance of international peace and security which are being dealt with by the Security Council, and shall similarly notify the General Assembly, or the Members of the United Nations if the General Assembly is not in session, immediately the Security Council ceases to deal with such matters.

Regulations concerning the Secretariat
Rule 50
The General Assembly shall establish regulations concerning the staff of the Secretariat.

VIII. LANGUAGES

Official and working languages
Rule 51
Chinese, English, French, Russian and Spanish shall be both the official and the working languages of the General Assembly, its committees and its subcommittees. Arabic shall be both an official and a working language of the General Assembly and its Main Committees.

Interpretation
Rule 52
Speeches made in any of the six languages of the General Assembly shall be interpreted into the other five languages, provided that interpretation from and into Arabic shall be made only in the Assembly and in its Main Committees.

Rule 53
Any representative may make a speech in a language other than the languages of the General Assembly. In this case, he shall himself provide for interpretation into one of the languages of the General Assembly or of the committee concerned. Interpretation into the other languages of the General Assembly or of the committee concerned by the interpreters of the Secretariat may be based on the interpretation given in the first such language.

Languages of verbatim and summary records
Rule 54
Verbatim or summary records shall be drawn up as soon as possible in the languages of the General Assembly, provided that such records shall be drawn up in Arabic only for the plenary meetings of the Assembly and for the meetings of the Main Committees.

Languages of the Journal of the United Nations
Rule 55
During the sessions of the General Assembly, the *Journal of the United Nations* shall be published in the languages of the Assembly.

Languages of resolutions and other documents
Rule 56
All resolutions and other documents shall be published in the languages of the General Assembly, provided that publication in Arabic of such documents shall be limited to those of the Assembly and its Main Committees.

Publications in languages other than the languages of the General Assembly
Rule 57
Documents of the General Assembly, its committees and its subcommittees shall, if the Assembly so decides, be published in any language other than the languages of the Assembly or of the committee concerned.

IX. RECORDS

Records and sound recordings of meetings
Rule 58
(*a*) Verbatim records of the meetings of the General Assembly and of the Political and Security Committee (First Committee) shall be drawn up by the Secretariat and submitted to those organs after approval by the presiding officer. The General Assembly shall decide upon the form of the records of the meetings of the other Main Committees and, if any, of the subsidiary organs and of special meetings and conferences. No organ of the General Assembly shall have both verbatim and summary records.

(*b*) Sound recordings of the meetings of the General Assembly and of the Main Committees shall be made by the Secretariat. Such recordings shall also be made of the proceedings of subsidiary organs and special meetings and conferences when they so decide.

Resolutions
Rule 59
Resolutions adopted by the General Assembly shall be communicated by the Secretary-General to the Members of the United Nations within fifteen days after the close of the session.

X. PUBLIC AND PRIVATE MEETINGS OF THE GENERAL ASSEMBLY, ITS COMMITTEES AND ITS SUBCOMMITTEES

General principles
Rule 60
The meetings of the General Assembly and its Main Committees shall be held in public unless the organ concerned decides that exceptional circumstances require that the meeting be held in private. Meetings of other committees and subcommittees shall also be held in public unless the organ concerned decides otherwise.

Rule 61

All decisions of the General Assembly taken at a private meeting shall be announced at an early public meeting of the Assembly. At the close of each private meeting of the Main Committees, other committees and subcommittees, the Chairman may issue a *communiqué* through the Secretary-General.

XI. MINUTE OF SILENT PRAYER OR MEDITATION

Invitation to silent prayer or meditation

Rule 62

Immediately after the opening of the first plenary meeting and immediately preceding the closing of the final plenary meeting of each session of the General Assembly, the President shall invite the representatives to observe one minute of silence dedicated to prayer or meditation.

XII. PLENARY MEETINGS

CONDUCT OF BUSINESS

Emergency special sessions

Rule 63

Notwithstanding the provisions of any other rule and unless the General Assembly decides otherwise, the Assembly, in case of an emergency special session, shall convene in plenary meeting only and proceed directly to consider the item proposed for consideration in the request for the holding of the session, without previous reference to the General Committee or to any other committee; the President and Vice-Presidents for such emergency special sessions shall be, respectively, the chairmen of those delegations from which were elected the President and Vice-Presidents of the previous session.

Report of the Secretary-General

Rule 64

Proposals to refer any portion of the report of the Secretary-General to one of the Main Committees without debate shall be decided upon by the General Assembly without previous reference to the General Committee.

Reference to committees

Rule 65

The General Assembly shall not, unless it decides otherwise, make a final decision upon any item on the agenda until it has received the report of a committee on that item.

Discussion of reports of Main Committees

Rule 66

Discussion of a report of a Main Committee in a plenary meeting of the General Assembly shall take place if at least one third of the members present and voting at the plenary meeting consider such a discussion to be necessary. Any proposal to this effect shall not be debated but shall be immediately put to the vote.

Quorum

Rule 67 [108]

The President may declare a meeting open and permit the debate to proceed when at least one third of the members of the General Assembly are present. The presence of a majority of the members shall be required for any decision to be taken.

Speeches

Rule 68 [109]

No representative may address the General Assembly without having previously obtained the permission of the President. The President shall call upon speakers in the order in which they signify their desire to speak. The President may call a speaker to order if his remarks are not relevant to the subject under discussion.

Precedence

Rule 69 [111]

The Chairman and the Rapporteur of a committee may be accorded precedence for the purpose of explaining the conclusions arrived at by their committee.

Statements by the Secretariat

Rule 70 [112]

The Secretary-General, or a member of the Secretariat designated by him as his representative, may at anytime make either oral or written statements to the General Assembly concerning any question under consideration by it.

Points of order

Rule 71 [113]

During the discussion of any matter, a representative may rise to a point of order, and the point of order shall be immediately decided by the President in accordance with the rules of procedure. A representative may appeal against the ruling of the President. The appeal shall be immediately put to the vote, and the President's ruling shall stand unless overruled by a majority of the members present and voting. A representative rising to a point of order may not speak on the substance of the matter under discussion.

Time-limit on speeches

Rule 72 [114]

The General Assembly may limit the time to be allowed to each speaker and the number of times each speaker may speak on any question. Before a decision is taken, two representatives may speak in favour of, and two against, a proposal to set such limits. When the debate is limited and a representative exceeds his allotted time, the President shall call him to order without delay.

Closing of list of speakers, right of reply

Rule 73 [115]

During the course of a debate, the President may announce the list of speakers and, with the consent of the General Assembly, declare the list closed. He may, however, accord the right of reply to any member if a speech delivered after he has declared the list closed makes this desirable.

Adjournment of debate

Rule 74 [116]

During the discussion of any matter, a representative may move the adjournment of the debate on the item under discussion. In addition to the proposer of the motion, two representatives may speak in favour of, and two against, the motion, after which the motion shall be immediately put to the vote. The President may limit the time to be allowed to speakers under this rule.

Closure of debate

Rule 75 [117]

A representative may at any time move the closure of the debate on the item under discussion, whether or not any other representative has signified his wish to speak. Permission to speak on the closure of the debate shall be accorded only to two speakers opposing the closure, after which the motion shall be immediately put to the vote. If the General Assembly is in favour of the closure, the President shall declare the closure of the debate. The President may limit the time to be allowed to speakers under this rule.

Suspension or adjournment of the meeting

Rule 76 [118]

During the discussion of any matter, a representative may move the suspension or the adjournment of the meeting. Such motions shall not be debated but shall be immediately put to the vote. The President may limit the time to be allowed to the speaker moving the suspension or adjournment of the meeting.

Order of procedural motions

Rule 77 [119]

Subject to rule 71, the motions indicated below shall have precedence in the following order over all other proposals or motions before the meeting:
  (*a*) To suspend the meeting;
  (*b*) To adjourn the meeting;
  (*c*) To adjourn the debate on the item under discussion;
  (*d*) To close the debate on the item under discussion.

Proposals and amendments

Rule 78 [120]

Proposals and amendments shall normally be submitted in writing to the Secretary-General, who shall circulate copies to the delegations. As a general rule, no proposal shall be discussed or put to the vote at any meeting of the General Assembly unless copies of it have been circulated to all delegations not later than the day preceding the meeting. The President may, however, permit the discussion and consideration of amendments, or of motions as to procedure, even though such amendments and motions have not been circulated or have only been circulated the same day.

Decisions on competence

Rule 79 [121]

Subject to rule 77, any motion calling for a decision on the competence of the General Assembly to adopt a proposal submitted to it shall be put to the vote before a vote is taken on the proposal in question.

Rule 80 [122]
A motion may be withdrawn by its proposer at any time before voting on it has commenced, provided that the motion has not been amended. A motion thus withdrawn may be reintroduced by any member.

Reconsideration of proposals
Rule 81 [123]
When a proposal has been adopted or rejected, it may not be reconsidered at the same session unless the General Assembly, by a two-thirds majority of the members present and voting, so decides. Permission to speak on a motion to reconsider shall be accorded only to two speakers opposing the motion, after which it shall be immediately put to the vote.

VOTING

Voting rights
Rule 82 [124]
Each member of the General Assembly shall have one vote.

Two-thirds majority
Rule 83
Decisions of the General Assembly on important questions shall be made by a two-thirds majority of the members present and voting. These questions shall include: recommendations with respect to the maintenance of international peace and security, the election of the non-permanent members of the Security Council, the election of the members of the Economic and Social Council, the election of members of the Trusteeship Council in accordance with paragraph 1 *c* of Article 86 of the Charter, the admission of new Members to the United Nations, the suspension of the rights and privileges of membership, the expulsion of Members, questions relating to the operation of the trusteeship system, and budgetary questions.

Rule 84
Decisions of the General Assembly on amendments to proposals relating to important questions, and on parts of such proposals put to the vote separately, shall be made by a two-thirds majority of the members present and voting.

Simple majority
Rule 85 [125]
Decisions of the General Assembly on questions other than those provided for in rule 83, including the determination of additional categories of questions to be decided by a two-thirds majority, shall be made by a majority of the members present and voting.

Meaning of phrase "members present and voting"
Rule 86 [126]
For the purposes of these rules, the phrase "members present and voting" means members casting an affirmative or negative vote. Members which abstain from voting are considered as not voting.

Method of voting
Rule 87 [127]
(*a*) The General Assembly shall normally vote by show of hands or by standing, but any representative may request a roll-call. The roll-call shall be taken in the English alphabetical order of the names of the members, beginning with the member whose name is drawn by lot by the President. The name of each member shall be called in any roll-call, and one of its representatives shall reply "yes", "no" or "abstention". The result of the voting shall be inserted in the record in the English alphabetical order of the names of the members.

(*b*) When the General Assembly votes by mechanical means, a non-recorded vote shall replace a vote by show of hands or by standing and a recorded vote shall replace a roll-call vote. Any representative may request a recorded vote. In the case of a recorded vote, the General Assembly shall, unless a representative requests otherwise, dispense with the procedure of calling out the names of the members; nevertheless, the result of the voting shall be inserted in the record in the same manner as that of a roll-call vote.

Conduct during voting
Rule 88 [128]
After the President has announced the beginning of voting, no representative shall interrupt the voting except on a point of order in connexion with the actual conduct of the voting. The President may permit members to explain their votes, either before or after the voting, except when the vote is taken by secret ballot. The President may limit the time to be allowed for such explanations. The President shall not permit the proposer of a proposal or of an amendment to explain his vote on his own proposal or amendment.

Division of proposals and amendments
Rule 89 [129]
A representative may move that parts of a proposal or of an amendment should be voted on separately. If objection is made to the request for division, the motion for division shall be voted upon. Permission to speak on the motion for division shall be given only to two speakers in favour and two speakers against. If the motion for division is carried, those parts of the proposal or of the amendment which are approved shall then be put to the vote as a whole. If all operative parts of the proposal or the amendment have been rejected, the proposal or the amendment shall be considered to have been rejected as a whole.

Voting on amendments
Rule 90 [130]
When an amendment is moved to a proposal, the amendment shall be voted on first. When two or more amendments are moved to a proposal, the General Assembly shall first vote on the amendment furthest removed in substance from the original proposal and then on the amendment next furthest removed therefrom, and so on until all the amendments have been put to the vote. Where, however, the adoption of one amendment necessarily implies the rejection of another amendment, the latter amendment shall not be put to the vote. If one or more amendments are adopted, the amended proposal shall then be voted upon. A motion is considered an amendment to a proposal if it merely adds to, deletes from or revises part of the proposal.

Rule 91 [131]

If two or more proposals relate to the same question, the General Assembly shall, unless it decides otherwise, vote on the proposals in the order in which they have been submitted. The General Assembly may, after each vote on a proposal, decide whether to vote on the next proposal.

Elections

Rule 92 [103]

All elections shall be held by secret ballot. There shall be no nominations.

Rule 93 [132]

When only one person or Member is to be elected and no candidate obtains in the first ballot the majority required, a second ballot shall be taken, which shall be restricted to the two candidates obtaining the largest number of votes. If in the second ballot the votes are equally divided, and a majority is required, the President shall decide between the candidates by drawing lots. If a two-thirds majority is required, the balloting shall be continued until one candidate secures two thirds of the votes cast; provided that, after the third inconclusive ballot, votes may be cast for any eligible person or Member. If three such unrestricted ballots are inconclusive, the next three ballots shall be restricted to the two candidates who obtained the greatest number of votes in the third of the unrestricted ballots, and the following three ballots thereafter shall be unrestricted, and so on until a person or Member is elected. These provisions shall not prejudice the application of rules 143, 144, 146 and 148.

Rule 94

When two or more elective places are to be filled at one time under the same conditions, those candidates obtaining in the first ballot the majority required shall be elected. If the number of candidates obtaining such majority is less than the number of persons or Members to be elected, there shall be additional ballots to fill the remaining places, the voting being restricted to the candidates obtaining the greatest number of votes in the previous ballot, to a number not more than twice the places remaining to be filled; provided that, after the third inconclusive ballot, votes may be cast for any eligible person or Member. If three such unrestricted ballots are inconclusive, the next three ballots shall be restricted to the candidates who obtained the greatest number of votes in the third of the unrestricted ballots, to a number not more than twice the places remaining to be filled, and the following three ballots thereafter shall be unrestricted, and so on until all the places have been filled. These provisions shall not prejudice the application of rules 143, 144, 146 and 148.

Equally divided votes

Rule 95 [133]

If a vote is equally divided on matters other than elections, a second vote shall be taken at a subsequent meeting which shall be held within forty-eight hours of the first vote, and it shall be expressly mentioned in the agenda that a second vote will be taken on the matter in question. If this vote also results in equality, the proposal shall be regarded as rejected.

XIII. COMMITTEES

Establishment of committees

Rule 96

The General Assembly may establish such committees as it deems necessary for the performance of its functions.

Categories of subjects

Rule 97

Items relating to the same category of subjects shall be referred to the committee or committees dealing with that category of subjects. Committees shall not introduce new items on their own initiative.

Main Committees

Rule 98

The Main Committees of the General Assembly are the following:

(*a*) Political and Security Committee (including the regulation of armaments) (First Committee);

(*b*) Special Political Committee;

(*c*) Economic and Financial Committee (Second Committee);

(*d*) Social, Humanitarian and Cultural Committee (Third Committee);

(*e*) Trusteeship Committee (including Non-Self-Governing Territories) (Fourth Committee);

(*f*) Administrative and Budgetary Committee (Fifth Committee);

(*g*) Legal Committee (Sixth Committee).

Organization of work

Rule 99

(*a*) All the Main Committees shall, during the first week of the session, hold the elections provided for in rule 103.

(*b*) Each Main Committee, taking into account the closing date for the session fixed by the General Assembly on the recommendation of the General Committee, shall adopt its own priorities and meet as may be necessary to complete the consideration of the items referred to it. It shall at the beginning of the session adopt a programme of work indicating, if possible, a target date for the conclusion of its work, the approximate dates of consideration of items and the number of meetings to be allocated to each item.

Representation of Members

Rule 100

Each Member may be represented by one person on each Main Committee and on any other committee that may be established upon which all Members have the right to be represented. It may also assign to these committees advisers, technical advisers, experts or persons of similar status.

Rule 101

Upon designation by the chairman of the delegation, advisers, technical advisers, experts or persons of similar status may act as members of committees. Persons of this status shall not, however, unless designated as alternate representatives, be eligible for election as Chairmen, Vice-Chairmen or Rapporteurs of committees or for seats in the General Assembly.

Subcommittees

Rule 102

Each committee may set up subcommittees, which shall elect their own officers.

Election of officers

Rule 103 [92]

Each Main Committee shall elect a Chairman, two Vice-Chairmen and a Rapporteur. In the case of other committees, each shall elect a Chairman, one or more Vice-Chairmen and a Rapporteur. These officers shall be elected on the basis of equitable geographical distribution, experience and personal competence. The elections shall be held by secret ballot unless the committee decides otherwise in an election where only one candidate is standing. The nomination of each candidate shall be limited to one speaker, after which the committee shall immediately proceed to the election.

The Chairman of a Main Committee shall not vote

Rule 104 [37]

The Chairman of a Main Committee shall not vote, but another member of his delegation may vote in his place.

Absence of officers

Rule 105 [32-34]

If the Chairman finds it necessary to be absent during a meeting or any part thereof, he shall designate one of the Vice-Chairmen to take his place. A Vice-Chairman acting as Chairman shall have the same powers and duties as the Chairman. If any officer of the committee is unable to perform his functions, a new officer shall be elected for the unexpired term.

Functions of the Chairman

Rule 106 [35]

The Chairman shall declare the opening and closing of each meeting of the committee, direct its discussions, ensure observance of these rules, accord the right to speak, put questions and announce decisions. He shall rule on points of order and, subject to these rules, shall have complete control of the proceedings at any meeting and over the maintenance of order thereat. The Chairman may, in the course of the discussion of an item, propose to the committee the limitation of the time to be allowed to speakers, the limitation of the number of times each representative may speak, the closure of the list of speakers or the closure of the debate. He may also propose the suspension or the adjournment of the meeting or the adjournment of the debate on the item under discussion.

Rule 107 [36]

The Chairman, in the exercise of his functions, remains under the authority of the committee.

Quorum

Rule 108 [67]

The Chairman may declare a meeting open and permit the debate to proceed when at least one quarter of the members of the committee are present. The presence of a majority of the members shall be required for any decision to be taken.

Speeches

Rule 109 [68]

No representative may address the committee without having previously obtained the permission of the Chairman. The Chairman shall call upon speakers in the order in which they signify their desire to speak. The Chairman may call a speaker to order if his remarks are not relevant to the subject under discussion.

Congratulations

Rule 110

Congratulations to the officers of a Main Committee shall not be expressed except by the Chairman of the previous session—or, in his absence, by a member of his delegation—after all the officers of the Committee have been elected.

Precedence

Rule 111 [69]

The Chairman and the Rapporteur of a committee or subcommittee may be accorded precedence for the purpose of explaining the conclusions arrived at by their committee or subcommittee.

Statements by the Secretariat

Rule 112 [70]

The Secretary-General, or a member of the Secretariat designated by him as his representative, may at any time make either oral or written statements to any committee or subcommittee concerning any question under consideration by it.

Points of order

Rule 113 [71]

During the discussion of any matter, a representative may rise to a point of order, and the point of order shall be immediately decided by the Chairman in accordance with the rules of procedure. A representative may appeal against the ruling of the Chairman. The appeal shall be immediately put to the vote, and the Chairman's ruling shall stand unless overruled by a majority of the members present and voting. A representative rising to a point of order may not speak on the substance of the matter under discussion.

Time-limit on speeches

Rule 114 [72]

The committee may limit the time to be allowed to each speaker and the number of times each representative may speak on any question. Before a decision is taken, two representatives may speak in favour of, and two against, a proposal to set such limits. When the debate is limited and a representative exceeds his allotted time, the Chairman shall call him to order without delay.

Closing of list of speakers, right of reply

Rule 115 [73]

During the course of a debate, the Chairman may announce the list of speakers and, with the consent of the committee, declare the list closed. He may, however, accord the right of reply to any member if a speech delivered after he has declared the list closed makes this desirable.

Adjournment of debate

Rule 116 [74]

During the discussion of any matter, a representative may move the adjournment of the debate on the item under discussion. In addition to the proposer of the motion, two representatives may speak in favour of, and two against, the motion, after which the motion shall be immediately put to the vote. The Chairman may limit the time to be allowed to speakers under this rule.

Closure of debate

Rule 117 [75]

A representative may at any time move the closure of the debate on the item under discussion, whether or not any other representative has signified his wish to speak. Permission to speak on the closure of the debate shall be accorded only to two speakers opposing the closure, after which the motion shall be immediately put to the vote. If the committee is in favour of the closure, the Chairman shall declare the closure of the debate. The Chairman may limite the time to be allowed to speakers under this rule.

Suspension or adjournment of the meeting

Rule 118 [76]

During the discussion of any matter, a representative may move the suspension or the adjournment of the meeting. Such motions shall not be debated but shall be immediately put to the vote. The Chairman may limit the time to be allowed to the speaker moving the suspension or adjournment of the meeting.

Order of procedural motions

Rule 119 [77]

Subject to rule 113, the motions indicated below shall have precedence in the following order over all other proposals or motions before the meeting:
   (*a*) To suspend the meeting;
   (*b*) To adjourn the meeting;
   (*c*) To adjourn the debate on the item under discussion;
   (*d*) To close the debate on the item under discussion.

Proposals and amendments

Rule 120 [78]

Proposals and amendments shall normally be submitted in writing to the Secretary-General, who shall circulate copies to the delegations. As a general rule, no proposal shall be discussed or put to the vote at any meeting of the committee unless copies of it have been circulated to all delegations not later than the day preceding the meeting. The Chairman may, however, permit the discussion and consideration of amendments, or of motions as to procedure, even though such amendments and motions have not circulated or have only been circulated the same day.

266

Decisions on competence
Rule 121 [79]
Subject to rule 119, any motion calling for a decision on the competence of the General Assembly or the committee to adopt a proposal submitted to it shall be put to the vote before a vote is taken on the proposal in question.

Withdrawal of motions
Rule 122 [80]
A motion may be withdrawn by its proposer at any time before voting on it has commenced, provided that the motion has not been amended. A motion thus withdrawn may be reintroduced by any member.

Reconsideration of proposals
Rule 123 [81]
When a proposal has been adopted or rejected, it may not be reconsidered at the same session unless the committee, by a two-thirds majority of the members present and voting, so decides. Permission to speak on a motion to reconsider shall be accorded only to two speakers opposing the motion, after which it shall be immediately put to the vote.

VOTING

Voting rights
Rule 124 [82]
Each member of the committee shall have one vote.

Majority required
Rule 125 [85]
Decisions of committees shall be made by a majority of the members present and voting.

Meaning of the phrase "members present and voting"
Rule 126 [86]
For the purposes of these rules, the phrase "members present and voting" means members casting an affirmative or negative vote. Members which abstain from voting are considered as not voting.

Method of voting
Rule 127 [87]
(a) The committee shall normally vote by show of hands or by standing, but any representative may request a roll-call. The roll-call shall be taken in the English alphabetical order of the names of the members, beginning with the member whose name is drawn by lot by the Chairman. The name of each member shall be called in any roll-call, and its representative shall reply "yes", "no" or "abstention". The result of the voting shall be inserted in the record in the English alphabetical order of the names of the members.

(b) When the committee votes by mechanical means, a non-recorded vote shall replace a vote by show of hands or by standing and a recorded vote shall replace a roll-call vote. Any representative may request a recorded vote. In the case of a recorded vote, the committee shall, unless a representative requests otherwise, dispense with the procedure of calling out the names of the members; nevertheless, the result of the voting shall be inserted in the record in the same manner as that of a roll-call vote.

Conduct during voting
Rule 128 [88]
After the Chairman has announced the beginning of voting, no representative shall interrupt the voting except on a point of order in connexion with the actual conduct of the voting. The Chairman may permit members to explain their votes, either before or after the voting, except when the vote is taken by secret ballot. The Chairman may limit the time to be allowed for such explanations. The Chairman shall not permit the proposer of a proposal or of an amendment to explain his vote on his own proposal or amendment.

Division of proposals and amendments
Rule 129 [89]
A representative may move that parts of a proposal or of an amendment should be voted on separately. If objection is made to the request for division, the motion for division shall be voted upon. Permission to speak on the motion for division shall be given only to two speakers in favour and two speakers against. If the motion for division is carried, those parts of the proposal or of the amendment which are approved shall then be put to the vote as a whole. If all operative parts of the proposal or of the amendment have been rejected, the proposal or the amendment shall be considered to have been rejected as a whole.

Voting on amendments
Rule 130 [90]
When an amendment is moved to a proposal, the amendment shall be voted on first. When two or more amendments are moved to a proposal, the committee shall first vote on the amendments furthest removed in substance from the original proposal and then on the amendment next furthest removed therefrom, and so on until all the amendments have been put to the vote. Where, however, the adoption of one amendment necessarily implies the rejection of another amendment, the latter amendment shall not be put to the vote. If one or more amendments are adopted, the amended proposal shall then be voted upon. A motion in considered an amendment to a proposal if it merely adds to, deletes from or revises part of the proposal.

Voting on proposals
Rule 131 [91]
If two or more proposals relate to the same question, the committee shall, unless it decides otherwise, vote on the proposals in the order in which they have been submitted. The committee may, after each vote on a proposal, decide whether to vote on the next proposal.

Elections
Rule 132 [93]
When only one person or Member is to be elected and no candidate obtains in the first ballot the majority required, a second ballot shall be taken, which shall be restricted to the two candidates obtaining the largest number of votes. If in the second ballot the votes are equally divided, and a majority is required, the Chairman shall decide between the candidates by drawing lots.

268

Equally divided votes

Rule 133 [95]

If a vote is equally divided on matters other than elections, the proposal shall be regarded as rejected.

XIV. ADMISSION OF NEW MEMBERS TO THE UNITED NATIONS

Applications

Rule 134

Any State which desires to become a Member of the United Nations shall submit an application to the Secretary-General. Such application shall contain a declaration, made in a formal instrument, that the State in question accepts the obligations contained in the Charter.

Notification of applicants

Rule 135

The Secretary-General shall, for information, send a copy of the application to the General Assembly, or to the Members of the United Nations if the Assembly is not in session.

Consideration of applications and decision thereon

Rule 136

If the Security Council recommends the applicant State for membership, the General Assembly shall consider whether the applicant is a peace-loving State and is able and willing to carry out the obligations contained in the Charter and shall decide, by a two-thirds majority of the members present and voting, upon its application for membership.

Rule 137

If the Security Council does not recommend the applicant State for membership or postpones the consideration of the application, the General Assembly may, after full consideration of the special report of the Security Council, send the application back to the Council, together with a full record of the discussion in the Assembly, for further consideration and recommendation or report.

Notification of decision and effective date of membership

Rule 138

The Secretary-General shall inform the applicant State of the decision of the General Assembly. If the application is approved, membership shall become effective on the date on which the General Assembly takes its decision on the application.

XV. ELECTIONS TO PRINCIPAL ORGANS

GENERAL PROVISIONS

Terms of office

Rule 139

Except as provided in rule 147, the term of office of members of Councils shall begin on 1 January following their election by the General Assembly and shall end on 31 December following the election of their successors.

By-elections

Rule 140

Should a member cease to belong to a Council before its term of office expires, a by-election shall be held separately at the next session of the General Assembly to elect a member for the unexpired term.

SECRETARY-GENERAL

Appointment of the Secretary-General

Rule 141

When the Security Council has submitted its recommendation on the appointment of the Secretary-Geneal, the General Assembly shall consider the recommendation and vote upon it by secret ballot in private meeting.

SECURITY COUNCIL

Annual elections

Rule 142

The General Assembly shall each year, in the course of its regular session, elect five non-permanent members of the Security Council for a term of two years.

Qualifications for membership

Rule 143

In the election of non-permanent members of the Security Council, due regard shall, in accordance with Article 23, paragraph 1, of the Charter, be specially paid, in the first instance, to the contribution of Members of the United Nations to the maintenance of international peace and security and to the other purposes of the Organization, and also to equitable geographical distribution.

Re-eligibility

Rule 144

A retiring member of the Security Council shall not be eligible for immediate re-election.

ECONOMIC AND SOCIAL COUNCIL

Annual elections

Rule 145

The General Assembly shall each year, in the course of its regular session, elect eighteen members of the Economic and Social Council for a term of three years.

Re-eligibility

Rule 146

A retiring member of the Economic and Social Council shall be eligible for immediate re-election.

Occasions for elections

Rule 147

When a Trusteeship Agreement has been approved and a Member of the United Nations has become an Administering Authority of a Trust Territory in accordance with Article 83 or Article 85 of the Charter, the General Assembly shall hold such election or elections to the Trusteeship Council as may be necessary, in accordance with Article 86. A Member or Members elected at any such election at a regular session shall take office immediately upon their election and shall complete their terms in accordance with the provisions of rule 139 as if they had begun their terms of office on 1 January following their election.

Terms of office and re-eligibility

Rule 148

A non-administering member of the Trusteeship Council shall be elected for a term of three years and shall be eligible for immediate re-election.

Vacancies

Rule 149

At each session the General Assembly shall, in accordance with Article 86 of the Charter, elect members to fill any vacancies.

INTERNATIONAL COURT OF JUSTICE

Method of election

Rule 150

The election of the members of the International Court of Justice shall take place in accordance with the Statute of the Court.

Rule 151

Any meeting of the General Assembly held in pursuance of the Statute of the International Court of Justice for the purpose of electing members of the Court shall continue until as many candidates as are required for all the seats to be filled have obtained in one or more ballots an absolute majority of votes.

XVI. ADMINISTRATIVE AND BUDGETARY QUESTIONS

GENERAL PROVISIONS

Regulations for financial administration

Rule 152

The General Assembly shall establish regulations for the financial administration of the United Nations.

Financial implications of resolutions

Rule 153

No resolution involving expenditure shall be recommended by a committee for approval by the General Assembly unless it is accompanied by an estimate of expenditures prepared by the Secretary-General. No resolution in respect of which expenditures are anticipated by the Secretary-General shall be voted by the General Assembly until the

Administrative and Budgetary Committee (Fifth Committee) has had an opportunity of stating the effect of the proposal upon the budget estimates of the United Nations.

Rule 154

The Secretary-General shall keep all committees informed of the detailed estimated cost of all resolutions which have been recommended by the committees for approval by the General Assembly.

ADVISORY COMMITTEE ON ADMINISTRATIVE AND BUDGETARY QUESTIONS
Appointment

Rule 155

The General Assembly shall appoint an Advisory Committee on Administrative and Budgetary Questions consisting of sixteen members, including at least three financial experts of recognized standing.

Composition

Rule 156

The members of the Advisory Committee on Administrative and Budgetary Questions, no two of whom shall be nationals of the same State, shall be selected on the basis of broad geographical representation, personal qualifications and experience and shall serve for a period of three years corresponding to three calendar years. Members shall retire by rotation and shall be eligible for reappointment. The three financial experts shall not retire simultaneously. The General Assembly shall appoint the members of the Advisory Committee at the regular session immediately preceding the expiration of the term of office of the members or, in case of vacancies, at the next session.

Functions

Rule 157

The Advisory Committee on Administrative and Budgetary Questions shall be responsible for expert examination of the programme budget of the United Nations and shall assist the Administrative and Budgetary Committee (Fifth Committee). At the beginning of each regular session at which the proposed programme budget for the following biennium is to be considered, it shall submit to the General Assembly a detailed report on the proposed programme budget for that biennium. It shall also submit, at such times as may be specified in the applicable provisions of the Financial Regulations and Rules of the United Nations, a report on the accounts of the United Nations and all United Nations entities for which the Secretary-General has administrative responsibility. It shall examine on behalf of the General Assembly the administrative budgets of specialized agencies and proposals for financial and budgetary arrangements with such agencies. It shall perform such other duties as may be assigned to it under the Financial Regulations of the United Nations.

COMMITTEE ON CONTRIBUTIONS
Appointment

Rule 158

The General Assembly shall appoint an expert Committee on Contributions consisting of eighteen members.

Rule 159
The members of the Committee on Contributions, no two of whom shall be nationals of the same State, shall be selected on the basis of broad geographical representation, personal qualifications and experience and shall serve for a period of three years corresponding to three calendar years. Members shall retire by rotation and shall be eligible for reappointment. The General Assembly shall appoint the members of the Committee on Contributions at the regular session immediately preceding the expiration of the term of office of the members or, in case of vacancies, at the next session.

Functions
Rule 160
The Committee on Contributions shall advise the General Assembly concerning the apportionment, under Article 17, paragraph 2, of the Charter, of the expenses of the Organization among Members, broadly according to capacity to pay. The scale of assessments, when once fixed by the General Assembly, shall not be subject to a general revision for at least three years unless it is clear that there have been substantial changes in relative capacity to pay. The Committee shall also advise the General Assembly on the assessments to be fixed for new Members, on appeals by Members for a change of assessments and on the action to be taken with regard to the application of Article 19 of the Charter.

XVII. SUBSIDIARY ORGANS OF THE GENERAL ASSEMBLY

Establishment and rules of procedure
Rule 161
The General Assembly may establish such subsidiary organs as it deems necessary for the performance of its functions. The rules relating to the procedure of committees of the General Assembly, as well as rules 45 and 60, shall apply to the procedure of any subsidiary organ unless the Assembly or the subsidiary organ decides otherwise.

XVIII. INTERPRETATION AND AMENDMENTS

Italicized headings
Rule 162
The italicized headings of these rules, which were inserted for reference purposes only, shall be disregarded in the interpretation of the rules.

Method of Amendment
Rule 163
These rules of procedure may be amended by a decision of the General Assembly, taken by a majority of the members present and voting, after a committee has reported on the proposed amendment.

Index

280

COLOPHON

Letter: Baskerville 11/12 and 9/10
Setter: Expertext, Alphen aan den Rijn
Printer: Samsom-Sijthoff Grafische Bedrijven, Alphen aan den Rijn
Binder: Callenbach, Nijkerk
Cover Design: Jan Jonkers